Preferring
Christ

Preferring Christ

A Devotional Commentary on the Rule of St. Benedict

Norvene Vest, Oblate OSB

Foreword by Dom Robert Hale, OSB Cam.

Afterword by Peter Brett, Canon Residentiary of Canterbury Cathedral

Translation of the Rule of St. Benedict Fr. Luke Dysinger, OSB

MOREHOUSE PUBLISHING

An imprint of Church Publishing Incorporated
Harrisburg—New York

First published in 1991 as *Preferring Christ: A Devotional Commentary and Workbook on the Rule of Saint Benedict* by Source Books and The Ravens Press.

Morehouse Publishing, 4775 Linglestown Road, Harrisburg, PA 17105

Morehouse Publishing, 445 Fifth Avenue, New York, NY 10016

Morehouse Publishing is an imprint of Church Publishing.

Translation of *The Rule of St. Benedict* Copyright © 1993 St. Andrew's Abbey, Valyermo, California.

Excerpts from the Jerusalem Bible, Copyright © 1966 by Darton Longman & Todd Ltd., and Doubleday, a division of Bantam Doubleday Dell Publishing Group Inc. Reprinted with permission.

Cover art courtesy of The Crosiers

Cover design by Wesley Hoke

Library of Congress Cataloging-in-Publication Data
Vest, Norvene.
  Preferring Christ : a devotional commentary and workbook on the rule
of St. Benedict / by Norvene Vest ; foreword by D. Robert Hale.
      p. cm.
Includes bibliographical references.
  ISBN 0-8192-1991-6 (pbk.)
  1. Benedict, Saint, Abbot of Monte Cassino. Regula. 2. Spiritual
life--Christianity--Meditations. I. Title.
  BX3004.Z5V47 2004
  255'.106--dc22
                    2003020501

Printed in the United States of America

08 09 10   5 4 3 2

This book is dedicated first to a place: the Our Lady Undercroft at Canterbury Cathedral, where I first had the idea that eventually resulted in this book;

and then to a community: the monks and oblates of St. Andrew's Abbey in Valyermo, California, who provided the rich soil in which these seeds could take root and produce fruit;

and finally to a guide: my husband, Douglas, who teaches me daily through his unselfconscious presence at my side the delightful art of preferring Christ in all things.

Contents

Foreword

This profound yet very practical volume speaks to an urgent spiritual need. Many people are yearning for an interior life deeply rooted in God, humanly balanced, and substantially founded in the Christian heritage. Norvene Vest offers a valuable resource in this regard by rendering much more accessible the spiritual wealth of the key text of the ancient Benedictine charism. These pages explore the solid, balanced wisdom of St. Benedict's Rule, which has nourished and guided innumerable Christians for nearly fifteen centuries.

Contemporary Christians from various denominations are feeling ever more attracted to spiritual classics such as the Rule. But it is not an easy matter to engage thoroughly a text of another age. Here, Norvene is singularly qualified to help.

With her husband, an Episcopal priest, she has ministered for ten years to the spiritual life of clergy and laity of the Episcopal Diocese of Los Angeles. The importance of the spiritual classics to this ministry has long been clear to them. And as chairperson of the Oblate Formation Committee of St. Andrew's Priory in California (a Roman Catholic Benedictine community), she has ongoing contact with monastic life and with those in the world who wish to share more directly in its ancient charism.

Norvene's participation in the direction of the Benedictine Experience programs at Bishop's Ranch, California, which draw people of several denominations, and her own long experience as spiritual director for many Christians of varied traditions—all this has enriched her own reflection regarding Benedictine spirituality and the heartfelt spiritual needs of people today.

I remember when Norvene first shared with me the central insight that made this book possible. We were walking down a rural road beyond Bishop's Ranch, with lovely vineyards to the right and left—a very Benedictine, sacramental setting! We were discussing the difficult issue of how an ancient text can be claimed for our own spiritual life, how to avoid a fundamentalistic approach on the one hand, and an arbitrary "adaptation" of the text to our own subjective tastes on the other. How can we authentically engage St. Benedict's Rule in a manner that is true to its profound insights, and also true to our own spiritual journey?

As we rounded the curve of the road, Norvene turned and said with intense enthusiasm: "The answer lies in the way we read the Rule. It shouldn't be studied like a book of regulations, or a school textbook. It should be read as *lectio divina!*" It was as if she had found the key to the front door of a wonderful and fascinating ancient cathedral. As true insights always are, once articulated, it was more than evident, and we monks have been reading the Rule this way for centuries. But I have never heard a monk put it that directly. And often we slip into other modes of reading, and lose contact with the deepest dimensions of the Rule's wisdom.

What precisely is the method of *lectio divina*? Basically, it means that we should read the Rule as we would meditate upon Holy Scripture or a spiritual classic. This means that we should first study the passage very attentively in order to grasp what is there. But then we should go on to meditate on it at a deeper, spiritual level, in our hearts. Even then, we are not halfway through the adventure. We need to go on to pray the text, to render it a vehicle for worship. And finally, we need to enable the text to lead us into a yet deeper level of contemplation of the ineffable God.

This is the way the monks and the faithful have read scripture and the great Christian spiritual writings through the ages. It is quite different from the "recreational" approach: speed-reading, skimming, then discarding and often forgetting a text. It is also quite different from anxiously studying a book for a test or a job requirement—the approach that is drilled into us at school.

Each page of this workbook is structured to support the reader in the ancient approach of *lectio*, enabling us to explore and assimilate, in a reverential and penetrating way, the riches of the Rule. If from this workbook we learn nothing other than this method of *lectio*, or if, already "knowing" it, we deepen our familiarity with it and our seriousness in using it, we shall have gained a great deal indeed, and come to know much about a foundational element of Benedictine spirituality. In fact, this volume offers a great deal beyond this. It provides numerous deep insights regarding other key elements of the wisdom of the Rule—of the author's own careful and prayerful *lectio.*

To use this method is not to force upon the Rule some foreign and artificial technique. Rather, it is to have prayerful recourse precisely to the approach that St. Benedict presupposes. *Lectio* is the way Benedictine monks endeavor to read any spiritual classic, in fact, to read their very lives. It is the way scripture itself presupposes that all of salvation history will be meditated, that every individual life journey will be pondered and prayed. For God is present, powerfully and effectively, in scripture, in the Rule, in the spiritual classics, and also in our lives. If we can carefully "read" that Presence, meditate that Presence, then go on to pray and contemplate that Presence, we shall be transformed.

But . . . do we have time for this? Do we have the energy? Can we muster the attention span? After all, we are frenetically busy, even with our "R & R" projects and hobbies. Not for nothing have we produced multibillion-dollar "entertainment" industries. In the words of T. S. Eliot, we are *distracted from distraction by distraction.* Thomas Merton notes the word's etymology: "Distraction" comes from the Latin, "pulled apart." Our rush alienates us from our deepest center—from that *still point of the turning world* (Eliot). But if we can find courage and open ourselves to the grace of following through with the discipline of *lectio,* of cleaving to the Rule (or another deep, spiritual text) until we have arrived at the heart of the matter—then we can finally start to heal and become transformed.

Some fourteen hundred years ago Pope Gregory the Great characterized St. Benedict's Rule as remarkable for its discretion. That last term is a rich one, rooted in scripture and the earliest Christian texts. It refers to Spirit-enabled discernment, carefulness, wise balance, deep insight. Perhaps our own age and each one of us could use more of that Benedictine discretion. We can all too easily become "charged-up," obsessed with something (it might be the latest spiritual craze). But to undertake carefully a journey that will xiv ♦ PREFERRING CHRIST

certainly lead to the heights if we keep moving steadily, taking nourishment from the Christian wisdom of the ages—that is something else. And so this workbook is something else.

The invitation one hears from these pages comes from far beyond the book itself, from far beyond St. Benedict. The source is ultimately The Beloved. And as the Rule observes, "What, dear brethren, is more delightful than the Lord's voice calling us? Behold, the Lord in His love shows us the way of life."

D. Robert Hale, OSB Cam.
New Camaldoli Hermitage
Big Sur, California
January 1991

Introduction

When I wrote this book for its first publication over ten years ago, I was writing primarily for lay people who wanted to know more about the Rule of St. Benedict as a spiritual document. I anticipated that readers would be oblates of Benedictine monasteries, or at least those who frequented Benedictine communities on personal retreat. At that time, there were not many resources available for persons who did not expect to become monks (a term referring to both men and women), because Benedictine spirituality was perceived as centered in the cloister and the vows. Yet even then, a growing number of lay people were sensing that Benedictine spirituality held a treasure helpful for life "in the world." The immense attractiveness of Benedictine life has continued to call hundreds of women and men worldwide and, thankfully, there are now many useful tools for Benedictine oblates as they try to apply the Rule in a vastly different time and culture than Benedict's.

As I have reviewed this devotional commentary for this current Morehouse publication, I realize that the Rule is more than a resource for people interested in Benedictine spirituality. Lingering page by page over Benedict's sixth century text, I see more clearly than ever its steady and practical wisdom for any Christian serious about faithfulness to the Gospel, indeed for anyone who deeply desires a more intimate life with God. A substantial portion of the Rule is direct and indirect quotations from scripture, as Benedict tries to share the wisdom of the book he knew by heart. On every page of the Rule, Benedict helps us reflect on the questions, "Do I love God?" and "Does God love me?" and to see what difference our responses make.

The problems and opportunities of every age of humanity bring with them the need for renewed concepts of the essence of the human spirit and the means of contact with the divine. Benedict's viewpoint seems to offer a profound affinity with the spiritual aspirations of our own time. Reaching out to us from the past, he brings a way of understanding and acting upon our desire for intimacy with the sacred that goes a long way toward healing the brokenness revealed by the isolation and cynicism so prevalent in our twenty-first century. What is the core of this viewpoint? Benedict combines a deep conviction of the abiding love of God with a constant call for a disciplined life.

Nothing is more important for human beings than learning to live in harmony with God's will, which is to say, with God's love. We are here for a purpose, which our deepest longing reveals to us. God places a longing in our hearts for relationship, and then takes the initiative in calling, urging, and caring about that relationship with each one of us. Furthermore, God is not dismayed when we neglect or ignore our deep longings, but continues in constancy to reach out, support, nurture, and draw us ever onward into that fullness of life which is only possible in loving union with God. Nothing can separate us from the love of God in Christ. (Rom. 8:38–9) While this abiding love of God is a foundational dynamic of Christian faith, Benedict helps make it real for us by teaching us how to live daily into that love.

Benedict's style is homely and pragmatic, rooted in the physical matters that consume so many of our waking hours—our work, relationships, food and clothing, environment, and community. A basic premise of the Rule is the principle that God is everywhere, all the time, and thus that every element of our ordinary day is potentially holy. Benedict places the primacy of spiritual discipline squarely into the midst of the ordinary: the consecrated life is not set-apart-ness but nearness to God in all we do and are. We cannot be whole without a specific commitment of our time, energy, attitudes, behaviors, and habits. Yet we can approach holiness with just such a commitment. The spiritual life consists in no more and no less than a repeated decision to be a certain kind of person in every waking moment, every given situation. There are no shortcuts; we must teach ourselves to be God's person, day by day and hour by hour. This discipline is real, constant, and fruitful.

The Rule is not full of moral dogmas nor packed with platitudes. Its form is simple and forthright, practical and applicable to every person. Benedict keeps raising questions for us to consider seriously: Do I really long for fullness of life? How do I go about living life grounded in the real and the important? Am I awake or asleep? What am I prepared to do for a healthy soul? Are there moral offenses that can jeopardize eternal life? What constitutes true repentance and how do I learn to accept forgiveness? What nurtures me? What is Christ asking me to do in my particular life circumstances today? What would spiritual maturity look and feel like in my life? As we move through the Rule with Benedict, we are urged to ask ourselves these questions, and discover where our answers lie. We can no longer live an unexamined life.

And these disciplines are always woven back into love. We are not allowed to hold back because of fear, nor lose heart under heavy judgment. Benedict is always reminding us that our motives and actions are a response to love. Our spiritual practices teach us to greet Christ in everything, and to bear the joy of that meeting. Every action becomes an offering: lifting up to God all that we hold (including our very selves), finding ourselves enfolded within the liberating will of God, and returning transformed into the very materiality of the world.

This book is designed to enable the reader to traverse this territory with Benedict in a pattern of daily devotion, taking a few verses from the Rule each day and meditating with them. This pattern is called that of *lectio divina* and imitates the way Benedict probably wrote the Rule, with slow, deep reflection on a single issue over a long period. *Lectio divina* literally means divine reading, and carries the same double meaning in Latin as in English: *what* is being read is divine/holy (usually the scriptures, but also in time we learn to read our own life as filled with the divine); and *how* it is being read is with the help of God's Holy Spirit. In order for this *how* to happen, we slow down our reading radically so we can be more open to what God's Spirit is telling us in it.

Traditionally, *lectio divina* (which is called lectio henceforth) involves four basic steps or elements.

1. *Lectio* (reading): Take a passage of scripture or other devotional/theological work and read a few verses aloud. The reading aloud engages more than just eyes and mind; it reminds us that we are reading with our whole being, not just for information, but for an encounter with the living God.

2. *Meditatio* (meditation): Allow yourself to be drawn by a particular word or phrase, pondering what it means, what the author might have meant in writing it.

3. *Oratio* (prayer): Apply the meaning to the present situation in your own life, allowing the words to penetrate your heart and address your concerns, and to evoke a prayerful response.

4. *Contemplatio* (contemplation): Turn the whole process back over the the Giver, allowing yourself to be deepened, guided, and transformed by the Spirit.

This book roughly follows that basic structure of lectio, with short chapters that encourage slowing down and engaging prayerfully with the text of the Rule as a spiritual guide. Each day's entry has four components:

1. *Text of the Rule itself.* A few verses are cited at the top of each section, moving sequentially through the seventy-three chapters of the Rule, in a translation made for this commentary by Fr. Luke Dysinger, O.S.B., of St. Andrew's Abbey in Valyermo, California.[1] You may wish to write out these verses in a paraphrase, and/or read the text aloud, slowly, experiencing its sound as a way of drawing you more deeply into the text.

2. *Comment.* This component contains a few paragraphs of commentary on the verses for the day, emphasizing what Benedict means by the passage, what he is asking, what he is doing here and why. While these comments are informed by wide acquaintance with secondary sources, they are not intended so much as scholarly commentary as rather an intuitive exploration of the basic spiritual themes being raised, especially as they might be applicable to the situation of contemporary readers.

3. *Reflection.* Here I make a shift from the objective to a more personal framework, asking of my own heart what this text means for me. This section involves my responses to the text as I prayed it myself over a period of a year and a half, exploring the individual issues with which I was struggling as I read and prayed. I was asking, how does this passage touch my own life? I have included this section in the book as a way of inviting your personal engagement with the ancient text, essentially modeling or stimulating the way I hope you will work with the text on your own.

4. *Prayer/Response.* This section is merely suggested by its title and left blank, as a more direct invitation for you to do your own reflection. I encourage using a notebook or journal alongside this book, supporting the daily time you set aside for prayer with the Rule. Before starting your own writing/reflection, you may find it helpful to set the book aside, close your eyes and breathe deeply, and in quietness listen to discover where God is leading you through this material on this day.

The intention of this pattern of presentation is to enable the Rule to come alive for you in your own movement toward deepening relationship with God. My experience is that praying the Rule in these slow *lectio* segments is an opening into its great riches, and a vital way of integrating personally the love of God and the life of discipline which the Rule teaches. For those readers quite new to this kind of experience, I offer "interludes" at the end of each major section of the Rule, as practical helps to the process. The interludes may be read all at once, or skipped altogether, according to your preference.

My desire is to present Benedict's sixth century text in such a way that its beauty and contemporary value can be appreciated, and I have tried to be faithful to his idiom and his intention, while yet making some adjustments that make it easier for a modern reader to enter fully into Benedict's "intuitive awareness of the unchanging realities"[2] of the soul. Occasionally the tension between these objectives—especially as regards inclusive language—results in a certain grammatical awkwardness, which I hope will be less of a distraction than retaining the original idiom intact. Benedict was very close to his twin sister, Scholastica, who headed a women's community very near his monastery, and from the beginning both men and women have lived under Benedict's Rule, with all major leadership roles being held by women, including that of abbess. Since the text itself does not tell us this, I have endeavored to make a few amendments so that the Rule's own inclusivity is not misconstrued.

The strongest feeling that comes to me as I have undertaken this journey of *lectio divina* through the Rule is that Benedict always keeps us focused on Christ. As he quotes extensively from scripture, it is almost always in response to the fundamental question in his mind: "How can I, this day, allow myself to be drawn more deeply into the mind of Christ, that I might be more and more the person

God has called me forth to be?" It is no accident that the best-known phrase of the Rule and its summary statement is:

Prefer nothing to the love of Christ!

The transformation of our whole selves toward that preference is the Rule's goal. May we all be blessed by Benedict's guidance in our transformation.

Norvene Vest
January 2004

The Prologue

Prologue

VERSES 1–2

*L*isten, *O my son to the precepts of the master, and incline the ear of your heart: willingly receive and faithfully fulfill the admonition of your loving father; that you may return by the labor of obedience to him from whom you had departed through the sloth of disobedience.*

Comment

In these first words of the Rule, Benedict communicates both a direct and personal relationship, and a sense of eager urgency. The phrases "my son" and "admonition of your loving father" are meant to show that the Rule is truly addressed to each one who reads or hears it; it is a personal word for each.

The phrases "listen," "willingly receive," "faithfully fulfill," and "that you may return" all convey energy and action, a kind of immediate personal application of what is spoken here.

The first word of the Rule is well known: listen! It is interesting indeed that this Latin word *ob-sculta* has the same root, and indeed almost the same meaning, as the Latin word *ob-oedire,* from which the English word obedience comes. There is a very important connection between true listening and deep obedience; both suggest a turning in order to receive more fully that which is being given.

Turning is really what the whole Rule is about. It presumes the first turning, or conversion, of Baptism; and it is then deeply interested in the second and lifelong turning of daily conversion to Christ. The question always in Benedict's mind is the question of Christian maturity: "How can we live out our commitment to God in daily life?" He is certain that God calls each one of us each day to respond more fully:

"Today if you would hear his voice, do not harden your hearts . . ." (RB Prologue 10, and Psalm 95, which is the *Venite*—opening psalm—of Vigils and Morning Prayer). Benedict's central concern is to ask what environment and what behavior will daily "bring us back" to God.

Thus Benedict begins with the practical questions of daily life.[3] He finds these clearly raised in Psalm 34:12: "Which of you wants to live to the full?" and in Psalm 15:1: "Yahweh, who has the right to enter your tent, or to live (with you)?" and he allows these psalms to broadly shape his call to a life of consecration to God, a call to take seriously the (second) ongoing turning of listening obedience.

Reflection

Benedict's challenge to return is issued personally to each one who reads or hears this prologue. Do I take the challenge seriously myself? I often struggle with the "sloth of disobedience," if by that is meant forgetfulness. All too easily, I can forget that I live even this minute in the sight of God. I forget that I am, even amidst this conflict or brokenness or joy or creative moment, empowered by the Spirit of God. I forget that I am, even and perhaps especially in my weakness and limitation, loved profoundly by my Christ.

I do know that I desire life and long to "dwell with the Lord," but I am often bewildered about how to respond to these longings. Yes, I could use a school for the Lord's service, a pattern or an environment that would help me live more fully each day in the heart of God. I am eager to see what fruit this *lectio* might produce in me. Lead on, Benedict!

Prayer/Response

Prologue
VERSES 3–7

*T*o you therefore, my words are now addressed, whoever you are, *that renouncing your own will, you take up the strong and bright weapons of obedience, in order to fight for the Lord Christ, our true King.*

In the first place, whenever you begin any good work, beg of him with most earnest prayer to perfect it; so that he who has now granted us the dignity of being counted in the number of his children may not at any time be grieved by our evil deeds. For we must always so serve him with the good things he has given us, that not only may he never, as an angry father, disinherit his children; but may never as a dread Lord, incensed by our sins, deliver us to everlasting punishment as most wicked servants who would not follow him to glory.

Comment

The images tumble out of Benedict's mind: King, father, manor lord, jumbled in a mixture of eagerness much like the letters of St. Peter when he seeks with such urgency to communicate to his hearers the majesty of the proffered gift and the danger of losing it. All Benedict's thought is centered upon salvation: the mystery of eternal life in God offered through Christ, and the possibility that we may refuse that glorious gift by our hardheartedness.[4] God has extended Godself in every way: by already counting us as children, by giving us good gifts within us, by aiding us even in our prayer, by cooperating with our beginnings (responses) to bring about completion.

But the choice is ours. Not once only, but every day in every action we take, we choose whether or not to follow God. This is what Benedict means by readiness to give up our own will: the intention to choose daily, to learn to choose habitually, to allow the deepening of our disposition to choose for God. It is not that our desires are inherently bad; indeed, sometimes they can be good.[5] Rather, it is necessary to train and discipline our desires toward the truly good choices of God's glory. The consecrated life is precisely the life of such discipline, set squarely in the context of ordinary, everyday choices. It is this life that the Rule endeavors to guide.

Reflection

I so appreciate one of C. S. Lewis's metaphors for God as "a smooth inclined plane on which there is no resting," so that given our present consciousness we are all day long "sliding, slipping and falling away."[6] I experience my intention like that. I intend to experience the day entirely as God's gift, and yet, before I am finished with breakfast, I have clutched at it, as if it were my possession, to be shaped and structured as I choose, closed off to any interruptions in my plan. Sometimes I wonder what I would say if Jesus decided to come in glory on this day . . . most likely I would urge him to go away until I am better prepared; I have certain activities I wish to finish first!

And I sense that the issue involved in my own willing is not simply a matter of conscious intention, but also a matter of my "spontaneous" responses. That is, what I truly will is revealed just as much in my habitual patterns as it is by my periodic conscious decisions. Thus, it seems likely to me that practice, moment-by-moment training of my responses in daily situations, might really bring me closer to God. When I look at it that way, how clear it is that I am not very good at habitually choosing God.

Prayer/Response

Prologue
VERSES 8–13

L et us then at last arise, since the Scripture stirs us up saying: It is time now for us to rise from sleep (Rom 13:11). And our eyes being open to the deifying light, let us hear with wondering ears what the Divine Voice admonishes us, daily crying out: Today if you hear his voice, harden not your hearts (Ps 95:7–8). And again, You who have ears to hear, hear what the Spirit says to the churches (Rev 2:7).

And what does he say? Come my children, listen to me, I will teach you the fear of the Lord (Ps 34:12). Run while you have the light of life, lest the darkness of death seize hold of you (John 12:35).

Comment

As so often in the Rule, when he introduces a subject Benedict piles one Scripture quotation on top of another, in a way quite bewildering to the modern reader. The essential reason for this lies in the ancient way of "knowing" scripture. In Benedict's time, even literate persons memorized large passages of scripture, with mouth as well as mind iterating verses over and over, so that the cadences and resonances of various passages evoked one another in a manner not disconnected from context, but not primarily dependent upon it.[7]

The key here is the matter of the word and truly hearing it. As far back as the times of the ancient Hebrews, the spoken word was understood as having an effective and inherent power of its own, which goes forth from the speaker, creating a response in those who hear. This is clear in the creation account in chapter one of Genesis, for example (God spoke and it was so!).

Benedict is bringing that concept to bear here, on the specific thing that happens every day with every Christian. God calls out (God's effective Word goes forth) each day, bringing us into immediate rela-tionship with God in the midst of our daily activity, if we will but hear. Benedict has offered these scripture passages that resonate in his deepest imagination, with the power of this daily word. It might be well to meditate directly on these passages, as he obviously has.

Reflection

In many ways, this is my favorite passage from the Rule. Partly that is because I live in one of the continuing "Benedictine" ecclesiastical traditions (that is, the Anglican church), where Psalm 95 is chanted every morning, so that each day I literally hear the call, "If only you would listen to God today, do not harden your hearts . . ." I rejoice in knowing that I belong to the community of saints, living and dead, who share that call.

And partly this is my favorite because I am strengthened by the idea that God's word is effective and potent: my role is to hear it and let it reside in me and do its work; my response is already evoked in the hearing. Some days it's easy and some days hard, but no matter how it feels, I am comforted by Benedict's sense that God's word is here every day, gently calling me forth.

Prayer/Response

Prologue
VERSES 14–18

*A*nd the Lord, seeking his own workman in the multitude of the people to whom he cries out, says again: Who is it who longs for life, and desires to see good days (Ps 34:12)?

And if you, hearing him, answer, "I am the one!" God says to you: If you long for true and everlasting life, keep your tongue from evil and your lips from speaking deceit. Turn aside from evil and do good; seek peace and pursue it (Ps 34:13–14).

And when you have done these things, my eyes will be upon you, and my ears will be open to your prayers; and before you call upon me, I will say unto you, Behold, I am here (Isa 58:9).

Comment

We see by Benedict's continued emphasis on the words of Psalm 34 that it carries a special meaning for him. Clearly, an essential element that he would impress upon us is the question and answer posed here:

Q. Do you long for eternal life with all your heart and soul?
A. I do!

So then, he continues, what is the practical and daily response/ behavior that is to be made and can be made? Crucial to this movement is the fear of the Lord and the disciplined moral behavior that is evoked by this awed regard. (A sense of fearful awe is often missing in modern experience, and is worth pondering for whatever relevance and value it might contain. There will be other opportunities in the Rule for such consideration.) An equally crucial element is the profound empowerment that happens by virtue of the Lord's active presence in our midst. The two—our awed regard and God's empowering presence—go hand in hand.

As always, Benedict presumes that a few verses will call to our minds the entire scriptural context. Both Psalm 34 and Isaiah 58 are concerned with the juxtaposition of human righteousness and God's glory that occurs in the life of one consecrated to God. What a lovely consideration is suggested by the first line of Psalm 34: "I will bless Yaweh at all times," because "bless" in that phrase has the same meaning as "benediction": both convey the desire to live out the good word of God given forth in one's very own creation and the renewing power of God's daily call.

Reflection

How well Benedict sets forth his goal (the yearning for Life!) and the purpose of his work (to provide a sound daily framework for our generous response to that yearning). In reading his words, I feel my own excitement build that even I am called to take my own life seriously enough to offer it to God. Such offering or consecration does not mean that I withdraw from the world, but, rather, that I recognize God's effective power in me and in the world in the midst of things as I find them. It is a double astonishment: 1) that it truly involves me; and 2) that God is empowering within things as they are.

Prayer/Response

Prologue

VERSES 19–22

What can be sweeter to us, dear brothers, than this voice of the Lord inviting us? Behold in his loving kindness the Lord shows us the way of life. Having our loins, therefore, girded with faith and the performance of good works, let us walk in his paths by the guidance of the Gospel, that we may deserve to see him who has called us in his kingdom (1 Thess 2:12).

And if we wish to dwell in the tabernacle of this kingdom, we shall never reach it unless we run there by our good deeds.

Comment

This is the basic stuff of faith: God is the One who calls (1 Thess). Humans are the ones who are called. The whole of human life can be summed up in the trusting response we make to that call. The whole goal of the monastic journey can be summarized by the phrase from Matthew 5:8 alluded to here: that we may deserve to see God.[8]

Notice that there is no opposition between faith and works. For Benedict, concerned with the practical questions of how best to carry out this response to God's call within the context of the given-ness of each unique life, turns immediately to the phrase "faith . . . and works." One without the other is empty. He never suggests that our own efforts alone bring us to God;[9] he always emphasizes that only the goodness of the Lord enables us to undertake this journey at all.

Yet, he urges us on: since God does call us, dare we refuse to respond with our whole beings? We are indeed called to participate in the sweetest joy we can imagine. Let's get on with it!

Reflection

At one level, I wonder why it is necessary to say this at all in the Rule, since it is so consistently the essence of the Gospel, so completely that which I already " know." In pondering this, I remember two of my foundational ideas: the first, that the heart of the Gospel can be told in a very few words, but it takes a lifetime or longer to learn to live the truth of those words. The second is that the Bible is one of the few books we read not because we don't know what is in it, but because we do.

In other words, the Rule is not intended primarily to inform me. Rather, it is meant to be formative: to provide a pattern with which I can begin to apply the Gospel fruitfully to my own daily life; to set forth an ordering framework that allows my heart to be enlarged so that it can more fully resonate with the glory of Love Itself.

Sometimes when I turn to the Rule this way—slowly and reflectively, a few verses at a time, inquiring of it from the quiet center of my spirit—I find that I want both to weep and to laugh with the unutterable joy of what God offers me.

Prayer/Response

Prologue
VERSES 23–28

ut let us ask the Lord with the Prophet, saying to him: Lord, who shall dwell in your tent, or who shall rest upon your holy mountain? (Ps 15:1). After this question, brethren, let us hear the Lord answering and showing us the way to his tent, saying: One who walks without stain and works justice; one who speaks truth in his heart, who has not practiced deceit with his tongue; one who has done no evil to his neighbor, and has not believed false accusations against his neighbor (Ps 15:2–3).

One who has brought the malignant devil to naught, casting him out of the sight of his heart with all his suggestions; and has taken hold of his bad thoughts, while they were still young, and dashed them down upon Christ (Ps 15:4, 137:9).

Comment

In general, in modern liturgical practice we simply avoid those sections of the Psalms or other scripture that seem to suggest uncivilized, not to say un-Christian, behavior. But Benedict does with scripture what we are seeking to do with the Rule: he approaches every verse of it sacramentally, even verses that at first seem repugnant or offensive. In other words, we always give the benefit of the doubt; we always ask: Is there here a deeper meaning than the obvious, which can lead me more truthfully to see my own life through God's eyes?

Evidently, Benedict found such a meaning in this "offensive" Psalm 137, because he refers to it twice in the Rule, both here and in Chapter 4 (verse 50). He understands the young who are dashed against the rock to be young temptations that are dashed at once at the feet of Christ, and thus destroyed before they have a chance to take hold in our souls. Modern psychological practice, especially in cognitive therapy, has rediscovered the wisdom of this advice. Today we are newly aware that we need not succumb to the pull of the many voices in our heads, not all of which are in our best interests. Centuries ago, Benedict asked us to consider this same possibility as a powerful dynamic of our journey toward and with God. The journey has its joy; it also has its risks. Christ is the surest foundation for both. Let us turn to him at once with whatever moves us.

A mood shift from "mercy" to "judgment" occurs at this point in the Prologue. God calls each person, and when that call is accepted, each one also accepts responsibility for his or her behavior. Yet that is a responsibility that no one can truly carry; the strength is not always in us to act as we would. This matter of daily living in such a way as to deepen the mind of Christ in our whole being, even and especially where "we can't"—that is the issue of Christian formation; that is the primary issue of concern in the Rule. Here Benedict begins to challenge us to accept certain disciplines, transmitted and supported within the community of faith.

Reflection

What touches me today is an invitation from Benedict to be attentive to, and to guide, those many "inner voices" that push and pull at me all day. I often think of these voices as "parent tapes" or use other psychological jargon to identify them, but fancy names don't minimize their harassment. As I ponder Benedict's intention in his language and in my experience, which I generally understand in psychological language, some connections appear.

I see a connection between the likelihood that I will speak sharply to my husband, or eagerly devour the latest gossip about a "friend," and the extent to which I have let myself become "hooked" by negative inner voices. If I am feeling rotten about myself, inadequate or confused, it is very easy to distract myself with external trivia or to discharge my emotions in a harsh outburst. I am not usually aware that these temptations keep me from the present awareness that God loves me, yet allowing myself to be caught by them may be one of the main ways in which I hold God off.

And if I teach myself to be aware of such temptations in their infancy, at the very first moment they appear, and at once offer them to Christ, I sense that I might find much greater peace of mind— and perhaps also much greater and genuine care for my neighbor.

Prayer/Response

Prologue
VERSES 29–34

*T*hese are they (dwelling in God's tent) who, fearing the Lord, are not elated over their own good works; but knowing that the good which is in them comes not from themselves but from the Lord, they magnify (Ps 15:4) the Lord who works in them, saying with the Prophet: Not unto us, O Lord, not unto us, but unto your name give the glory (Ps 115:1). In this way the Apostle Paul imputed nothing of his preaching to himself, but said: By the grace of God I am what I am" (1 Cor 15:10). And again he says: He who glories, let him glory in the Lord (2 Cor 10:17).

Hence also the Lord says in the Gospel: The one who hears these words of mine and does them is like a wise person who built his house upon a rock: the floods came, the winds blew and beat upon that house, and it did not fall; because it was founded upon a rock (Matt 7:24–5).

Comment

We can read Benedict with joy, as we discover him to be a person asking serious questions about (and proposing guidelines for) the life of commitment to the Lord—a consecrated life, in other words. In our culture, it is not easy to find concrete guidance for the issues that arise when one has embarked upon a consecrated life. Benedict clarifies what is essential and tells us how to shape a faithful response. We realize at once that temptations will be an issue, but it is perhaps less clear to us that elation may equally be a problem. Yet Benedict sees it as important enough to mention very early in the

Rule. The issue is this: How do we handle the awareness that we are being used as an instrument and partner of God's own spirit?[10] The committed Christian will often find himself or herself lifted up, empowered in the strongest and most harmonious way to carry out a given work. The temptations here are very great—either to refuse the work altogether because of the overwhelming sense of being carried (i.e., "out of control" or "beyond capacity"), or to claim the work as our own, as if God had nothing to do with it.

Benedict sets this issue in two contexts: 1) Psalm 15 (continuing from above)—that fundamentally our orientation must be toward God, in fear and praise; and 2) Matthew 5–7 (the Sermon on the Mount)—that we must, and will, do those things that astonish the world, because we belong to Christ and our lives are founded on him.

Reflection

The quotations from St. Paul emphasize grace and glory . . . I could profitably spend years pondering these two fundamental concepts of the Christian life. I imagine that Benedict is urging me to do just that—and to live in such a way as to allow those "concepts" to be embodied in my life!

I often wonder about giving God glory. Exactly how do we undertake an action in such a way that people see it and give glory to God? Benedict suggests it has something to do with fear of God and praise . . . but maybe the key is in the house built upon a rock. If I love Christ above all things, and try to allow that to be more and more true in the way I actually live each day, then both my actions and other people's responses will ultimately be as they should be.

Recently I had an experience that later struck me as an experience of God's glory. I was making a presentation to an eager and interested group, and together in that moment we had an experience of God in our midst. We all felt high and lifted up—and also empowered to be better people. Afterward it came to me: that's what God's glory is like! That realization enabled me to carry the joy of the moment with me for a time. I offered up the whole experience, delighting in it even more because I knew it to be the touch of God.

Prayer/Response

Prologue
VERSES 35–44

With these (admonitions) concluded, the Lord is waiting daily for us to respond by our deeds to his holy guidance. Therefore, in order that we may amend our evil ways, the days of our lives have been lengthened as a reprieve, as the Apostle says: Do you not know that the patience of God is leading you to repentance? (Rom 2:4). For the loving Lord says: I do not desire the death of a sinner, but that he should be converted and live (Ezek 33:11).

Since then brethren, we have asked of the Lord who is to dwell in his tent, we have heard his commands to those who are to abide there, it remains for us to complete the duties of those who dwell there. Our hearts, therefore, and our bodies must be prepared to fight in holy obedience to his commands. And let us ask God to supply by the help of his grace what by nature is hardly possible to us. And if we wish to reach eternal life, escaping the pains of hell, then—while there is yet time, while we are still in the flesh and are able to fufil all these things by the light which is given us—we must run and perform now what will profit us for all eternity.

Comment

With these verses, Benedict brings the body of his prologue to a close. The whole tone of the prologue has been that of invitation. Do you wish life? Do you long to dwell in the Lord's tent? Do you hear the Lord calling out to you today?

This invitation comes through Benedict, but clearly he means to convey that the invitation is God's own; Benedict is just the messenger. God assures us in love that we are each invited to life, not death. Indeed, God will supply to us what is lacking in nature, so that we may respond to the invitation so generously, so consistently offered.

The invitation must receive a response. In fact, it does receive a response from each one of us, whether intentional or not. We have asked the Lord who may dwell with him, and we have heard his answer. God awaits our response. What will we do now? How important is all this to us? How much will we invest?

Benedict concludes his Prologue with a heightened exhortation to each Christian to accept the baptismal promise with life-and-death earnestness. Our response to God's gift in Baptism must involve a daily turning toward the Creator of all life, to claim our gift of life within God's "tent." That turning involves offering ourselves in each moment to Christ, consecrating our lives. Such a consecration does not take us far off or high up, but happens with the materials—indeed with the very life—we each one are given. As in eucharist, we bring forth bread and wine as symbols of the daily stuff of life, so a spiritual consecration involves offering the specific elements of our daily life.

Is the longing in us so great that we will consecrate ourselves? That is the question Benedict poses, and each of us must answer it for ourselves.

Reflection

Is it more difficult for people of our time than of Benedict's to offer themselves wholly to God? It seems clear to me that such self-offering does not mean running away to somewhere else, but offering myself here and today, where I am. In some ways it does seem to me that it is harder to do that today than in Benedict's day. Today we feel we know so much more about "the way things are." God seems more remote and impersonal, sort of detached from normal everyday life; or alternatively, God in Christ is often understood so personally that we lose our fear/awe regarding the hereafter. Today there is a greater sense of complexity and of the many things on earth that need doing by people. There is a greater sense of individualism, of the urgency to use one's own gifts effectively.

But I am wandering away from the question of how I am touched by this passage. I am avoiding the real issue: Will I offer myself to God today? I doubt that there was ever a time when it was "easy" to give oneself wholly to God; yet, in some ways it is the most "natural" thing in the world to do. So, today, do I accept both the difficulty and the naturalness and plunge in? Will I simply make the offer of my life to God in this moment? I want to . . . as I wait, I realize I have given a big sigh . . . breathed out and up myself . . . given what I can in this moment!

Prayer/Response

Prologue

VERSES 45–50 (END)

We have therefore, to establish a school of the Lord's service. In the institution of it we hope to establish nothing that is harsh or oppressive. But if anything is somewhat strictly laid down, according to the dictates of equity and for the amendment of vices, or for the preservation of love; do not therefore flee in dismay from the way of salvation, which cannot be other than narrow at the beginning.

For as we progress in this our way of life and in faith, our hearts shall expand, and we shall run the way of God's commandments with the unspeakable sweetness of love. So that, never departing from his guidance, but persevering in his teaching in the monastery until death, we may by patience participate in the sufferings of Christ; that we may deserve also to be partakers of his kingdom. Amen.

Comment

This rich text may be fruitfully reflected upon many times at length. It is a summary of the purpose of the ascetical program set forth in the Rule, and thus an abbreviated commentary on the purpose of Christian spiritual discipline.

Notice particularly that the school for the Lord's service is both a continuing place of learning and a place for the exercise of the journeyman's skills. The spiritual life always involves learning, as well as action congruent with faith in the concrete opportunities presented by community life. Notice, too, that the basic text for this school is "his guidance"—not primarily the Rule itself, but rather primarily the Word of the Lord, made known in scripture and in daily revelation, and secondarily in the Rule, the abbot, and one's fellow pilgrims insofar as they are expressions of that Word.

But it is nonetheless true that we must choose where we will stand in order to follow "his guidance." For each of us there must be a place to which we are committed, and a path to which we give our obedience, or we have not truly incarnated our commitment to God. And to some extent, that means choosing something blindly, giving ourselves to something we do not fully understand, trusting that in the faithful self-offering we will be transformed so that our understanding as well as our loving is gradually deepened and enriched.

Perhaps the most powerful of these sentences is verse 49 ("For as we progress in this our way of life."). The "our way of life" is a translation of the Latin *conversatio*, the third monastic vow, representing the moment-by-moment conversion in response to God which is at the core of the Rule. Growth involves growth in *conversatio* and in faith, that is, in ever more intimate relationship with God. Benedict acknowledges that this relationship may involve fear and discipline, a darkness of vision from which one can only proceed in faith or simple obedience. But he also insists that the relationship involves the "unspeakable sweetness of love," even in this life.

Reflection

I have reflected at length upon spiritual discipline, what it is, what motivates it at best, what it is oriented toward. I have concluded that I cannot "capture" it with my mind, because it inevitably involves what I regard as opposites—strictness and fear as well as generosity and delight. It seems to me that at some point I must simply give up my struggle to understand and give myself to a regimen that has been tested by others of faith.

One of the very difficult things about such self-giving (submission) for a person like me is the sense in which it must involve a leap of faith. At some points along the journey, it is not permitted to me to ask "why." That is not because I cannot or do not want to ask, but because I haven't yet the capacity to receive the true answer. I have discovered that the very essence of spiritual formation is that it involves encounter and engagement with something/Someone of whom I am profoundly ignorant. It seems right that initially I test the path I wish to consider for its reasonableness and its compassion. But it is equally appropriate for me to realize that there are times in which my present worldview is totally inadequate for me to receive the response I seek. So I must simply continue to give myself to that which I do not understand. In such a journey, how very much I value the guides of tradition and authority that give me occasional markers, letting me know that others have trod here before me.

Prayer/Response

Interlude I

A NOTE TO THE READER

How are you doing on reading in the mode of *lectio divina?*

Perhaps you have been following Benedict's Prologue in the format outlined here, reading the words in a daily rhythm but not finding it easy to get into the additional rhythm of the reflection and prayer components. These occasional interludes at the end of major units of the Rule are intended to provide additional help to strengthen your process of *lectio.*

First, be aware that my reflection process is intended as a model, but not a rigid mold for your own. You may discover that the content of my reflection on any given day is simply out of sync with what is in your heart. Feel free to follow your own inclinations.

Perhaps the most important element in *lectio* is allowing yourself to be drawn by the specific words or phrases that attract you this day. The living Word addresses each person each day. Its method is that of attraction. Some word or phrase not necessarily central to the whole passage is calling, reaching out to you, inviting your attention. That word or phrase has a particular message, integrating the theme of the passage with some specific component of your life at this moment. So, the key to effective *lectio* is to listen for and respond to the personal attraction.

For example, in the *lectio* segment for the Prologue, verses 8–13, I was attracted by the phrase "If you hear his voice today, do not harden your hearts." But perhaps as you read over the passage reflectively, a quite different phrase jumps out at you. Perhaps "It is time now" or "ears to hear" or something else. As you say this phrase repeatedly to yourself, suddenly a connection is formed with something in your own life that you had not been aware of. Or perhaps you will gain insight about an area in which you had been resisting God, or a sense of great joy will steal over you.

The idea is to stop for a few moments, read the text slowly and expectantly, and be attentive when something "clicks." Hear what the words say to you, perhaps jot down a few notes so you don't forget, offer a short prayer, and then go on with your day. Be aware that your *lectio* will continue to nourish your heart all day. Why not try it right now?

Foundational
Matters

(Note: Before the chapter title, there is a parenthetical note as follows: *Here begins the text of the Rule. It is called a Rule because it directs the lives of those who obey it.*)

Chapter 1, The Various Kinds of Monks
VERSES 1–2

*J*t is plain that there are four kinds of monks. The first are the cenobites: that is, those who do their service in monasteries under a rule and an abbot.

Comment

There is much misunderstanding and variation in opinion about who monks are and what they do, as well as what a Rule of Life is and how to use it. In these "Comment" sections, we look closely and prayerfully at the language of the Rule itself to see what it tells us in its own terms about such questions. We ask: What is Benedict trying to say to us through his choice of language and emphasis?

Two items of note appear here. The parenthetical phrase at the beginning of the chapter may not have been in the earliest manuscripts, but it is a helpful reminder about the linguistic roots of the word "rule." Regula literally means "straight edge," as in a plumb line or carpenter's edge that sets a measure or boundary that is "true," or properly aligned. The Rule serves that purpose for the community of monks—in Benedict's case, by pointing consistently toward the Gospel and its daily applicability.

The reference here to cenobitic monks is brief, chiefly because the balance of the Rule is addressed to them. There was in Benedict's time, and still is, a tendency to think of a solitary individual engaged in heroic ascetical feats, works of charity, or spiritual heights, as the culmination of the religious life. However, taken overall, Benedict's Rule suggests something quite different: that the optimum setting for the true Christian life is in community—in the daily, committed, face-to-face interaction of very different people who share a love for God. Not only does Benedict express his preference by listing the cenobites first (community monks, the sort for whom he writes), but in verse 13 of this chapter, he calls them "the strong kind." For all practical purposes, Benedict defines the true monk this way: as one who lives in monastic community, serving under an abbot and a rule. He goes on (after this preliminary chapter) to provide a rule for the cenobitic monk that powerfully articulates the nature of the optimum communal setting for the consecrated Christian life.

Reflection

Both rule and community are severe and constant tests of my willingness to be a part of something bigger and more important than my ego. There are days when the idea that I really belong is so exhilarating that I give myself generously and with joy, and days when I feel so grumpy that I would like to withdraw from the constant pressure of otherness and incompleteness that is so exasperatingly manifest in human interaction. I guess it is precisely that tension which makes the Rule a sound and practical ascetical system, subtle as it sometimes seems. To let my ego be given away, daily and bit by bit, but intentionally: that surely is even harder work than regular fasting! Well, Benedict, I'll walk with you a while to see what you want to teach my heart.

Prayer/Response

Chapter 1
VERSES 3–5

*T*he second are the anchorites—hermits: that is, those who, not in the first fervor of monastic life, but after long probation in the monastery, have learned by the help and experience of others to fight against the devil. They go forth well-armed from the ranks of their brethren to the solitary combat of the desert. They are now able to fight safely without the support of others, by their own strength and with God's assistance, against the vices of flesh and thoughts.

Comment

This short chapter sketches a brief history of the cumulative Christian wisdom about the best ways to live the consecrated life. In the first centuries after Christ, serious Christians often found themselves embracing martyrdom. After Christianity became the official religion of the Roman Empire, many earnest Christians found faith lukewarm at best "in the world" and thus chose the way of the hermit. As generations of Christians experimented and observed carefully the results of those experiments, the awareness grew that certain forms of monastic life enhance spiritual progress, and certain forms hinder it. Consensus developed that one who is serious about the Christian life "needs training, a training that aims at absorbing the wisdom and profiting from the experience of many previous generations."[11]

Benedict's Rule clarifies the emerging idea that the cenobitic or community life is at least equally as important as the eremitic, or solitary calling. The language in this paragraph reveals much of Benedict's thinking on this matter.

The real battle is the devil's war against God for human souls. This battle is fought in every setting on earth, but becomes particularly intense whenever a human spirit determines to turn to God. The methods of the devil are subtle and carefully designed, so that one unacquainted with these tactics in general may incorrectly interpret them as personal doubts, desires, or incapacities. In any case, two things (in addition to prayer) are very helpful in combating these tactics: 1) knowledge of them, shared by those who themselves have struggled; and 2) the continual support of those now engaged side by side in the struggle.[12]

Living in community itself is often a source of temptation, when irritation, comparisons, and conflicts invite ego isolation from one another. Yet Benedict consistently treats such temptations as opportunities for self-giving in the context of the community of faith.

Reflection

I often wonder whether Christian community really exists in the contemporary parish setting. Yet, I am compelled to admit that I am given opportunity to experience the support of community far more than my pride lets me see or respond to. It seems to me that true community grows only over a long period of shared intimacy and explicit acknowledgement of Christ's empowering presence. Yet I feel that seldom either have I had or taken the opportunity to truly grow in faith and love (and trials!) with other committed Christians. What might be the reasons for this—both in me and in my environment? Even my present-day monastic friends struggle with this issue. For me, community is indeed a strenuous discipline—

and a gift of grace. I look forward to the hard interior work of exploring this discipline of community further with Benedict and in the communal contexts of my life.

Prayer/Response

Chapter 1
VERSES 6–9

A third and detestable kind of monks are the sarabaites, who have been tried neither by rule nor by experience as gold by the furnace (Prov 27:21); but, being as soft as lead, still keep faith with the world in their behavior, lying to God with their tonsure. Living in twos or threes, or even singly without a shepherd, they enclose themselves not in the Lord's sheepfolds but in their own. Their law consists in their own pleasures and desires: whatever they think fit or choose to do, that they call holy; and what they do not like, that they consider unlawful.

Comment

Strong language here! In Benedict's day the Roman world as it was known was falling apart. Many persons were intensely seeking roots, something that would give security and stability in a time of great change. Yet Benedict suggests that there are those who try to fool themselves—or others—into believing that they have found something worthwhile, but it is really a vast illusion, and a cynical one at that. When someone pretends to believe in God and is quite without inspiration, he or she either doesn't believe there is a God or believes that God has no power.

True commitment to God demands submission both to tradition and to authority. Both tradition and authority have their limits, but we are only qualified to speak to those limits after being tested. At first and for a long time we must submit to the wisdom contained in tradition and in the elders. We must find a good school and undergo strenuous training—training that will often demand something different than what we would "freely" choose. Even our wills must be taught to recognize the good, and to choose it in daily situations.

Make no mistake: there is real and awesome power here! It is a fearful thing to fall into the hands of the living God, and while we may do so gladly, it behooves us to do it with the utmost respect and obedience.

Reflection

Again I hear the phrase: "still keep faith with the world in their behavior"—and I am indicted and humbled by it! I keep forgetting how deeply my most "personal" desires have been formed by the crass, egoistic, and consumptive culture in which we live. What are most damning are those moments I realize how utterly incapable I am of choosing for myself that which (even) is my own good. I don't yet know enough to make such choices; more profoundly, I don't yet love enough. I am often aware of what a puny thing my loving is!

There is great comfort in the possibility that I can rest in and be formed by something I can trust which is "bigger" and wiser than I am. Something incarnated, something that belongs to the human community as God's gift. There is also great risk in the vulnerability entailed in giving myself to such tradition and authority. But perhaps the power of my need and my longing is now great enough to allow me to take that risk.

Prayer/Response

Chapter 1
VERSES 10–13 (END)

*T*he fourth kind of monks are those called gyrovagues, who spend their whole lives seeking hospitality in province after province, monastery after monastery, staying three or four days at a time; always wandering and never stable, they are slaves to self-will and the snares of appetite: they are in all things worse than the sarabaites.

Of the most wretched life of all these it is better to remain silent than to speak. Leaving these behind us, therefore, let us proceed, with the help of God, to make provision for the cenobites—the strong kind of monks.

Comment

Benedict has told us that he proposes a school for the service of the Lord, and in this chapter he makes clear that the school does call for some definite training. In this section, he gives a clue about the training—it is a training of the will; it is designed to liberate us from slavery to the will. One who calls himself a monk dares not be a slave to appetite/willfulness.

"Will" is a word very narrowly conceived in our culture: we think of it as kind of an executive, decisive and controlling; it almost has the features of an "iron fist." In contrast to this concept, however, the mainstream of Christian tradition has generally conceived will as a matter of the heart—not in a sentimental, flaccid way, but as a passionate harmony of one's entire being. What Benedict is opposed to is allowing ourselves to be moved by the superficial forces of appetite, which prevent our deep discovery of authentic inner necessity.

Here Benedict spells out that monks in community are the strong kind. He writes to those of us willing to explore our own experience for the ways in which community brings us into fuller life. One commentator has suggested that Benedict understands cenobites to be the "strong kind" because they are willing to recognize and to act on their needs, their weaknesses, and their longings.[13] In some essential way, Christians in community belong to and supplement one another. Thus, in community it is as important to offer our needs as it is to offer our gifts. Strength is found in the combination.

Reflection

Many times I have thought about what will is (especially when I start a new diet), and I cannot say that I know, in the sense of knowledge that wells up out of me from within.

But I believe Benedict is right, that in order to discover (and train) my will, I must be stable; that is, "stay put." I need to stay quiet for a time, undistracted by multiple stimuli and competitions for my attention, undistracted by the noisy inner cravings that would mentally draw me here and there. I need to stay put until I enter quiet, and know the greatness of God and the terrible inadequacy of myself. I need to stay put until I have passed beyond even that, and know the enduring power of love. And there, finally, I discover a depth and passion that must flow over and spend itself in compassion, charity, and adoration.

Prayer/Response

Chapter 2, What Kind of Person the Abbot Ought to Be
VERSES 1–5

An abbot who is worthy to govern a monastery must always remember what he is called, and fulfill his title through his deeds. For he is believed to hold the place of Christ in the monastery, since he is addressed by a title of His (Christ's), as the Apostle has said: You have received the spirit of adoption of sons by which we cry, "abba, father" (Rom 8:15).

Therefore, the abbot should never teach or enact or command anything contrary to the teaching of the Lord; rather let his commands and his teaching, like the leaven of divine justice, suffuse the minds of his disciples.

Comment

The word abbot is obviously taken from the intimate word of prayer that Jesus taught his disciples, "abba." St. Paul reminds us that we are enabled to use this word only when empowered by the Spirit, and that the nature of that empowering is to know ourselves to be children of God, and heirs of the promise made manifest in Christ. (Rom 8:15b–17).

What is Benedict up to with this "abba"? He has made two major shifts in the biblical tradition, but those shifts tell us not so much about a theology of abba, as about Benedict's idea of what is a monastery.[14] First, he calls Christ "Abba," as well as God the Father. Second, he applies the place of Christ to the one in charge of the monastery, and therefore calls him abbot.

The abbot is always to remember what his title signifies and act accordingly. The monks believe the abbot represents Christ to them, that he exercises the spiritual parenthood that will bring them forth into the fullness of eternal life.[15] He is the mystical head as the monks are the mystical body of the glorified Christ, who brings all things to perfection in himself.

The abbot bears the responsibility to help form the monks into Christ's way. This spiritual formation is communicated by word and example. It is rooted in the Gospel and is best communicated by a guide as well as by a "map." The abbot is this guide.

One cannot understand the role of the abbot without understanding something of the work to be done in taking on the "mind of Christ." True, the abbot has sole responsibility and authority, to which the monks are required to submit in willing obedience. But this responsibility carries with it the need to give life, ongoing even into eternity. Each monk cannot know what this life is or how to receive it except as the abbot and the Spirit help open the spaces inside him that are designed as places where God can dwell.

Reflection

How does this passage touch my life today? I realize that only recently I have begun to be aware of questions for which I am not yet capable of receiving the answers. What I must do first is to allow a capacity to be created inside me that will permit me to discover what I seek. This is humbling and frustrating. Especially because I see myself as a competent adult, sometimes I resent having to slow down, to turn off all my analytical apparatus and evaluation criteria, and simply to submit myself to a new thing as a babe—innocent, unknowing, receiving it on its own terms, until I belong enough to it and it to me for creative dialogue to begin. In a sense, an artist goes through this process in learning a craft. It is, I think, the continuing process of becoming part of Christ.

Prayer/Response

Chapter 2
VERSES 6–10

*L*et the abbot remember always that at the fearful judgment of God both his (the abbot's) teaching and the obedience of his disciples— both of these matters—will be examined. The abbot must, therefore, know that the shepherd will be considered at fault if the father of the household (paterfamilias) finds that the sheep have yielded no profit. If, on the other hand, he has exercised all pastoral diligence over a restless and disobedient flock, always striving to heal their unhealthy ways; then the shepherd will be acquitted at the Judgment of the Lord, and will say to the Lord with the prophet: I have not hidden your justice in my heart;

I have declared your truth and your salvation (Ps 40:11), but they condemned and spurned me (Isa 1:2, Ezek 20:27). Then at last the sheep disobedient to his care will be punished by overpowering death.

Comment

What obligation do we owe to our God? To speak forth God's truth when we know it; to listen for God's truth when we do not. (And to know the difference!) Obedience is one of three key vows in the Benedictine way of life, and Benedict's concept of obedience is rooted in the ancient notion of listening. Here Benedict draws from Old Testament sources: both Isaiah and Ezekiel are told to speak forth the Word, for the people have refused to listen; they are disobedient and rebellious.

The whole point of the Benedictine life is to train the heart to listen for the Word that matters, and when it is heard, to allow it to take creative root in one's heart and then burst forth, "giving growth to provide seed for the sower and bread for the eating" (Isa 55:10). Thus, at various cyclical points in life followers of the Rule are either listening, nurturing, or proclaiming. Each of these tasks is a kind of stewardship for God.

In order for God's whole work to be done, each must perform his or her part faithfully and at the right time, the abbot no less than the novice. No one is responsible for what the other refuses to do, but each is responsible not only to do his or her own part, but also to encourage others mightily to do theirs. Yet, finally it is God's work and God's ultimate judgment under which all rest.

It is often said that the Benedictine abbot is the *paterfamilias*, the head of the family, with ultimate power and authority. However, that Roman word/concept appears only once in the Rule: here, where it refers explicitly to God, to whom the abbot is accountable. Rather, the abbot is a father primarily in the sense of one who has nurtured the seed of God's Word in himself and now must proclaim it, thus mysteriously begetting it in his spiritual sons and daughters.

Reflection

Often I wonder when to speak and when to listen. The analytical part of my head wants precise rules to tell me when I am at which stage. But Benedict's helpfulness to me is on pointing out that relationships are always better than—or perhaps essential supplements to—rules.

To be faithful to the growing life of the Spirit in me, I do much better when I entrust myself to a guide who has traveled at least part of the path before me. And to be faithful to Godself, I do much better when I continue to listen for God's own living Word than when I think I have heard all that is necessary and stop listening/relating.

How to discern? First, I wonder when to speak and when to listen. If the answer to that question is to find a guide, the next question is how to find a guide. And then how to relate to a guide, once such a person is found. All this takes discernment. Again, I ask for rules, and all I get is relationship! Relationship is much harder work, and often seems very ambiguous. Perhaps the answer lies in verses 2–4 above, wherein the abbot is told to belong to Christ, and let Christ live in him. The first step is to soak myself in the gifts of God: scripture, Eucharist, tradition, and human guides. I am to train my heart to listen for the Word, and to receive it gladly. Then, as Christ comes more fully to dwell in me, my questions will begin to sort themselves out more readily. This is a school Benedict is guiding. And how much I need to be a student!

Prayer/Response

Chapter 2
VERSES 11–15

*T*herefore, when anyone receives the name of abbot he is to govern his disciples by a twofold teaching: that is, he must show forth all that is good and holy more by deeds than by words; declaring to receptive disciples the commandments of the Lord with words, but demonstrating the divine precepts to the stubborn and the simple-minded by the example of his deeds. And it should be seen in his teaching and in his own actions that those things contrary to the law of God are not to be done, lest while preaching to others, he himself be found reprobate (1 Cor 9:27); and God say to him in his sin: How is it that you recite my justice and declare my covenant with your mouth, when you hate discipline and cast my words behind you (Ps 50:16–17)? And also this: How is it that you can see a speck in your brother's eye, and not notice the plank in your own (Matt 7:3)?*

Comment

The Lord's commandments, those lessons about the good and the holy that come to us in the Christian tradition—these must be lived. They are empty words unless we take them in and allow them to form our hearts, minds, spirits, and behavior.

In ancient cultures, the main task of the parents was understood to be teaching children how to live. The orphan was bereft because he or she had no land to inherit and no skills to be learned in apprenticeship.[16] The most important gift parents gave their children was their values, their convictions about life and how it was to be lived in practice. This inner formation is truly a gift of life, in which every person needs the help of others.

The Benedictine abbot models parenthood in this sense. He is to have received what he has been taught in such a manner that he is able to pass it along through his very presence. The essence of the Christian life, represented in these passages of scripture, is that it is not enough simply to hear the Word: one must allow it to enter deeply into one's body and soul, shaping it and pouring forth fruitful response. The abbot cannot teach the Lord's commandments unless he himself has been so formed and is so living. The abbot himself must be obedient to the Word or he has nothing to teach.

A modern author puts it like this: "So few understand; because where they know, they do not obey . . . If Christ's words seem true, obey them with your whole strength and might. This is the way of life."[17]

Reflection

I find I am getting increasingly impatient with my urge to go on and on reading more "spiritual books." It is true there are many good ones; it is also true that fundamentally they all say the same thing, and it can be said in very few words indeed. What I am trying to teach myself is that my knowledge is not worth anything until it begins to become lived knowledge.

And so I long—with all my heart—simply to be true to Christ, true to the one Christ calls me to be. And I sense this calls me to less rather than more. This calls me to simplicity, gentleness, prayer, silence.

Oh, I know I will always fall short. And I know that very few will see what I am doing. And I know that the nearer to Christ I am, the more appalled I will be at my lack of charity. Even so, I long to be more drawn into the mind of Christ, and I find myself more and more allowing this longing to be my prayer.

Prayer/Response

Chapter 2
VERSES 16–22

*T*he abbot is not to make any distinction of persons in the monastery. He should not love one more than another unless he finds one better in good actions and obedience. A free-born man is not to be put before a slave who becomes a monk, except for some other reasonable cause. Although, if justice requires it, the abbot may see fit to change anyone's rank. Otherwise let each keep to his regular place, because whether we are slaves or free, we are all one in Christ (Gal 3:28, Eph 6:8) and serve alike in the army of the one Lord; for with God there is no partiality among persons (Rom 2:11).

Solely in this only are we distinguished in his sight: if we are found to surpass others in good works and in humility. Therefore, let the abbot show equal love to all and impose on all the same discipline, according to their merits.

Comment

In a sense, these verses are a lesson in discernment. Given that wisdom of the heart and the person's inner formation are the goals of the monastic life, how is the abbot to discern who is progressing well and who is to be rewarded with positions of responsibility, authority, and respect? (Benedict's evident familiarity with the Sermon on the Mount no doubt shaped his thought that all persons do indeed have their reward, but the issue is primarily that of right rewards for right motives and right actions in such a way that the kingdom of God is drawn near.)

First, and radically, the world's exterior standards—slavery or freedom, wealth or poverty, title, education, and so on—are clearly irrelevant. Each person has an important place in Christ's body.

Second, nonetheless, there are standards that we can use. Implicit here is the fact that interior dispositions do show themselves exteriorly, especially in the interactions of community. The work of the heart, the hidden action of amenability to the Spirit's graces, the evolving disposition toward the mind of Christ—all of these are manifest for the one who has eyes to see and ears to hear. And they will be manifest in two ways in particular: 1) good works, and 2) humility/obedience. Within a very few pages, Benedict will present his thinking on both these topics (Chapters 4, 5, and 7).

But something else is here. The purpose of the abbot's discernment is to know how to "discipline" and give favors to all the members of the community. This discipline/favoring is to aid the members' ongoing formation, to aid their ongoing conversion into the life of Christ, and to aid the whole community to become Christ's body. Each and all are called to the extraordinary communion characteristic of the members of the body of Christ. The abbot's work is to build toward this communion, especially by noticing and nurturing the Christ-life growing inside each member of the community.

Reflection

Benedict uses the phrase "the abbot may see fit." I wonder how I see. As my prayer deepens, I feel that many shifts occur of which I am only partly aware. Certainly some of these shifts affect my response to and even my basic perception of what is there to be seen.

I realize as I reflect on this passage that one of the key ingredients of discernment is indeed what I see—not only where my focus is, but how superficially or how deeply I am looking. For a long time, I saw only with the world's eyes; I was impressed by wealth and power and repelled by poverty and weakness. Sadly, I have not lost such perceptions altogether.

But I sense also that I am learning to see with God's eyes. What great joy it is to notice and celebrate the Christ-life growing inside so many persons! I realize that often I see that new life in others more clearly than they do "from the inside," and it is a great encouragement for me to lift it up and help them see and celebrate it too!

Prayer/Response

Chapter 2
VERSES 23–29

*F*or in his teaching the abbot should always observe the recommendation of the Apostle, in which he says: Reprove, convince, rebuke (2 Tim 4:2). That is, he should suit his action to the circumstances, mingling gentleness with sternness; showing now the rigor of a master, now the loving affection of a father, so as sternly to rebuke the undisciplined and restless, and to exhort the obedient, mild, and patient to advance in virtue. And such as are negligent and haughty we charge him to reprove and correct. Let him not shut his eyes to the faults of offenders; but as soon as they appear, let him strive, as he has the authority for that, to root them out, remembering the fate of Eli, the priest of Shiloh (1 Sam 2:11–4:18). Those of good disposition and understanding let him correct, for the first or second time, with words only; but such as are troublesome and hard of heart, proud or disobedient, let him chastise with bodily stripes at the very first offense, knowing that it is written: The fool is not corrected with words (Prov 29:19), and again, Strike your son with a rod and you will have freed his soul from death (Prov 23:14).

Comment

Usually in our *lectio*, it is well to turn first to those matters that disturb us or seem repugnant to our ways of thinking. In this passage, there are two such ingredients. One is the physical punishment, which nowadays is not something we condone for any reason. But the other, deeper issue is that of any punishment. In today's "democratic" and "modern" society, it is fashionable to believe that no one has any right to judge anyone else, nor to take action based on that judgment.

Benedict has dealt with the issue of what standards or criteria we may use in the immediately preceding verses of this chapter. But here he is dealing with the more fundamental question: Why use any standards at all?

In Chapter 4, he makes clear that one of the essential tools of the spiritual craft is to "Fear the day of judgment," and in this passage he demonstrates that the abbot must also live in such fear. Note that the 2 Timothy passage quoted here begins with the admonition: "Before God and before Christ Jesus who is to be judge of the living and the dead, I put this duty to you . . ." And Eli in 1 Samuel pleads with his sons: "[I]f (one) sins against Yahweh, who will intercede for him?" The point is, there is a day of God's judgment, and the abbot bears the heavy responsibility to account not only for his own actions, but for the souls of those entrusted to him. Often a sharp rebuke or blow, or even an honest verbal confrontation of the truth about what one is doing, will "bring a person to his senses." The abbot's responsibility is such that he may not refuse these useful tools for the purpose of God's work of converting love.

Reflection

There's a lot to chew over here. Often part of me knows that I really should speak to those I love plainly and honestly about what I see them doing to themselves. But that is so hard, because it involves at least two ingredients quite beyond my "control": one is that I must do it because of my deep love for that specific person (and I never am "naturally" utterly pure of heart in my loving). So, I usually have to go back to my prayer for a while before I can even consider such a step. The other difficulty is that their response is really wholly up to them and the Holy Spirit, and if I have got up my courage to speak at all, then I want the outcome to be what I desire (and I begin to get a vested interest, which causes me to try to control the result rather than simply speak what I see). I am driven back to prayer yet again, that I may truly release the situation and the person to God.

And yet I am acutely grateful when a true friend has spoken in this way to me, even though my first reaction is usually angry denial!

Prayer/Response

Chapter 2
VERSES 30–36

*T*he abbot ought always to remember what he is, and what he is called, and to know that to whom more is committed, more is required. And he must consider how difficult and arduous a task he has undertaken, of ruling souls and adapting himself to many dispositions. Let him so accommodate and suit himself to the character and *intelligence of each, winning some by kindness, others by reproof, others by persuasion, that he may not only suffer no loss in the flock committed to him, but may even rejoice in their virtuous increase.*

Above all let him not, overlooking or undervaluing the salvation of the souls entrusted to him, be more solicitous for fleeting, earthly, and perishable things; but let him ever bear in mind that he has undertaken the government of souls, of which he shall have to give an account. And that he may not complain for want of worldly resources, let him remember what is written: Seek first the kingdom of God and his justice, and all these things shall be added unto you (Matt 6:33), and again: Nothing is wanting to them that fear him (Ps 34:9).

Comment

The abbot has been given the name of Christ; he is entrusted with the most precious of treasures. By his scriptural allusion in verse 30, Benedict makes clear that though the abbot is a servant, he is highly placed—perhaps like the one in Luke 12:47 to whom much was committed but who did not prepare himself. If such a one defaults, there is severe punishment indeed.

What does the master's will call for the abbot to do? First, he or she is to have great regard for the unique qualities of each, dealing with each according to his or her need or capacity. This goes against our modern instinct, by which, in the name of equality/fairness, we treat all the same. It takes both discernment and skill to regard and treat each according to who they are in God's eyes.

Second, the abbot is not to allow himself to become so burdened with administrative duties that he defaults on spiritual formation responsibilities. The abbot has considerable responsibility to provide for food, clothing, housing, and security—none of which in Benedict's time (nor often since) could be taken for granted. It is easy for us to carry these burdens so heavily that they preoccupy us and consume all our energy, especially today when most human economies function on the principle of relative scarcity. But here Benedict recalls the abbot (and us!) to the radical way of the Sermon on the Mount, and reminds us that there is only one fear that is important—the fear of God. When that one fear is properly in place, all the rest falls into order. "How good Yahweh is—only taste and see! Happy the (one) who takes shelter in God!" (Ps 34:8).

Reflection

The phrases that seem most to touch me today are these: "remember who I am and what I am called" and "may not complain for want of worldly resources." It seems very important for me to remember who I am (a child of God) and what I am called (Christian). Usually I forget. In fact, recently I participated in one of those exercises in which you fill out ten slips of paper, each one completing the sentence "I am . . ." When I finished the exercise, I had listed ten different "identities" of myself. I did not even think to put down Christian on the list. Many days pass without my recalling that I am a baptized person and a child of God. How would my days be different if I were regularly to meditate on that identity of mine? For I do believe it is my most important identity.

I suppose that one of the reasons I don't take it more seriously is actually because I don't think I have the resources. I am, after all, just an ordinary human creature, with the usual quota of neuroses. I get "stuck" in many ways in my days: in the blues, in physical dis-ease, in preoccupation with my activities and engagements. There is so much to occupy me, and so little to uplift me. How could I possibly take very seriously a call God gives me to become "a holy person"? (I don't even have a good vocabulary for it.) But Benedict does take it seriously on my behalf. Even more astonishing to me than his continual lack of surprise in encountering human limitation is his constant emphasis on the ultimate human vocation. He never forgets that God longs for every one of us to "dwell in his tent." Nothing is more precious or more valuable to Benedict than my soul. Can I say the same?

Prayer/Response

Chapter 2

VERSES 37–40 (END)

et the abbot know that he who has undertaken the government of souls, must prepare himself to render an account of them. And whatever may be the number of the brethren under his care, let him be certainly assured that on the Day of Judgment he will have to give an account to the Lord of all these souls, as well as of his own. And thus,

being ever fearful of the coming judgment of the shepherd concerning
the state of the flock committed to him, while he is careful on others'
accounts, he will be solicitous also on his own. And so, while correcting
others by his admonitions, he will be himself cured of his own defects.

Comment

Here Benedict is drawing on Hebrews 13:17: "Obey your leaders
and do as they tell you, because they must give an account of the
way they look after your souls; make this a joy for them to do, and
not a grief—you yourselves would be the losers."

In this chapter, Benedict has been establishing the authority and
responsibility of the abbot. Indeed, he has actually defined monks
(cenobites) as those who "do their service in monasteries under a
rule and an abbot" (RB 1:2). So the abbot's role and functions are
foundational to the whole monastery's faithfulness to its call in
Christ. Throughout, Benedict's image of the monastic community
seems very like St. Paul's image of the "body of Christ": many members, each with his or her own gifts and weaknesses, interdependent, drawn into being by Christ the head. While the abbot plays the
incarnated role as head in Christ's name, it is always clear that the
abbot is also under Christ's sovereignty. And that the abbot is interdependent as well—his life, indeed his very soul, is deeply entwined
with the life of the members whom he serves.

Thus it is fitting to close this chapter with a reference to the profound importance of the daily deepening in the abbot's own conversion to Christ, as he grows in the Spirit even as he also conforms
his monks to the mind of Christ.

Reflection

Several years ago, a very honest retreat participant came up to me
after a conference I had conducted and said to me, "Do you dare to
speak like that without every day living that way?" It was a serious
question and not an accusation, and I was touched by it, because it
is exactly to the point. Sometimes I get so carried away with the
beauty and the power of who I am in Christ that I forget who I am
without Christ. I am so often tempted to say, "Okay, Lord, now I
understand. I can go it on my own for a while." And I neglect my
own work of humility and obedience as I allow my energies to be
focused solely on my care of and for others.

Perhaps, though, the other extreme is equally bad: to be so aware of who I am without Christ that I refuse to act when and where I am called to, because I know I can't do it alone. Obedience calls me to take authority when appropriate, even though it may cause me to carry a burden for other souls that I know I am not adequate to carry alone.

Prayer/Response

Chapter 3, Summoning the Community for Counsel
VERSES 1–6

As often as any important matters have to be transacted in the monastery, let the abbot call together the whole community, and himself declare what is the question to be settled. And, having heard the counsel of the brethren, let him weigh it within himself and then do what he shall judge most expedient. We have said that all should be called to council, because it is often to the younger that the Lord reveals what is best. But let the brethren give their advice with all the restraint of humility, and not presume stubbornly to defend their own opinion; but rather let the matter rest with the abbot's discretion, that all may submit to whatever he shall consider best. Yet, even as it becomes disciples to obey their master, so does it behoove him to order all things prudently and with justice.

Comment

In the previous chapter, we recognized the abbot's responsibility to discern and act, and noted the guidance Benedict offered in that area. This is another instance of guidance in discernment.

From a human point of view, these are astonishing verses: Why should one with sole authority consult those he supervises? And in what manner do those consulted give their opinions? Not in Benedict's time nor in ours is there anything comparable to this consultation in a secular setting, and it occurs infrequently enough in religious ones. This is a matter of listening for God's will in the recognition and expectation that in matters affecting the life of the community, God speaks not only through scripture and in the wisdom of the praying seniors, but also through the insights of every member of the body. The key phrase is "the Lord reveals . . ." Everyone in the consecrated community is listening (and learning to listen, a lifelong task) for what the Spirit is saying, aware that each person may carry the Spirit's voice.

Therefore, far from being an exercise in which a majority opinion is sought or defended, this is a case in which there is attentiveness by all gathered in this moment, to internal whisperings as well as to external voices, that the Spirit of God may be made manifest and then discerned and then acted upon.

The abbot is to choose that which is salubrious (health-giving) for the body, his community.

Reflection

Learning to listen for the will of God is quite a task. Oddly, I seldom discover it in myself when I approach it directly. Usually it is revealed more readily when my approach is indirect. If I say to myself, gritting my teeth, "Today I will listen for the will of God," it rarely produces fruit. But if instead I pray, willing to wait and be silent and give up the initiative . . . and if I am very attentive to each thing or person I encounter during the day, just enjoying the wonder that each is . . . and if I give thanks for all that is given so abundantly to me in that day (air and warm water and birds singing and good smells and a phone call from dear Aunt Sally), then, unaccountably, I find myself more attuned to the presence of God's kingdom in this place and in this moment. And I find the "big decisions" are naturally and easily birthed in such a presence.

Prayer/Response

Chapter 3
VERSES 7–13 (END)

*L*et all, therefore, follow the Rule in all things as their guide, and *from it let no one rashly turn aside. Let no one in the monastery follow the will of his own heart: nor let anyone presume insolently to contend with his abbot, either within or without the monastery. But if he should dare to do so, let him be subjected to the Rule. The abbot himself, however, must do everything with the fear of God, and in observance of* *the Rule: Knowing that he will have without doubt to render to God, the most just judge, an account of all his judgments.*

If it happens that less important matters have to be transacted for the advantage of the monastery, let him take counsel with the seniors only, as it is written: Do all things with counsel, and you will not afterwards repent of it (Sir 32:24).

Comment

The cenobitic monastery is defined as monks living together under a Rule and an abbot (RB 1:2). Throughout the Rule, there is an effort to balance these three essential components of the life: the Rule, the abbot, and mutual obedience within the community. In each case, both an authority and responsive obedience to that authority are involved. Both of these are matters that are very elusive in our time. Rather than trying to define authority and obedience, let us simply pay attention to the way Benedict describes them in context, and reflect on possible relevance for us. At the minimum, as used here, obedience seems to involve relinquishment of personal willfulness.

Even the abbot is to be obedient to the Rule. Perhaps the passage Benedict quotes from Sirach helps clarify what is intended here:

> The (one) who fears the Lord will accept his correction . . . Those who fear the Lord will have justice done them, and make their good deeds shine like a light . . . If (one) fears the Lord, evil will not come his way, again and again he will be rescued in his trials. (Sir 32: 14, 16; 33:1)

The key is fear of the Lord–knowing that we are in fact under authority, a steward of the God of creation. Stewardship involves thought and care, but also obligation, and finally, freedom, because full responsibility lies with Another, one we can call upon in time of trial for deliverance.

Reflection

I turn "obedience" over and over in my mind, wondering about it. How does it apply to my life? Perhaps the idea of stewardship helps, because stewardship seems to involve obedience in two directions. The steward must care for that which has been placed in his or her charge. He or she must know its essential qualities and what it requires for health and optimum growth, being attentive and responsive to it. This careful listening to the nature of a thing or a person is a kind of obedience, and might, for example, involve watering the lawn when I would rather be reading a book.

However, another direction is involved, because stewardship implies also an obedience to one who assigns or gives responsibility, a Giver. That would seem to imply recognizing that what I have is gift and then caring for it accordingly. Perhaps it suggests my being responsible in the care of my own body, mind, and spirit so that I am able to care for my charges. And certainly, it involves knowing that I have help: there is someone I can call when I'm in "over my head." I don't have to know all or be everything, but just do the best I can.

And yet I sense obedience to a Giver goes even deeper than that. Perhaps careful attentiveness to all I have been given, "charges" and capacities included, eventually allows me to see into them so fully that I discover the mystery they embody, and find myself lost in wonder. Surely the joy and gratitude evoked at such a time are part of obedience!

Prayer/Response

Chapter 4, The Instruments of Good Works
VERSE 1

In the first place to love the Lord God with all your heart, all your soul, and all your strength (Ex 20:2; Matt 22:37–39; Mark 12:30–31; Luke 10:47).

Comment

In a sense, this chapter of the Rule is an icon for the entire Rule itself, a summary, a window opening onto the whole vision of the life to which the Christian is called. Benedict sees the world as God's gift; not as something external and separate, but rather as a gift filled with God's own self shared with us in all the moments of the day. Paradoxically, the way we respond best to God's presence within the ordinary occasions of each day is to offer each of those occasions to God. God is involved in everything; we come to know that by offering everything to God.

This work of offering or consecrating every moment to God is the basic work of Christian formation. It is thus practiced and learned and deepened in us within every moment. This simple task is a life-long one.

The Rule is designed to help us discover and be faithful to ways to undertake this daily task of consecration. This chapter of the Rule in particular is a special and privileged *lectio*, the type we are undertaking in this book. This chapter, culled from scripture, is a poem; especially in the Latin, the rhythmic cadences allow it to be memorized, taking root in the person's heart. Thus, it can be carried throughout the day as a way to hold priorities before our eyes so we are never separated from God. It becomes a way to bring our grounding in prayer into our daily actions.

Benedict begins with the first Hebrew commandment—the one Jesus himself lived by and passed along to us, transformed by what his life teaches us.

Perhaps we wonder how the emphasis of Benedictine spirituality can be characterized as distinct from other Christian forms. This first central tool gives us an important clue. Here Benedict offers his summary of what he learns through prayer about how to live life. We might ask him: What is the basic reality which you meet/encounter at the deepest point of your prayer life? We might expect an answer something like this: "I am a worm. And how astonishing, God, that you should redeem me." Yet pondering Benedict's spirit in the Rule, we sense that his answer moves in quite a different way, rushing forth like this: "Oh, God, what a wonder you are! My heart cannot encompass the Glory you give forth, and yet I rejoice to join in your praises with all the angels and saints!"

Obviously, both responses are essential to the Christian life, but they involve very different emphases. It is enormously revealing of Benedict's spirituality that this crucial list of instruments begins with these four words: LOVE THE LORD GOD!

Reflection

Love the Lord God! Sometimes I let this short phrase be my prayer word for the day, repeating it over and over to myself as I wash the dishes, drive to work, talk with associates, brush my teeth, work on the computer.

When I think of the phrase with my mind, as a command, I get confused and I don't know where to start. But when I let it be the prayer of my heart and my body, I am comforted (in the old sense of being both heartened and strengthened), because I know this phrase to be something the Spirit does in me. I know it to be one of those "effective words" of God, whose empowering presence is taking root in me.

Prayer/Response

Chapter 4
VERSES 2–9

*T*hen, to love your neighbor as yourself. You are not to kill, not to commit adultery, not to steal, not to covet (Rom 13:9). You are not to bear false witness (Matt 19:18; Mark 10:19; Luke 18:20). You must honor all (1 Pet 2:17). You must not do to another what you would not have done to yourself (Tob 4:16; Matt 7:12; Luke 6:31).

Comment

Much might be said about loving neighbor as self, and Benedict does say much throughout the Rule as he instructs us how to receive Christ in ourselves and in others. Indeed, this loving is an essential dimension of the Benedictine way of loving God and inevitably involves the related commandments that follow. Here Benedict is concerned as a first priority to state the practical commandments that bear immediately upon life in a voluntary community.

We notice that Benedict slightly shifts the order of presentation of the Ten Commandments.[18] In this way, he presents us with three pairs of rules, first stipulating the negative and then the positive aspect. He writes:

1. Do not steal from anyone; but more, do not even covet something another has.

2. Do not lie about anyone; but more, honor each person's essence.

3. Do not kill anyone; but more, do not violate their integrity and yours by adultery or even the avoidance of charity.

These are practical ways of loving our neighbor and ourselves, essential as the foundational elements of community life, summed up finally in that phrase used by Jesus in the Sermon on the Mount to capture the essence of the Law and the Prophets:

Treat others as you would like them to treat you.

Reflection

On many days I feel like a rotten person, and it's not so easy for me to value myself as God does. At such times, I am very hard to live with! The great comfort of these simple, practical rules is that they are doable. Simple intention suffices to be kind to one's neighbors, friends, family, and acquaintances. It is not difficult to be kind; indeed, it is a great relief simply to decide that's your intention and to act upon it. Oftentimes, indeed, that is all I would ask of others for myself . . . They don't need to be deeply sensitive to the inner qualities of my soul if they are simply willing to be kind. And it is helpful to remember that on this little, unostentatious basis, the Christian life is founded. Kindness is faithfulness to God in little things, on which any deeper level of commitment must be based.

Prayer/Response

Chapter 4

VERSES 10-19

*T*o deny yourself, in order to follow Christ (Matt 16:24; Luke 9:23). To chastise the body (1 Cor 9:27): not to seek after delicate living; to love fasting. To relieve the poor; to clothe the naked, to visit the sick (Matt 25:36), to bury the dead. To help in affliction; to console the sorrowing.

Comment

Having set forth the basic commandments, Benedict turns to the central motive of this Christian life—Christ himself. He reflects on Peter's confession, realizing that when we know who Jesus is, the knowledge requires radical changes in the orientation and in the outcome of our daily lives. Those of us who follow Christ would gain life; we must then "deny ourselves." What, in practical terms and from the gospel perspective, might this mean? This is Benedict's question, and what follows is the fruit of his reflection and his integrated tradition.

He begins with the great Jewish triad, so much a part of Jesus' own life: prayer, fasting, and almsgiving. Prayer, because that is how we come truly to know and be nourished by Christ. Fasting and other such bodily disciplines to train our bodies as servants and fellow workers, rather than as instruments so delicate as to lack the capacity to serve wholly. Almsgiving and service to the sick or afflicted in order to discipline our spirits toward generosity and habitual self-giving.

Reflection

I reflect on these principles of the ascetical life, wondering how they apply to me. What do I think these fundamental disciplines mean for me?

Prayer: openness to communication with God, sometimes in words and sometimes in silence; nourishment;

Fasting: "breaking the cycle between hunger and satisfaction long enough to receive whatever it is I desire."[19]

Almsgiving: teaching myself the freedom to share the best of my life; generosity.

I remember how central these three were in Jesus' life, and I can sense how important they are to life under Benedict's Rule. I have not thought much about how they can be integrated into my own life in a practical way, and I see that as necessary. Preliminarily, I notice that prayer becomes increasingly important to me. The more I do it, the more I need it! It also seems that as my prayer grows, a natural generosity opens up in me, so that "almsgiving" seems naturally to follow prayer. I have less need to cling to any possessions; I am freer to give away what I know to be gift. However, I still do not feel a natural disposition to fasting. Perhaps I am unnecessarily anxious about getting enough; in any case, there is unfreedom in me in that connection at present. Here is room to grow.

In all these spiritual disciplines, Benedict seems to me to offer a balanced approach. Above all, he looks at spiritual disciplines insofar as they show up in daily activities. He seems be aware that daily habits are important things. What I actually practice, over the long haul, day in, and day out, profoundly forms my spiritual capacity. I never know when I will be called upon to undertake some important task. So often the key issues in the spiritual life are those moments calling forth a spontaneous and immediate response. The way I have trained myself through my daily habits will make a great deal of difference in my capacity to receive the grace God will give me in such moments.

I feel that Benedict advises me that any temporary or extreme behavior is less helpful for my spiritual as well as for my physical well-being than a simple, steady, day-by-day response.[20] I want my spiritual disciplines to be based on this observation.

Prayer/Response

Chapter 4
VERSES 20–21

*T*o keep aloof from worldly actions; to prefer nothing to the love of Christ.

Comment

This book is titled *Preferring Christ* because that phrase captures the essence of the Benedictine spirit. This phrase—to prefer Christ, to let the love of Christ come first—occurs both here and in the penultimate chapter (72:11), almost like bookends framing all that is carried within these pages.[21] The preference for Christ in the Rule is much deeper than the few verses specifically using this phrase; throughout the whole Rule, preference for Christ is implicit in everything.

We might begin to explore this preference by asking: Who is Christ? How does Benedict understand the nature of Christ? Perhaps surprisingly to our way of thinking, Benedict seldom refers to Christ as "friend," though there is clearly an intimate relationship. Yet for him, Christ is primarily one to be respected—Lord, Father, King: one who carries authority over us.[22] Christ is also one who can be trusted. Benedict often thinks of Christ as the Good Shepherd, or the tender and loving pastor, the one who lays down his life for us. And Christ is also Rock, the steady one who has power over all the powers of darkness and light, showing us the right way.

It is fundamental to the Rule that this Christ (our Lord, Shepherd, Rock) is embodied in the many people we greet each day. That is especially true of those we serve—strangers and the sick—but also of those to whom we owe obedience—the abbot. The nearness of Christ in the word of God as well as in the very pots and pans (31:10) means that all things may reveal Christ as we learn reverence and gratitude for the world God has given.

If this is who Christ is for Benedict, what does it mean to prefer this One? To prefer someone is to wish to be with him or her, to choose him or her over all other options. It is to give the loved one top priority, to put the beloved ahead of everything else. It is simply to find the person desirable. As always, Benedict is less interested in theory than in practice. Throughout the Rule, he gives hundreds of examples of what preferring Christ means in practical ways: it is no more complex than that every encounter presented to us each day is an opportunity to give and receive the love of Christ. And it is every bit that demanding.

Because Christ is who he is, the demand is matched by a gift. It is the love of Christ that we are to prefer. And fortunately, that phrase carries a double meaning, in English as well as in Latin: the love of Christ means both Christ's love for us as well as our love for him! The burden of preferring Christ does not rest solely on our shoulders. In everything we do, Christ's love has first moved toward us, helping us prefer him. Let our lives be centered in the awesome fact of this love. This preference is at the heart of the Rule.

Reflection

Almost every time I think about it, I feel that I don't know Christ nearly well enough. Yet I also have a deep hunger to know more about him. Perhaps it is like any love relationship: the more I know of someone, the more I feel there is yet to know! A person is a great and wonderful mystery, more so when he or she is deeply loved. And this person, Christ, is the best mystery of all.

I like the idea that this love is a matter of desirability, a matter of almost erotic loving. Because the part of me that draws me forward, that attracts and pulls me so strongly toward another, causes me to run in eagerness to be with my beloved. It is quite a different feeling than the heavy "I ought to" kind of feeling, in which I am primarily conscious of how unworthy I am. And, I do think there is room in erotic longing for great respect and regard, a deep awe and reverence for the wonder of another.

Preferring Christ . . . might I actually live each day in such a way that I look with eagerness to discover my beloved Christ greeting me within each ordinary moment of it? I'm reminded of that silly song fragment: "It's a lovely day today, and whatever you've got to do, I'd be so happy to be doing it with you!"

Prayer/Response

Chapter 4
VERSES 22–28

Not to gratify anger: not to harbor a desire of revenge, not to foster guile in your heart, not to make a feigned peace, not to forsake charity. Not to swear, lest perchance you perjure yourself; to utter truth from your heart and your mouth.

Comment

If Christ is the center, that has practical applications in the way we live each day. In the modern world, so concerned with motives and with concepts, there is often almost a contempt for practical lists of good works such as those we find in the latter part of Paul's letters or in the Sermon on the Mount. Such New Testament sources are Benedict's favorites, and his mind turns toward them far more often than to such passages as the poetic first chapter of the Gospel of John.

Partly this is because of his practical nature. Largely it is because he truly believes that our sanctification is realized in our daily choices and habits.

As humans, we often feel strong passions such as lust, anger, or profound impulses for ego protection that cause us to puff ourselves up. A large part of standard Christian ascetical practice is devoted to the rooting out vices such as these, and strengthening the corresponding virtues.

Notice the simplicity of Benedict's ascetical pattern: let it go. It is a sort of mundane meditation-on-the-spot: be attentive to impulses within yourself and when you notice their presence, release them at once. Simply live the day, being attentive to yourself, to God, to your family; and trust that if you are aware and attentive—and prayerful!—the Spirit will be free to move powerfully within you and your setting. It is an asceticism whose dynamics are rooted in the practice of humility and trust.

Reflection

Recently I have become aware what a demanding spiritual discipline is this simple practice of attention to the present moment! At times of stress, I find myself enmeshed in a complex pattern of self-denunciation, guilt, frustration, and weariness, which effectively blocks me from being aware of what is actually going on.

Basic simplicity of the heart, rooted in the truth about what really is, turns out to be the disposition of profound spiritual maturity. I find myself having to begin over and over, needing to start yet again as a novice, in humility. Yet, oddly, there is often a greater gentleness and self-care in such simplicity than there is in complex psychological assessment. Both are needed, of course, but how liberating it is to be able to imagine and hope for the possibility of simplicity as the truest reality of my being!

I think the key here is keeping my focus on Christ. If I forget that focus in an exclusive attention on my own impulses, it is easy to become buried in the quicksand of my own fears and imaginings, losing my capacity to be authentic, spontaneous, indeed, present to the here and now, where Christ is.

Prayer/Response

Chapter 4
VERSES 29–33

*D*o not render evil for evil *(1 Thess 5:15, 1 Pet 3:9). Do no wrong to anyone; rather, bear patiently the wrong done to yourself. Love your enemies (Matt 5:44; Luke 6:27). Do not render cursing for cursing, but rather blessing. Bear persecution for justice's sake (Matt 5:10).*

Comment

Love your enemies. Why is this theme so frequent in the New Testament and emphasized here by Benedict as direct guidance for our lives? We have heard it often, but find it very difficult to practice.

Not only is it hard work: it often seems quite foolish. Why then does it reappear repeatedly as something fundamental to Christian life? Its advocates seem to imply some sort of conviction about the way things really are, as distinguished from the way things seem to be. Benedict suggests not simply an expression of a moral duty, but rather an awareness of the way goodness comes into being in a situation that needs reconciliation.

His awareness seems to hint at something like this: if evil is brought into a situation, it appears to have great power to provoke and evoke evil response from others in the situation. But if even one person resists that instinctive reaction and gently but firmly offers a response of goodness (that fragile flower of tenderness and well-wishing), if even one continues to look for and find Christ in an evil situation or person, then, in some mysterious way, goodness is not only released there but also prevails!

This awareness is also reflected in 1 Peter 3: "Instead pay back with a blessing. That is what you are called to do." Cooperation with the fundamentally powerful force of goodness in the world must be what Benedict is affirming and encouraging here.

Reflection

I have often thought recently about the "entitlement ethic"—the idea that each person is entitled to (has by right of birth) things like a comfortable home, a good job, several cars and TV sets, rich food, good health, dutiful children, and so on. At first encounter, the entitlement ethic seemed to me to be a shocking point of view, but gradually I have come to realize how very pervasive it is, even in myself. When I don't get what I want or expect, when people aren't nice to me, when I feel I have done my part and others aren't cooperating (on my scheme), I am often resentful and inclined to "hit back."

I especially notice such resentment when I feel I am not liked or appreciated, or when someone seems very different from me, or when another "gets in my way" when I'm doing something "important." There are hundreds of situations in a week that cause me to feel unjustly put upon, and I want to "give back" to others the baloney I feel has been given to me.

And I think Benedict is saying to me here that each one of these impulses is a golden opportunity for my sanctification. Each time I am tempted to strike back, I can choose instead to bless. And if I do bless, I am helping to bring about not only my own sanctification but, infinitely more importantly, God's kingdom on earth—whether or not I can see it!

Prayer/Response

Chapter 4
VERSES 34–38

*D*o not be proud, nor given to wine (Titus 1:7, 1 Tim 3:3). Do not be a glutton, nor given to much sleeping, nor slothful (Rom 12:11).

Comment

What is the relationship between serious commitment to God and physical or bodily disciplines? In our time, we might well ask: Is there any relationship? Throughout the ages, Christian practice has involved some physical austerity, but its nature has varied widely. Benedict's response to this question, as to so much else, is moderation.

At first, we might wonder at the combination in this listing of pride, alcoholism, gluttony, and sloth, until we realize that they are alike in taking a good thing too far. In themselves, self-regard, pleasures of food and drink, and rest are all gifts of God and to be enjoyed. But when they become excessive and addictive (controlling us instead of our controlling them), then they are severe barriers to the consecrated life.

One of the most difficult issues we have to face in living out the consecrated life is the right balance between enjoyment of the good things of earth and the longing for possession of them, which results in our very souls being possessed by them. There are more serious and evil barriers to the spiritual life than these physical excesses, but few are more widespread or persistent. Perhaps the key to balance here rests in the discovery that exaggerated involvement with the physical is often a frantic effort to hide from ourselves or from others the realization of our basic incompleteness. By physical excess, we are frequently ignoring or refusing the interdependence of relationship with God.

Benedict's citation from Romans reminds us of the importance of such a relationship: Never flag in zeal (not slothful); but on the contrary, allow the Spirit to fill you, realizing that you are engaged in service with/for the Lord (paraphrased, Rom 12:12). In daily life, the material and the spiritual are interpenetrated, because the whole created world expresses its Creator.

Reflection

The spread of material excesses and addictive behavior in our society today is awesome. Indeed, I find myself struggling from time to time with compulsive consumption. The more I try to "kick the habit" (cigarettes, alcohol, food), the more strenuous the resistance I encounter. Or, I find myself developing an addiction to some disciplinary practice as a substitute for another addiction. (There is some evidence that people who use biofeedback machines to reduce stress addiction become "addicted" instead to the machine's feedback!)

What is at issue here? I don't know for sure, but gradually my experience moves me in the direction of Benedict's thought. At the bottom of all this compulsive consuming is a painful awareness that I am incomplete, like half a clamshell, or a couple of notes apart from a musical phrase. My addictions help me drug myself away from this awareness. If instead I choose to live with my incompleteness, entering it fully, I discover in the heart of my longings the truth that I am partial because complete only in relationship with God. The key to any spiritual discipline for me is this willingness to experience the pain of my present inadequacy, allowing myself to know it as a reminder of my true wholeness-in-love.

Prayer/Response

Chapter 4
VERSES 39–40

*D*o not murmur or speak evil of others.

Comment

Here Benedict is concluding a section on personal behavior begun at verse 10, "To deny oneself in order to follow Christ." What follows is a group of key issues in learning to place God first, minute by minute, each day:

1. fasting and almsgiving

2. preferring Christ

3. dealing with strong emotions

4. confidence in God

5. dealing with excesses of every type; and now,

6. basic disposition.

We notice the interaction between practical issues and attitude toward God. We notice too that "disposition" sums up both, with its focus on the prevailing quality of one's actions and character. Personal disposition is revealed in murmuring, a term often used by Benedict in the Rule.

What is it to be a murmurer or a grumbler? Fundamentally, it is a refusal of the present moment, a refusal of what has been given in this time and place as adequate for me and/or worthy of God. There are many ways to refuse the present moment. One mode is always to be seeing the kingdom of God "out there" or "elsewhere." Another is always to be dissatisfied with what is here. One may also ignore God by keeping one's vision on the far horizons, or by rejecting what is given in the present vicinity.

Implicit in murmuring is the idea that things "should be" different: "should" because I deserve or need better, or even "should" because God deserves or needs better. But to impose on the present my idea of some different possibility is to miss the fullness of this present moment. C. S. Lewis captures this problem so well in *Perelandra*, where he refers to the clinging of the memory to something past, thus refusing the pleasure of the given present.[23]

In a sense, to speak ill of others involves the same kind of dynamic—to lay upon them some sort of expectation of what they "should" be like, and to judge them against that, instead of being fully present to who they actually are, in their uniqueness before God, in their similarities to me, and in their differences from me. If I am truly present to another person, I cannot fully penetrate his or her uniqueness, so he or she remains mysterious and attractively unknowable/unfolding to me. If I am really present to another person, I cannot separate myself from him or her, that is, set myself up as "objective" judge, for I have entered into the person's experience in such a way that I share his or her essence.

Obviously, there is a place for "envisioning" possibilities, but murmuring and detracting are ways of saying "no" to what is, and thus of closing off rather than opening up God's emerging kingdom. They are ways of refusing what God offers abundantly in this sanctified place and time—sanctified because Godself is revealed in it, if only we are open to receive.

Reflection

Last week I found myself half-listening to the dinner-table conversation of the person across the table from me, neglecting what he was actually saying, so that I could place him in a neat category in my mind. ("Oh, ho! He is such-and-such a type, and I always can expect certain behavior from that sort. I am of course in a more distinguished category than he, so nothing of value can occur here . . . etc., ad nauseum.") And I realized with a start just how much I was closing myself off from any possibility of meeting God—or even my dinner companion—in that moment.

And grumbling is like that, too: when I am busy complaining about how hard this work is or how tired I am, I am gaining "control" of the situation—fitting it into my "known" categories—at the expense of seeing any newness breaking through. A hundred times a day I catch myself dreaming of the past or planning the future, effectively closing myself off from the mystery of the present. I think Benedict hopes I will learn to see this and practice making the shift back to the moment. My desire to have order and to be in control is to confine the present into an unnecessarily restricted channel that cannot contain the extravagant abundance of the daily gifts of God. When I can shift to full presence in the here and now, I often find my heart full and my spirit high and lifted up. How much more God longs to give than I to receive!

Prayer/Response

Chapter 4

VERSES 41–43

*P*ut *your hope in God. Attribute any good that you see in yourself to God and not to yourself; but recognize and always impute to yourself the evil that you do.*

Comment

The metaphor that comes to mind is that of an accounting ledger. On one side is God's account, with its debits and credits. On another side is the Christian's account, with its debits and credits. Benedict is saying that every time something good happens, even if it seems you have achieved it on your own, credit it to God's account. And every time evil or sin occurs, debit it to your own account. Thus, all the credits go to God and all the debits go to you. It is a very out-of-balance ledger.

At first, this seems grossly unfair. But as we enter more deeply into the reflective life, it increasingly seems to reflect the true situation. If the quality of goodness is revealed in our predisposition, our first impulse, then self-honesty forces acknowledgment of the poverty of our own intentions. Over and over we realize how weak is our will to goodness, how greatly we are dependent on the grace of God in even the most minor matters.

If the first response to the unbalanced ledger is anger at its unfairness, the second response is often that of great fear or utter despair. For we are quite simply nothing in the only measures that count. This realization is the first essential movement toward salvation, because salvation requires us to know how profoundly we need God. It is this realization that prompts the whole of Chapter 7 and the Rule's continuing emphasis on humility.

But there is a parallel movement, also essential to salvation, and that is the willingness to give up, to hand over, our fear and despair as well as our pride. God has come to us in Christ and is now one of us; God gives us God's own Spirit as inner resource, assuring us of God's desire that we share fully in the reconciliation and wholeness of the world. Hope is warranted!

Reflection

To know how best to be God's partner in daily life is one of the most difficult tasks I have. Perhaps someday it will be easier, but at this moment I find it confusing and awkward. I keep falling off the path in one direction or another. Some days I feel so important, so good, so righteous, so effective for God; I can do it all myself! Some days I feel unable even to love my family, I feel so utterly remote from love and sunk in despair. My sense is that I do best when I give up thinking primarily about how I'm doing and focus my attention instead on God's overwhelming generosity. Then my heart overflows with gratitude, tears, and responsive love that seem to bring all things into harmonious relationship quite naturally.

Prayer/Response

Chapter 4
VERSES 44–47

*F*ear the day of judgment: be in dread of hell. Ardently desire everlasting life with deep spiritual longing. Keep death daily before your eyes.

Comment

Benedict is shifting to another issue. Until now, he has given a variety of instructions about the daily conduct of life. Now he begins to probe more deeply: he is exploring directly the reasons why our daily conduct matters and the spiritual dimensions of daily action.

At first, most of us tend to slide quickly over these verses because the language feels "out of date." Generally we moderns do not often think of the "four last things,"—that is of sin, death, hell, and judgment—and when we do, it is with a curious mixture of discomfort and puzzlement. And yet, as we reflect upon Benedict's words here, it occurs to us that underneath these seemingly obsolete concepts there must be something relevant for us.

The underlying point here is that what we do with our lives really does matter; in some way far beyond our conscious understanding, each action of each day does cumulatively draw us either closer to God or further away. Each of us is invited to ponder more deeply for ourselves how we understand the nature of that motion. The pondering helps us discover the reality. And then we need to keep the awareness of this reality foremost in our minds and hearts as a guide for our every action. Jesus' way of saying this is "Stay awake" in Matthew 24:42–25:13: "Stay awake, because you do not know either the day or the hour."

Reflection

I have often tried to imagine what heaven or hell might be like, in some terms that might make sense to me, and I always have to give up, because they are beyond my imagination. But what I can begin to glimpse is what Benedict suggests in the intense phrases: "dread" and "deep spiritual longing." As I grow in faith, I realize increasingly that do I exist in fullness only because God is near. And my longing for the nearness of God deepens and my dread of being without God grows. I think heaven and hell must be somewhere along that continuum.

How odd that one small act of kindness or indifference has anything to do with eternal life! And yet, once I begin to see it that way, how comforting the sense that there is some continuity between the fact of charity here and whatever life is like there. My hunch grows that it is by these daily acts that I begin to build habits or dispositions that draw me closer to God or take me further away, until one day I will realize that the kingdom has already come and I did not know it.

Prayer/Response

Chapter 4
VERSES 48–49

*K*eep guard at all times over the actions of your life, knowing for certain that God sees you everywhere.

Comment

These verses suggest one of the key principles of the Rule: the awareness that we are always in God's presence.[24] This foundational element of the consecrated life has been called "habitual recollection" —the habit of being collected (brought together) into the truth about ourselves and about God. Such a habit is not "natural" in the sense that it is not the normal state of consciousness for most human beings. But it is natural in the sense that it is the fullest and most accurate awareness of what it is to be human. It is that state of being in which our hearts overflow with the unspeakable sweetness of love (Prologue 49).

The next few verses of the Rule go on to describe how this constant presence can be a source of strength in times of temptation, but it is well to dwell here for a moment to allow these verses in their fullness to enlarge our hearts. God's constant gaze is profoundly an expression of God's unutterable love, tenderness, and care for us, against all expectation. The Holy One of Israel is our Shepherd, and we are God's people! (Ps 95: RB 9:3).

In this sense, keeping guard at all times means not only living in faithfulness to those disciplines that curb excesses and guide intentions, but also watching with eager expectancy for the ways in which God will love us this day. One of the best ways to develop the practice of the presence of God is to reflect afterward upon the events of the day, with your eyes open to see and your ears open to hear God's presence and voice within those events. Discovering how God has loved us by reflection upon the last hour gives us greater longing to watch for God's presence in the next one!

Reflection

For some time now I have developed a rhythmic pattern of reflection on and expectancy for the Spirit's presence in my life. But I confess myself to be periodically overwhelmed by the power and purposefulness with which I seem to be carried ever deeper into the divine life. I begin to suspect that as I reflect upon past experiences, God uses that process to enlarge my heart so that I am able to receive even greater "doses of love" in future experiences. As I reflectively appreciate the work of God that has been done in me and for me, the value and the capacity are made greater in me as God "appreciates" me. My attention is the method God uses to help me become a more effective channel of God's presence within the ordinary. So, to me, "watch" means not only "watch out," but also "watch for" and celebrate!

Prayer/Response

Chapter 4
VERSE 50

*D*ash down at the feet of Christ your evil thoughts, the instant that they come into your heart; and lay them open to your spiritual father.

Comment

Again Benedict refers to Psalm 137, as in the Prologue (see *lectio* on verse 28): at the first instant, dash temptation against the feet of Christ! It has a kind of quaint ring about it, and yet what a simple and practical device for so much that is made so complicated in so many forms of Christianity (and psychology).

At once give it to Christ. Do not let it take root.

This particular foundational element flies in the face of much that many modern "twice-born's"[25] seem to experience. Such sensitive spirits seem burdened by pain and sin, haunted by continuous temptations, drawn back again and again into the whirlpool of pain and suffering from which there often seems no relief. And it only makes it more frustrating when the "once-born" brothers and sisters blithely speak of "thinking positively" or "letting go and letting God." And yet, without superficiality, all can sense the rich beauty in Benedict's assurance that we are all God's children, constantly in God's care, with Christ's protection at every moment.

This attitude is well demonstrated in one of the stories told of Benedict.[26] Apparently one day a young novice was assigned to hold a light while Benedict dined. It is said that the novice found himself thinking angry and resentful thoughts about why a person as important and valuable as he should be required to undertake such a menial task. He had not quite realized that the thoughts were an unbidden and powerful temptation to pride, when Benedict looked up gently and admonished firmly, "Brother, cross yourself at once!" Gentle but firm; loving while realistic; insistently pressing the call to every person to share God's own life: such is the Rule.

Reflection

Lately I have been so moved by the idea that all the many fears that beset me need to be put in context by the greatest fear of all: the fear of God! I've seen the possibility of letting the other fears assume their proper proportion in relation to that one. The fear of God contains within it the deepest charity; indeed, it is the "negative face of charity."[27] Perhaps this is an odd way to understand the meaning of the phrase "perfect love casts out fear," but it is one that has more power for me than the sentimental sort of love I previously envisioned. I need a strong and powerful antidote to the strong and powerful fears and temptations that beset me. I am slowly learning that these negative pulls are puny things compared to God's great love. But what a great practice to keep setting the two side by side in my own experience, and to learn their relative value!

I long to let everything in my life find its natural order in relation to the one thing necessary. To remember that Christ has won the final victory, and that victory is actually available for me in this moment, because God never ceases to watch over me. I am hungry not just to believe in, but also to live in, the reality of that.

Prayer/Response

Chapter 4
VERSES 51–54

*K*eep your mouth from evil and wicked words. Do not be excessively talkative. Do not speak vain words or words intended only to provoke laughter. Do not love excessive laughter.

Comment

How little we know about silence today! We think of it as the absence of noise, rather than as a fertile soil for the development of wisdom. Compared to other rules of this time, Benedict's Rule is relatively moderate about silence. Yet Benedict firmly insists on the importance of a harmonious relationship between words and silence. Benedict seems to be suggesting that there is an economy of words and laughter, that the fewer they are, the more apt they are to contain wisdom.[28] Indeed, there is a suggestion that we can become captive to excess with words and laughter, as with other good things.

Everything in the Rule is oriented toward the Word and the obedient hearing of the Word. When language contributes to that, it is honored, even in the humble routines of the workshop.[29] When language claims our attention for its own sake, drawing us away from Christ, then it is to be quickly curtailed.

It is for this reason that silence finds its place along with these other foundational elements of the consecrated life: it provides a rich fertilizer facilitating the growth of the fragile bud of the soul toward God. It contributes greatly to our capacity to hear the daily Word of God addressed to us.

Reflection

I am aware that often so-called humor carries a considerable weight of anger and prejudice. I have tried to teach myself neither to offer nor to encourage such humor, but occasionally I find myself caught up again by the realization that I have been cruel, when I thought all I wanted to be was entertaining.

"To be entertaining". . . maybe that is the crux of it for me. One of my truly painful childhood memories involves such an incident. I had become friends with a neighbor girl, a shy and kind but not very popular person, who was also the niece of our classroom teacher. On several occasions when I visited her, he was also at her home. One day on the playground, I found myself the center of a group of the "popular kids" and I was "entertaining" them by exaggerating stories about our teacher's behavior at her home. Suddenly I saw her stricken face on the edge of the crowd, and I called out boldly, "Isn't that so, Carol?" I think the teacher himself might have taken the ribbing in stride, but I deeply regret the impulse that caused me to "buy" the interest of the others at the cost of her dignity and affection.

I don't need to eliminate humor from my life; I need to allow Christ to take away those tendencies of my ego to puff itself up at the expense of others. It is not so much a matter of not speaking: I need to allow myself to enter the school of silence in such a way that I encounter true self-knowledge, to learn my true value, not at the expense of others, but in loving relationship to my Source.

Prayer/Response

Chapter 4
VERSES 55–58

*L*isten willingly to holy lectio; apply yourself frequently to prayer. Daily confess to God in prayer your past sins with tears and sighs, and amend them for the future.*

Comment

For Benedict, there is no separating the response from the listening. Here he implies an attitude and a behavior somewhat foreign to our modern, analytical way of doing things. He does not list a series of separate and discrete steps: read scripture *(lectio)*, pray, weep, and change; rather, it is all one fluid motion. Benedict takes it for granted that we come to our reading of scripture eagerly, convinced that here is a word of life for us now, that we listen with expectancy that our lives will be changed by what we hear. Quite naturally, then, we move from such listening to praying: "Lord, what are you saying to me here?" And our prayer naturally turns then to an examination of conscience: "How far short I fall from what I would be! How deeply I yearn to be closer to God, yet I seem always to be falling away from the life/love/relationship to which I am drawn! Oh, Lord, forgive me and help me!" And so, from tears and sighs to repentance: "By God's grace, may I this day be more faithful to God and to the self I know God longs for me to be and indeed is already drawing me toward."

Reflection

I am acquainted with the procedure described above, but what a remote acquaintance it is! I know it as a thing separate from my being; not often enough as a lived knowledge, true of me and in me. I ponder: How does repentance and transformation actually happen?

Sometimes I play with the idea that what God longs for me to be already exists somehow and somewhere, and is actually a force that has a drawing power, attracting me now by the fullness of its reality. Possibly the force of that existence is as compelling, as influential in shaping the person I am today, as is any past action or memory or parental influence. Perhaps my unknown future is as important for me this day as my all too well-known past. Perhaps the effectiveness of this simple scheme of *lectio* is that it accesses such a reality in me and for me.

I always sense in myself some resistance to such an idea, perhaps because I want to "stay in control" of my life. Such a power for good (in me!) seems somewhat like a rollercoaster: once I board, it might take me to places and in ways I did not "intend"!

And yet, the resistance is balanced by desire. I want the abundant life that is mine. God has given me a glimpse of what it is like, to belong to my Lord in mind and body and heart and spirit and strength, and I like it. It's better than anything I know. I pray today to say "yes" with all my being.

Prayer/Response

Chapter 4
VERSES 59–61

*D*o not fulfill the desires of the flesh (Gal 5:16): hate your self-will. Obey in all things the commands of the abbot, even though he himself (which God forbid!) should act otherwise, being mindful of that precept of the Lord: Do what they say, but not what they do (Matt 23:3).

Comment

Here Benedict places a finger on what is in many ways the key to his asceticism: pride or self-will is the great danger of the spiritual life; it is wanting to "play God" rather than to adore God. But pride is subtle and pervasive in human experience. How to combat it?

In a sense, the whole Rule consists of guidelines to harness and channel the ego for God. Benedict offers many ways to discipline pride, including: attention to the daily interactions in community, even-handed assignment of humble tasks to all persons, and the limitation of bodily and spiritual disciplines to moderate actions shared by everyone. But the fundamental method to combat pride, undergirding everything else, is simple obedience. Obedience in the scandalous, incarnational way of the cross: obedience to flawed human beings who have been given to us as our superiors; obedience in the form of cheerful submission in daily routines to the necessarily limited people who have been given to us as our family and our community. These are hard words for a twenty-first-century American individualist!

Reflection

For several years now, I have deeply pondered this "odd" vow: obedience. Benedict insists on it, usually quite literally, again and again. Of course, he acknowledges the need for checks and balances: there must be change, there must be opportunity for all gifts to flower—and leaders are to be restrained lest they "run amok." But obedience is the rule, and civil disobedience the exception. Whereas, for us—for me—it's usually the other way around: I protest/disobey first, and only later wonder about what obedience might have brought.

What does obedience teach me? My hunch is that as I learn to be obedient to the people given to me, I will discover a much deeper trust in God's will, in God's own plan working itself out as God intends it. In some contexts, my addiction to what I think of as a rational process of equity and fairness is probably a misleading illusion, masking my own pride and need for control. I suspect that by my refusal of obedience, I severely discount the possibility of the work of the Spirit in the real arenas of my life.

As I have explored obedience in my own life, my discoveries are interesting. First, I find that my initial desire is to assess and evaluate the rightness or wrongness of those in authority over me. Second, I prefer my judgment to theirs, and it is a long, hard struggle interiorly before I am willing to submit to their authority. Third, I discover that as I do submit, in some way I don't understand, God uses my gentle and cheerful cooperation to bring out of the situation as a whole what needs to happen. It mystifies me and runs counter to my instincts. I have begun to suspect that the interior work I must do in order to humbly and honestly be obedient is exactly what God needs me to do at this moment, almost in a way that seems entirely independent of the external circumstances . . . And yet, it also seems to affect those circumstances positively.

Prayer/Response

Chapter 4
VERSES 62–73

*D*o not wish to be called holy before you are so; but first be holy, that you may be truly called so. Daily fulfill by your deeds the commandments of God: love chastity; hate no-one; do not be jealous, nor give way to envy. Do not love strife. Flee from vainglory. Reverence your seniors; love your juniors. Pray for your enemies in the love of Christ. Make peace with your adversary before the setting of the sun.

Comment

These verses conclude Benedict's guidance on the tools of the spiritual craft. In the first part of this chapter, he emphasized daily actions; in the latter part, he has turned more explicitly to the spiritual foundations of those actions. The image with which he is working is the artisan using the tools of the craft for the slow forming of a work of art, which is the soul in God. This slow formation is concerned with the simple routines of the ordinary day, with the ongoing conversion of our lives into their most exquisite shape. Just like any good tools, the instruments enumerated in this chapter make easier that difficult work of discovering God in our dailiness, in our duties, in our doldrums, in our successes.

These verses highlight the performance of daily actions in relation to their spiritual dimensions. Key to all is the first verse here, and the one that follows (in the next section):

1. "Not to wish to be called holy before you are so" implies that each one is indeed on the path to holiness and can look forward with expectancy to the growth of holiness;

2. "Never despair of God's mercy" reminds us that the essential meaning of holiness is nearness to God/consecration for and by God. So holiness is not primarily a matter of our own virtue (for who can hope to love one's enemies except in Christ's love?), but primarily a matter of God's ever-present love and power. We may depend upon this nearness, and live within it.

Reflection

Today I feel very far from holiness indeed, and far from God, too, because I allow my own cares and fears to preoccupy me and take up the spaces in my mind and heart.

And I am acutely aware of the value of carrying on in faith that God is here and Christ is forming me, even when I least feel it, even when my experience does not confirm what my head and heart know.

So, I go on with my day, trying to be recollected. I find that I am seeking to practice presence to whatever is in front of me. I look for ways to choose to be gentle rather than to be confrontational with myself and with others. Even so, I have to remake those choices every five minutes, because I keep forgetting! Yet, throughout the moments of my day, I am seeking to trust in the mercy of God. In all this, I am thankful for the wisdom of Benedict, who sounds to me as if he also had been in this "place" of yearning and falling short.

Prayer/Response

Chapter 4
VERSE 74

*A*nd never despair of God's mercy.

Comment

Benedict invites every person to take seriously the call God makes to each one of us to be holy. He asks for a lifelong commitment, lived out daily, in the context of community life, governed by an abbot and a Rule. He spells out a list of fundamental attitudes and behaviors that the committed one is to strive to express in every moment of life. And he draws all together in this reminder that we must never despair of God's mercy.

Why is such a reminder necessary and appropriate?

As a generalization, there seem to be two main temptations that beset the committed Christian: self-righteousness and despair. The former is the temptation of the mind, and the latter of the heart. As we begin to enter seriously into life with God, discovering how much fruitfulness is possible, it is easy at first to be self-satisfied with our "progress" and our perfection. The quality of life is vastly improved, and self-congratulation comes naturally. We may find ourselves judging others unfavorably by comparison.

But the organic rhythm of the spiritual life is such that this first phase tends to be followed by a period of discouragement. Perhaps the discouragement comes when you encounter an obstinate refusal in another to accept the glorious liberty of the children of God. Perhaps it comes when some daily incident forces an uncomfortable admission that your ego is still quite a healthy "monster." Perhaps it comes when inner voices assault you with a reminder of just how unworthy you are. These are temptations of the heart; in them, there is a realization that, even though you have come so far and worked so hard, there remains deep within you a basic refusal of the divine life. This may deflate your spirits, and remorse may lead to self-pity and despair.

That is why the fundamental and final tool of the spiritual craft must be to never despair of God's mercy. For indeed, this is the truest expression of the first tool—to love God with the whole heart—even and especially when you know yourself to be nothing.

Reflection

There are days when hope in God's mercy seems impossible to me. I am quite accustomed to having my mind "play tricks" on me, and so long as I am attentive, it is not terribly difficult to tell myself there is another perspective than the one that seems so persuasive at this moment. But it is much harder for me to cope with the fact that my heart (or rather, my feelings) leads me astray. It is very difficult for me to weave the fine emotional line between self-pity and true repentance, between an overwhelming sense of sadness and willing-ness simply to offer my whole life (again!) to God, knowing it is never as much as I wish it were.

Prayer/Response

Chapter 4
VERSES 75–78 (END)

ehold, these are the tools of the spiritual craft, which, if they are constantly employed day and night, and duly given back on the day of judgment, will gain for us from the Lord that reward which he himself has promised: "what eye has not seen nor ear heard, God has prepared for them that love him."

And the workshop where we are to labor diligently at all these things is the cloister of the monastery, and stability in the community.

Comment

So much richness in a few sentences! Everything we have is given to us, even those basic tools by which we do our part to participate in the formation of our souls. For these tools, as for life itself, we will be held accountable on judgment day. Thus, we are responsible for being good stewards, even of such things as governance of our tongues, constructive release of anger, and reverence for those with whom we live (Luke 19:12–28) .

We will be rewarded for these efforts; indeed, Matthew too speaks of "reward" in heaven (Matt 6:2–4). What good insight Benedict has that our reward will be more than we can even imagine—more than our hearts can even conceive. So we are not to waste time worrying about what heaven will be like; just to go on living each day as faithfully as we can.

The work of this life in Christ is an art, not a science. Certain tasks are basic, but their application day by day in a specific setting must vary, and it takes a keen eye (fixed on Christ) and a generous heart (finding Christ in the midst) to make that application. But Benedict is clear that the workplace is simply right here and now. We need not be seeking elsewhere: God is here, and if not here, then nowhere else. So we are to make the commitment to what we are given, and stay with it until death, as the best way to exercise the spiritual craft: just here and just now.

Reflection

It almost seems that my "instincts" run counter to Benedict's guidance in every case:

- I often want my spiritual tools to remain shiny and bright, looking pretty on the wall; but I don't use them nearly as often as I have occasion to!

- To give all this effort for some reward completely unknown—how unfair! Wouldn't it be more reasonable of God to let us know ahead of time what the reward is (so I could have more control over it)? I want to be a participant (manager), not a recipient (subject)!

- As much as I have thought about stability, I still can't believe it. God here? In the midst of this broken, unreconciled, bitter, and manic place? Here?

Prayer/Response

Interlude II
A NOTE TO THE READER

Is your *lectio* beginning to bear fruit for you?

Perhaps there are times when you find a word or phrase at once, but also times when nothing seems to come at all. Even more troubling, perhaps there are days when repugnance or anger at some verse is so strong that you can't get past it to anything else.

It is just as helpful, if not more so, to "go with" something that repels or angers you as to go with a positive attraction. The strong negative response may be a signal about a major area in your spiritual life, and may open up something that until now has been quite hidden from you.

Several years ago, my husband joined a spiritual reading group. He and the others in the group read passages from one of the Christian "classics" and then came together to discuss their insights. (They discovered that they were able to tap the riches of the older texts much more effectively when they combined their individual reactions.) At one point Doug mentioned that he was marking his text in the margins with pluses and minuses: a plus when he liked and agreed with the point, and a minus when he disagreed with it.

One of his colleagues pointed out that the pluses probably were unimportant markings, because they merely recorded his acknowledgment of what he already knew. In contrast, the minus marks were extremely useful to him, because they noted areas in which new growth was already underway. The point is not that we are necessarily going to make a 180-degree turnabout in our opinions. Rather, wherever there is strong emotional energy, some personal engagement is signaled that is worthy of attention and care.

The Rule abounds with examples of things we are likely to find repugnant: obeying the abbot, always giving credit to God, confessing sins every day, being forbidden to do our own will, avoiding even good speech and laughter, physical punishment, and so on. While there are good reasons to oppose some of the Rule's provisions, there are always also good reasons to include them. Are we free to consider both sides, and if not, what does our lack of freedom tell us about areas of blindness or pain we are carrying?

Our *lectio* is a graceful opportunity to explore our energies and emotions in these areas, gently and with care, in light of God's call to each one of us to become whole. The insights opened by our dislikes are invitations to release unnecessary baggage in ourselves. As you explore these negative attractions, remember this: the Christian life is intended to lead us through death to resurrection. And death—even of unnecessary baggage or strong ego identifications—feels like death; it is costly. But it is not the last word.

Monastic Virtues

Chapter 5, Obedience
VERSES 1–9

T   *he first step of humility is obedience without delay. This becomes those who hold nothing dearer to them than Christ, and who on account of the holy servitude which they have taken upon them, and for fear of hell, and for the glory of everlasting life, as soon as anything is ordered by the superior, just as if it had been commanded by God himself, are unable to bear delay in doing it. It is of these that the Lord says: upon hearing me with his ear he has obeyed me (Ps 18:44). And again, to teachers he says: he who hears you hears me (Luke 10:16).*

Such as these, therefore, leaving immediately all that is their concern, and forsaking their own will, with their hands disengaged and leaving unfinished what they were about, with the ready step of obedience, follow by their deeds the voice of the one who commands. And so, as it were at the same instant, the bidding of the master and the perfect work of the disciple are together more perfectly fulfilled in the swiftness of the fear of God.

Comment

The subjects of Chapters 5, 6, and 7 of the Rule (obedience, silence, and humility) have often been called the monastic virtues, they are so central to the spirit of the consecrated life for which Benedict legislates. Here we turn to obedience, already encountered in the Rule several times as a major element of Benedict's thought, and we note that obedience is also one of the three primary monastic vows. (See Chapter 58, verse 17.)

Earlier we observed that Benedict's concept of obedience is rooted in the ancient notion of listening.[30] The Latin root words upon which obedience is based mean hearing in a way that involves meeting/encounter. The foundation of true obedience is deep attention in order to receive more fully that which is being spoken/given. The whole point of the Benedictine life is to train your heart to listen for the Word that matters, and when it is heard, to respond with all your being, so that life springs forth. And indeed, in his reference here to those who "leave immediately all that is their concern," Benedict clearly is thinking of the disciples, who put aside their nets immediately in order to follow Christ when he called them.[31] The point is that each of us receives similar opportunities to follow Christ within the context of our own daily interactions. To be obedient is to listen to our life contexts in such a way that we develop sensitivity to this call.

It is essential to the Rule that obedience be rooted within the specific, limited, and incarnational setting given to each life.[32] We practice obedience by giving ourselves humbly—not just to the uncreated God, but also to the specific superiors and teachers God gives us.

Sometimes the simplicity of the Rule lulls us into forgetting just how countercultural it is. The modern American temper not only celebrates individualism, but also encourages a rationalistic spirit in which each person is at all times responsible solely for himself or herself. It is considered a fundamental human right to think through things and decide for yourself. Obviously, obedience can be taken too far, and individual reason is a gift to be exercised by each of us.[33] But in our time, we attribute little or no value to obedience, and Benedict assigns it primary importance. How does he ground such importance?

Observe first that here as elsewhere, the key is holding nothing dearer than Christ. So it is Christ and our love for him that motivates our obedience. Second, we see that as a practical matter, the superior (and the poor and the stranger) is seen as Christ and must be obeyed with a ready heart. Third, the objective of obedience is an attunement of wills in relationship so that the command and the obedient deed have almost the aspect of a single movement. In other words, there is a profound union that is being created in the eager obedience, a relationship integral to both parties.

Reflection

What a long way I am from a spirit of obedience! It is very difficult for me to set aside my own concerns and tasks when my husband asks me for something, for example—at all, much less at once. I remember a time when I was a teenager. My father asked me to do something and I stopped and asked him "Why?" He was outraged, and I shouted back, "Why are you paying all that money to send me to college, if you don't want me to ask why?" I felt entirely in the right.

Apart from the normal teenage issues of asserting a separate identity from one's parents, it occurs to me that another issue here touches the core of obedience. The goal of a harmonious union of mind, heart, and spirit is utterly shattered by an insistence that each request/instruction be evaluated to determine if it is reasonable and appropriate. It is a form of insisting on separation that is poor training indeed for life in Christ. There must, at some point, be a simple willingness to do what the other asks out of love for the other—simply because he or she asked. And, painfully, that willingness must be expressed with a real live person, one whose frailties I see all too well!

Prayer/Response

Chapter 5
VERSES 10–13

*T*hese therefore choose the narrow way, upon whom presses the desire to attain eternal life, of whom the Lord says: Narrow is the way which leads to life (Matt 7:14). So that living not by their will, nor obeying their own desires and pleasures, they walk according to the judgment and command of another: thus they live in community, and desire to have an abbot over them. Such as these without doubt fulfill that saying of the Lord: I came not to do my own will, but the will of him who sent me (John 6:38).

Comment

What is Benedict doing here? What he is *not* doing is advocating "fancy" or extreme physical austerities like those undertaken by many in the desert. Instead, he actively discourages such ascetical feats. Benedict's essential ascetical discipline is different, summed up in two deceptively simple words, "obedience" and "humility." It is clear to Benedict that the great enemy of the spiritual life is pride, and the best antidote to pride is a genuine submission to another human being. The humiliations likely to originate from such a submission are great—our own wills are repeatedly put in second place.

We all like to think highly of our own opinions and judgments, but Benedict makes clear that often such judgments are mere whims and appetites for self-promotion. He is not, of course, talking about overthrowing our deepest will—that movement of strong passion in our hearts that draws us ever more closely to our true center in God.

What is our model of the human psyche, and how do we understand the various movements of our thoughts and emotions? It is important for us to begin to ask ourselves what we know, not only of obedience, but also of humiliation, opinion, appetite. Are those the same or different from passion and will? How are they connected and interrelated?

Benedict is working from a model largely developed by Cassian,[34] which in turn was a synthesis of much Christian thought of the time. It is less important for us to understand the details of that model than to consider the assumptions of our own culture in light of what we are discovering in our spiritual journey. Do the standard formulations of our culture square with what we are beginning to experience as we ponder Benedict's meanings in light of our own spiritual journey?

Most of all, it is important for us to begin to uncover the capacity enabling us most fully to respond to the call of Christ to us, and to explore how we train that. These are the questions that the Rule encourages us to ask ourselves and expects us to shape our behavior accordingly.

Reflection

How is my life touched by these considerations? My first response to these questions is to be perplexed. It had not occurred to me that the model of the human person current in our time might not be the only workable model. How do I even start to consider another?

Well, let's see. So far in these reflections, I have observed that sometimes my thoughts are illusions, and that sometimes even my feelings are merely superficial in relation to my deepest self. I have noticed that sometimes what I want is on the level of what might be called "appetite," and that does not feel the same to me as the great hunger I have for God. I know that sometimes my will is self-centered (protective, anxious, clutching, even greedy or lazy); and sometimes my will is a thing like a song, when I am deeply in harmony with Something-I-can't-name. It seems an odd thing, but maybe obedience ("walking according to another's decisions and directions") might help me learn to do God's will.[35]

Prayer/Response

Chapter 5
VERSES 14–19 (END)

*B**ut this very obedience will be acceptable to God and sweet to others only if what is commanded is done, not fearfully, tardily, nor lukewarmly, nor with murmuring, nor with an answer showing unwillingness: for the obedience which is given to superiors is given to God, since God Himself has said: The one who hears you hears me (Luke 10:16). And this obedience ought to be given with a good will, because God loves a cheerful giver (2 Cor 9:7).*

For if the disciple obeys with ill will, murmuring not only with his lips but also in his heart, even though he fulfill the command he will not be acceptable to God. For God sees the heart of the murmurer. And for such action he will gain no reward; rather he will incur the punishment due to murmurers, unless he amends and makes satisfaction.

Comment

Benedict never fully tells us his mind, since he favors succinctness. But here he suggests a very important distinction—almost lost in our time—between compliance and obedience. Compliance is a cringing and sluggish response to a command by someone reacting as if the command and the master were alien things, unrelated to him- or herself. Obedience is something different, a response given freely and gladly, a response involving love and thus deeply embedded in a relationship of care. Do we today have a concept of obedience that means more than compliance, a concept of allowing a command to come into our hearts and be welcomed there?

In some respects, it seems almost foolish for Benedict to contrast something so important as obedience with something so paltry as grumbling. We have already considered that grumbling is fundamentally a refusal of what is given, a refusal to be present here and now.[36] And here we see further into Benedict's insight about grumbling: that it gives us a little "safe place" where our egos can blossom. With that runaway vine in the corner, all the other pruning turns out to be ineffective. Grumbling cherishes the "bottom line" conviction that I really know best . . . even better than God.

Reflection

A part of me is most uncomfortable with the way these issues are framed. Is there no third alternative to the evil of compliance/grumbling on the one hand, and the good of obedience to a human superior on the other? I am enough of an individualistic American to feel that as a real pinch.

To whom must I be obedient, anyway? Not living in a monastery, I don't have an official "superior" in the sense of an abbot. Not working in an office, I don't have a "boss." Who has God given to me to obey in the specifics of my life?

Well, there is my husband . . . but we have a "modern" marriage, and obedience is not an issue. Or is it? I often find myself unwilling to accept the simplest possible action on his part without an explanation. He must justify to me leaving the mail in an odd place or taking a different route home or hundreds of other actions in which I find I am not simply and cheerfully present to him, trusting in his good will and sound judgment without knowing specifics. True, some of my questions are based on a desire to share his life, but it's a fine line between that and wanting to "improve/fix" him.

And what about the chairperson of that voluntary association I belong to? She's a wonderful person, but her style is very different from mine, and I'm always itching to change her, rather than allowing myself to be obedient to her leadership. And often I grumble that meetings didn't go the way the great "I" thinks they should have. True, there is a place for collaboration between two different viewpoints, but it's a fine line between that and refusal of an authentic relationship with another.

Perhaps if I watch my grumbling, I'll discover new areas in which I need to learn the freedom of obedience.

Prayer/Response

Chapter 6, Restraint of Speech
(ENTIRE)

*L*et us do as the prophet says: I said, I will take heed to my ways that I not sin with my tongue: I have placed a watch over my mouth; I became dumb, and was silent, and held my peace even from good things *(Ps 39:1–3). Here the prophet shows that if we ought to refrain even from good words for the sake of silence, how much more ought we to abstain from evil words, on account of the punishment due to sin! Therefore, on account of the importance of silence let permission to speak be seldom granted even to perfect disciples, even when their conversation is good and holy and tending to edification, because it is written:* In much speaking you shall not avoid sin *(Prov 10:19); and elsewhere* Death and life are in the power of the tongue *(Prov 18:21).*

For it is appropriate for the master to speak and to teach; but the disciple is to be silent and listen. And therefore, if anything is to be asked of a superior, let it be done with all humility and deferential reverence, lest more be said than is proper. But as for buffoonery or silly words, such as move to laughter, we utterly condemn them in every place, nor do we allow the disciple to open his mouth in such discourse.

Comment

In Chapter 4, verses 51–54, Benedict talked about silence, but here we encounter it as a statement of one of the three key monastic virtues. A key commentator on silence in the Rule[37] makes clear that silence, obedience, and humility are inseparable in Benedict's thought. These three characteristics are considered central monastic virtues. Perhaps we can readily understand obedience and humility as virtues. But why is silence so important?

Silence is so foreign to our lives that it makes many of us jumpy. Occasionally, on silent retreats, a person will compulsively burst out talking; and periodically in a public setting, we will see an otherwise quite normal person talking nonstop to him- or herself. Most of us know people who turn on the radio or television the moment they walk into the house, simply to have the "noise." Even in churches, after a full minute of silence during the service, people begin to cough and shift nervously. Many of us have never had the opportunity to experience an hour of silence. So it is difficult for us to imagine why and how silence might be a major virtue.

Benedict knows silence as the fundamental state of things: full, rich, nourishing, and creative; and words are interruptions of this underlying rich texture. Perhaps the key is in Proverbs 18:20–21, where the clear suggestion is made that someone who loves words will tend to let him- or herself be satisfied by them, thus stopping short of the true satisfaction. Notice especially that Benedict emphasizes the word "disciple" in this chapter. It is the disciple's task (the one who follows Christ) not to make words, but to let hunger for the Word lead him or her creatively into daily silence. Human words distract and deflect from this relationship unless and until they are born out of the silence.

Reflection

Just yesterday I became aware of myself rattling on and on, and I was suddenly ashamed and embarrassed. I think my need to talk came from two sources: one, that I had just shared some very deep thoughts with my friend, and I was a little anxious about so much intimacy, so I tried to cover it up with a flood of words (deny it?). And the other was that I had also drunk too much caffeine and was unconsciously "wired." I wonder how direct the relationship is between caffeine, noise, sugar, and the frantic rushing around so typical of the environment in which I find myself daily. Am I aware of the Lord in all of that?

Prayer/Response

Chapter 7, Humility
VERSES 1–8

*T*he Holy Scripture cries out to us, brothers, saying: *Everyone who exalts himself shall be humbled, and one who humbles himself shall be exalted (Luke 14:11; 18:14). In saying this, it teaches us that all exaltation is a kind of pride, against which the prophet shows himself to be on his guard when he says: Lord, my heart is not exalted nor my eyes lifted up; nor have I walked in great things, nor in wonders above me (Ps 131:1). And why? If I did not think humbly, but exalted my soul;*

then like a child that is weaned from its mother—so you would treat
my soul (Ps 131:2).

Therefore, brothers, if we wish to arrive at the highest point of humility,
and speedily reach that heavenly exaltation to which we can only ascend
by the humility of this present life, we must by our ever-ascending actions
erect a ladder like the one which Jacob beheld in his dream, by which
the angels appeared to him descending and ascending. This descent and
ascent signifies nothing else than that we descend by exaltation and
ascend by humility. And the ladder thus erected is our life in the world,
which, if the heart is humbled, is lifted up by the Lord to heaven.

Comment

Benedict's method of introducing any major subject is to turn to
scripture, known by most of the monks "by heart." In a sense, it is a
confusing method for the modern reader because Benedict seems to
pile image upon image without really explicating any of them. A
helpful—perhaps essential—way to understand his method ourselves is to turn to the referenced scriptures and ponder them in our
hearts for what meaning they may reveal.

At minimum, Benedict has a simple and straightforward point:
the problem of the spiritual life is pride (or self-exaltation); the
remedy is humility. Before he goes into the steps of humility, he
wants us to think about this, comparing what we notice in our lives
with the words of scripture.

The scriptural verses he has selected elaborate this point. We
notice that the Gospel of Luke uses the same quotation twice in five
chapters—a rare occurrence and an important emphasis ("Everyone
who exalts himself . . ."). We notice too that in both these Lukan
citations, Jesus is talking to Pharisees, those spiritually "adept" persons who tend to be comfortable in their conformance to external
religious requirements, that is, self-righteous. And we realize at once
that for those of us who seriously commit our lives to God, self-
righteousness may be a major trap. So, whatever humility is and
however it may be gained, we probably need it more than we know!

Reflection

Self-righteousness is a very comfortable bed, and I find myself slum-
bering in it far more often than I would like to admit. At the
moment, I feel it as a dis-ease in one particular way. I have been

noticing that the more I pray and the deeper I come into God's heart, the more I am acutely aware of the terrible gluttony, dishonesty, and self-centeredness of our culture. Perhaps in itself that is not bad, but I fear I am developing a very critical spirit, because I am feeling as if "they" are alienated from God, while "I" am superior to them. I am tending to see myself as somehow exempt from these cultural forms of isolation from God, and therefore to see others as inferior to me. It troubles me, but I don't know quite how to take hold of it. I sense that compassion may be an important key, and probably humility is as well. I look forward to what Benedict will say about humility.

Prayer/Response

Chapter 7
VERSES 9–13

*T*he sides of the same ladder we understand to be our body and soul, in which the call of God has placed various steps of humility or discipline, which we must ascend. The first step of humility, then, is that a person always keeps the fear of God before his eyes (Ps 36:2), avoiding all forgetfulness: that he is ever mindful of all that God has commanded; that those who despise God will be consumed in hell for their sins; and that he always considers that life everlasting is prepared for those who fear God. And keeping himself at all times from sin and vice, whether of thoughts, tongue, eyes, hands, feet, or his own will, let him thus hasten to cast away the desires of the flesh. Let him consider that he is always beheld from heaven by God, and that his actions are everywhere seen by the eye of the Divine Majesty, and are every hour reported to God by the angels.

Comment

Various commentators trace elements of this ladder of humility to Cassian and the Rule of the Master, or compare it with the elaborated versions of Bernard or Aquinas.[38] Several points may help illuminate these introductory verses of Benedict for us. First, the monastic tradition seems to trace the progressions in the ladder from the internal cultivation of humility to its external manifestations. Thus, it may appear to us that the list moves from the harder step to the easier one. Benedict no doubt would insist that outer action be congruent with internal motive, so he begins with work in the heart, knowing that progress there takes time.

Second, there is an apparent conflict between this verse: "the first step of humility is . . . the fear of God," and the first verse of Chapter 5: "The first step of humility is obedience without delay." Obviously, there is a close connection between obedience and the fear of God; yet, they are not the same.

We can imagine that as Benedict began to think about humility as a whole, his thoughts turned to the fear of God as its fundament. This foundation grounds humility in the recognition that ultimately it is not our work that builds the ladder, but God's work in us. Humility is oriented toward wisdom, and that can come only as gift, not as due wage. However, it is interesting that Benedict does not choose to cite Proverbs 9:10, where this point about wisdom is made, but instead uses the psalm (36), where the emphasis is negative: "Transgression speaks to the wicked deep in their hearts; there is no *fear of* God before their eyes" (verse 1, emphasis added). The choice of this Psalm to introduce humility makes clear not only that humility is God's gift, but also that humility is fundamentally motivated by a recognition of who God is: "For *with you* (O God) is the fountain of life, in your light we see light" (verse 9, emphasis added).

Reflection

What a good reminder Benedict always is to me! I cannot count the number of times I have undertaken or practiced a discipline, only to become aware that I am preoccupied with what I am doing, losing sight of to Whom I am going.

Partly, of course, that's because I wish I could do it myself (could become perfect myself), rather than love and praise the One who is truly perfect. Humility is a long time coming, but I can at least see that it begins with the breathtaking recognition of who God is. It is astonishing to me to consider the utter contrast between God and me, while at the same time realizing that God wants a relationship with me. It's hard even to hold that in my mind, much less to learn it by heart.

Prayer/Response

Chapter 7

VERSES 14–22

*T*his the prophet tells us, when he shows how God is ever present to our thoughts, saying: God searches the heart and the mind (Ps 7:10). And again: The Lord knows the thoughts of men, that they are empty (Ps 94:11). And God also says: You have understood my thoughts from afar (Ps 139:3); and The thought of man shall confess to you (Ps 76:11). In order, therefore, that he may be on his guard against evil thoughts, let the humbler brother always say in his heart: Then shall I be without stain before God, if I have kept myself from my sin (Ps 18:24).*

We are, indeed, forbidden to do our own will by Scripture, which says to us: Turn away from your own will (Sir 18:30). And so too we beg of God in prayer that God's will may be done in us. Rightly therefore are we taught not to do our own will, if we listen to the warning of Scripture: There are ways which to people seem right, but the results of them lead to the depths of hell (Prov 16:25); or again, when we tremble at what is said of the careless: They are corrupt and have become abominable in their pleasures (Ps 14:1).

Comment

Benedict continues to search his memory of scripture, endeavoring to form and clarify his thinking on this topic. If we follow the content carefully, it contains a tightly woven theological argument that invites us prayerfully to enter more reflectively into awareness of who God is and who we are. Because true fear of God is motivated not solely by a sense of who God is, but also by a sense of who we are, self-knowledge is needed; self-knowledge that we are created beings, with motives that often lead us astray.

In these last two quotations, Benedict points toward an understanding of the human will as exceedingly limited. We cannot choose rightly because our knowledge is vague, and our desires pull us in all directions. The only ultimately freeing choice is to choose God, over and over each day, as Lord of our will. Interestingly, St. Paul chose this same passage from Psalm 14 to make a very similar point: all we can do is throw ourselves upon the mercy of God (Rom 3:10–11).[39]

Reflection

Can I really know the truth of this argument in my heart? One way to learn it, of course, is to find myself embroiled in some disaster that forces me to look clearly at my motives. But short of that, can I really know it as my own reality? I suppose part of its truth is revealed in my very resistance to seeing my own will as being truly limited. What a cherished dream I carry that one day I shall be all knowing, all good, and so on!

And yet, in a positive sense, I do often find myself in situations in which I have an acute sense that I have no business doing what I'm doing alone, because I haven't the capacity. When I seek to comfort a bereaved friend . . . When I offer to confront and challenge one who needs to break through to her own true beauty out of the mess in which she is embedded . . . When I try to forgive a dear friend who has wounded me greatly . . . When I sense just how contentedly I am caught in the greedy, self-satisfied narcissism of my culture . . . In all these and other moments, I can only throw myself on the mercy of God.

Prayer/Response

Chapter 7
VERSES 23–30

And in regard to the desires of the flesh, we must believe that God is always present to us, as the prophet says to the Lord: O Lord, all my desire is before you (Ps 38:10). Let us be on our guard then against evil desires, since death has its seat close to the entrance of delight; thus the Scripture commands us, saying: Do not go after your desires (Sir 18:30). Since, therefore, the eyes of the Lord behold good and evil (Prov 15:3); and the Lord is ever looking down from heaven upon the children of humans, to see who has understanding or is seeking God (Ps 14:2); and since the works of our hands are reported to God, our Maker and Creator, night and day by the angels appointed to watch over us; we must be always on the watch, brothers, lest, as the prophet says in the psalm, God should see us at any time fall into evil and become

*unprofitable (Ps 14:3); and lest, though God spare us now because he
is merciful and expects our conversion, God should say to us hereafter:
These things you did and I remained silent (Ps 49 [50]:21).*

Comment

Here Benedict seems to be describing the "pull" or attraction that is
opposed to the fear of God. Our own desires and appetites, if freely
pursued, lead toward death and away from God. But notice that the
fear of God is likewise an attraction or a desire. What Benedict seems
to be suggesting here is that the love of God—that sturdy and virile
love which is known in scripture as fear—is the most effective antidote to our base desires. What keeps our desires pure is the continuous recollection that God sees us and longs for our response toward
him in each moment of every day. What keeps us from succumbing
to the "desires of the body" is the stronger desire for the only One
capable of truly satisfying us. So desire itself is not a negative thing,
nor is the body. Rather the struggle is the movement toward or away
from God as it is manifest in our desires.[40]

Reflection

Generally, I think of peacefulness as the "right" attitude to have
when I am at ease with God. So it has been difficult for me to consider the possibility that sometimes I might feel passionate in God's
presence and with God's grace. Gradually, however, I have begun to
realize that often my appetites or desires were merely diluted and
misdirected longings for "the Real Thing," for God's own self. As a
result, I have begun to experiment in exploring my own desires; I
ask myself: "What do I really want here?" letting the longing deepen
in me. And I have been graced with some moments in which I felt
my heart pounding and my whole soul engaged in such a way that I
could not mistake the work of the Holy Spirit. I have come to know
that God doesn't always want me to be calm and bordering on the
passive; there are indeed moments when God actually calls forth
my strong passion. Essential here is remembering God, staying recollected to the truth of God's ongoing presence, at all times. So both
my passion and my calm can be offered in love to the One who is
my creator.

Prayer/Response

Chapter 7

VERSES 31–33

*T*he second step of humility is that a person does not love his own will, nor delights in gratifying his own desires; but carries out in his deeds that saying of the Lord: I came not to do my own will, but the will of the one who sent me (John 6:38). And again it is written: "Self-will deserves punishment, but necessity wins a crown."

Comment

The issue is not doing away with one's own will for its own sake, rather living within the flow of the Will that created us. We are to imitate Christ in this. As we look at Christ described by John in his sixth chapter, we see a man of great "personal" power. He has done mighty healings; he has walked on the sea; he has fed the five thousand. And the people have asked him, "What must we do, to be doing the works of God?" This, indeed, is the question Benedict poses to us this day: what must we do to be doing God's will? And Benedict points us to the answer Jesus gives:

1. let me nourish you: believe in me and feed on me;

2. and (here Benedict focuses us), imitate me as you see me do not my own will, but the will of the One who sent me and who loves abundantly.

Benedict asks us to ponder and pray about how well we can make this scripture our own.

Interestingly, he supplements the gospel with a quotation that refers to the martyr Irene (AD 304).[41] The meaning intended is that there is a punishment for self-will, but a crown for pursuit of what might be called obligation/duty or "inner necessity." We are like kings and queens when we are acting in harmony with our own deepest willing, an "inner necessity."[42] What is the content of such inner necessity as intended by Benedict? There is some promise of reward, so the willing is motivated by a longing for something known to be valuable. How might we moderns understand the content of this "eternal reward" that invites our passionate response? Such reward must involve a sense of ultimate fulfillment or completion, which perhaps comes with a sense of deep intimacy or union with One who loves us and is the source and goal of our desire. If such intimacy or union is the reward promised us, then we might begin to sense that to be alone or separate or without such intimacy is unbearable. Even today we would do what we could to move toward that relationship of deep love, and eternity without it would be merely gall and ashes. We are made for love, for completion in union with our God, and the longing movement toward that union is the truest movement of our inner selves. Thus, the "necessity" of deepest will and desire is to allow ourselves to respond to this heart-felt longing to be who we truly are, to belong to the One whose we are, to actually imitate our Lord using the power of the nourishment he provides us.

Reflection

Already I find myself caught up in a song of praise, drawn beyond comment and reflection to prayer! Surely doing God's will must be something like that: to find yourself caught up in a mighty movement in which you are an integral part, but which is much larger than simply the result of your singular contribution.

It is perplexing and difficult and often downright impossible to make these subtle distinctions in my own life between self-will and God's will, between unworthy desire and the desire that leads to Life. I know I need to struggle with it, because that is one of the main ways I discover a workable response. But I also find that the more I struggle with it in my head alone, the more I find myself in quicksand: stuck and getting more stuck. When I allow my heart to lead, living in the present (with my eyes on Jesus), almost without realizing it, I find myself responding as I would, to God.

Prayer/Response

Chapter 7
VERSE 34

*T*he third step of humility is that for the love of God a person submits himself to his superior in all obedience; imitating the Lord, of whom the apostle says: He was made obedient even to death (Phil 2:8).

Comment

What depth in a few words! We have observed previously that Benedict regards obedience to God as operating on the incarnational
principle, that is, it is practiced best in relation to other human and
flawed beings just like ourselves.[43] True obedience is not the same
thing as a reasoned judgment that a request is sound and then following it. On the contrary, it is a willingness to follow/respond to
what is asked, particularly when you don't see the sense of it; so you
act in faith that God is working out what needs to be, even in the
obscurity or seeming wrongness of the present situation.

Perhaps we often think of Jesus' obedience as being given to
God, who is good, and therefore it made sense. But in practice, Jesus'
obedience to God caused him to submit humanly to things that
didn't make sense—even to things that seemed wrong or evil—
always in faith that God's power was present and effective, in part
because of Jesus' faithful obedience. Surely Gethsemane must have
been something like that: it must have looked to Jesus the man as if
the devil were triumphing, and every bit of his reason must have
urged him to fight the Pharisees and the other petty and vicious
human forces arrayed against him. But instead, he consented—"in
the dark," so to speak, in his human knowing—trusting that God
was working in ways he could not guess to bring about God's purpose precisely in this thing that seemed so wrong.

Both Benedict and St. Paul (in Phil 2) make the connection
between Jesus' obedience on the cross and our obedience to each
other in community. Often it must seem to us that a great wrong is
being done, but we can also be acutely aware of God's power fully
present in the situation, because "in (our) minds we must be the
same as Christ Jesus" (Phil 2:5).

Reflection

I can say those words, and realize that I don't have any idea what they
might mean in my life. I must look for them: keep open to the opportunities God presents to show me what such obedience can do.

I have been thinking a great deal recently about the "unimagin-
able." Sometimes I have a sense that when I freely invite God into a
situation or a relationship (even if I do so because I'm at the end of
my rope), it blossoms into something so precious I could not have
even imagined it. And if I couldn't imagine it, I certainly couldn't

create it. So when I insist on staying in control—or insist that my judgment always be favorable before I proceed—then I limit the possibilities to those I can envision. I close myself from God's gracious surprises.

What deep trust it requires to consent "in the dark," though!

Prayer/Response

Chapter 7
VERSES 35–38

*T*he fourth step of humility is that if in this very obedience hard *and contrary things, even injuries, are done to him, he embraces them patiently with silent acceptance, and does not grow weary or give in, as the Scripture says: He who perseveres to the end shall be saved (Matt 10:22). And again: Let your heart take courage, and wait for the Lord (Ps 27:14). And showing how the faithful ought to bear all things, however contradictory, for the Lord, [the Scripture] says in the person of the afflicted: For you we suffer death all day long; we are counted as sheep for the slaughter (Rom 8:36; Ps 44:22).*

Comment

Benedict is a realist regarding human nature and social interactions. While elsewhere he makes stringent demands upon the abbot and other monastic officials to take their stewardship earnestly and in the name of Christ, here he emphasizes to each monk that it will often be the case that the decisions made by our superiors (those decisions over which we have no control, which nonetheless form the circumstances in which we must live) may often have harsh or difficult effects upon us.

He is suggesting, in short, that the committed Christian must not expect external circumstances generally to be cheerful, prosperous, and aptly suited to our fondest desires, skills, and temperaments. We may suffer, and greatly, even—and perhaps especially—when our commitment to Christ is deepest.

But the point Benedict emphasizes here by his careful selection of scripture is not our suffering (or even our happiness), but only our love of Christ. No one is to suffer for the sake of suffering. We are simply to live—as fully and as deeply in love with Christ as we can be this day—and accept whatever comes for his sake. The passage from Matthew emphasizes allegiance to Christ, the lovely Psalm 27 emphasizes the goodness of the Lord, and the final passages emphasize the key: "for you."

Reflection

Perseverence . . . endurance . . . I think often of such qualities, realizing afresh how little developed they are in me. I am so little practiced in waiting in trust that Christ is already present. I was reflecting just this morning on our three cats: how well they get along now, but how much bitter violence there was among them when the aggressive stray kitten first came. For a long period (or so it seemed to me: it was about fifteen months), the violence continued, and then one day it seemed to have passed. I had by then seriously considered killing the stray ("putting him to sleep") to restore peace.

So it is in my life in many respects. When there is a hard patch, I want to "do something" to fix it or change it. The last thing I think of is to endure through it, for Christ's sake, and in trust that his goodness is already victorious.

Prayer/Response

Chapter 7
VERSES 39–43

*A*nd secure in their hope of the divine reward, they go forward with joy, saying: But in all these things we overcome, through the one who has loved us (Rom 8:37). And so in another place Scripture says: You have tested us, O God; you have tried us as silver is tried by fire; you have led us into the snare and laid tribulation on our backs (Ps 66:10–11). And in order to show that we ought to be under a superior, it goes on to say: You have placed people over our heads (Ps 66:12).

Moreover, fulfilling the precept of the Lord by patience in adversities and injuries, they who are struck on one cheek offer the other; to someone *who takes away their coat they leave also their cloak; and being forced to walk one mile, they go two (Matt 5:39–41). With Paul the Apostle they bear with false brothers, and bless those who curse them (2 Cor 11:26; 1 Cor 4:12).*

Comment

What is Benedict saying in this tapestry he weaves of scripture? We are reminded of the "prayer" attributed to Teresa of Avila: "If this is how you treat your friends, Lord, no wonder you have so few of them!" And that truly does focus the point: this is how God treats friends! How often have we read or heard this, and yet when it comes to our own experience, we really don't believe it or accept it. Surely, we think, it will be different with me. But Benedict gently layers one quotation after another to remind us it is not and will not be different—even for the monk consecrated to God. Especially for the person consecrated to God!

First, St. Paul: "God has put us apostles at the end of his parade, with those sentenced to death . . ." (1 Cor 4:9). "So many others have been boasting of their worldly achievements, that I will boast myself" (2 Cor 11:18): and he lists the tremendous human suffering he has endured.

Then, the image from the Psalms, which is a favorite of holy ones through the centuries, even before Jesus until now: we are being "tried" as silver in a fire. In some way beyond our understanding, these sufferings purify us. They seem—and often are—manifestly unfair, and yet our simple obedience to the hardships and unjust treatment that come to us somehow brings us nearer to Christ.

Indeed, Benedict almost makes this explicit in his free paraphrase of the Matthew quotation. He has suggested that our superiors are often given to us precisely to serve as trials. And when he uses the word *angariati* ("pressed into service") to elaborate on how such superiors may treat us, he is choosing it not from this verse of Matthew, but rather from Matthew 27:32, which refers to Simon of Cyrene, pressed into the service of carrying the Lord's cross.[44] Benedict is suggesting that we look with expectancy to meet and serve the Lord in everything that happens to us, however difficult or unjust it may seem.

Reflection

It goes without saying how far I am from living according to these verses. But I have been struggling much with it just lately, when it seems to me that everything the Lord has trained me for and prepared me to do is so unwelcome and unwanted in the situation in which I find myself. And I am angry and resentful and I want to change things (not to change *me*, but to change things). And I find instead that I must simply endure invisibility and my sense of worthlessness and helplessness—simply endure. And while I am enduring, I am also to be aware of God's intimate presence both in the situation and in me. For that is the focus Benedict offers me: God in the midst of it all!

Prayer/Response

Chapter 7
VERSES 44–48

*T*he fifth step of humility is to hide from one's abbot none of the evil thoughts that beset one's heart, nor the sins committed in secret, but humbly to confess them. Concerning this the Scripture exhorts us, saying: Make known your way to the Lord and hope in God (Ps 37:5). And again: Confess to the Lord, for God is good; for God's mercy endures forever (Ps 106:1; Ps 118:1). So also the prophet says: I have made known to You my offence, and my iniquities I have not hidden. I said, I will confess against myself my iniquities to the Lord; and You have forgiven the wickedness of my heart (Ps 32:5).

Comment

Private confession has largely fallen into disuse today. Theologians argue about why someone should confess, when God already knows everything, and why confess to another person or a priest, when the sin is between yourself and God.

Benedict suggests to us that confession, even of thoughts and temptations, is one of the key steps in humility. Why does he think so? These passages suggest several major points:

1. "Confess" to God, in Psalms 106 and 118, is sometimes translated today as "give thanks" to God. This suggests the wonderful ambi-

guity about the meaning of confession, so well encapsulated in the phrase "the confession of St. Peter": to confess is to realize one's own sinfulness and, at the same time, to realize and appreciate the terrible awesomeness of God (Matt 16:15–17; Luke 5:8–9). To confess is to acknowledge that God is creator and lord, in charge of the universe and of me.

2. Such a God, of course, need not also be a good God or a loving God. It is our faith, within the Judeo-Christian tradition, that although God is indeed awesome, God is even more so trustworthy, a loving parent. So in Psalm 118, the constant refrain is "God's mercy endures forever." So in Psalm 37, confession implies trust in the One who guides and governs all. Confession embodies such trust.

3. The first scripture passage Benedict chooses here asks us to make our way known to God: to let God's light fall upon all that is in our hearts and illumine it. We think of this action as being the whole of confession. But the third passage suggests the other half of it as well. A few verses later, Psalm 32 speaks in the Lord's voice to the one who has confessed, saying, "I will instruct you and teach you the way to go; I will watch over you and be your adviser" (Ps 32:8). Thus we see that in some implicit manner, when we offer our way to God in confession, it is gradually conformed to God's own way, and we are ennobled and empowered to move serenely in the way that we should go and that we long to go—with Christ.

Reflection

Again and again I am mystified and left in wonder by this conviction of Benedict's that our tiny movement in the direction of God (a simple obedience "in the dark," so to speak) should be met by the glorious and transforming impulse of God's love. Benedict is so certain that the process of transformation is real, immediate, and effectively present in the ordinary events of every day—if we are willing simply to act "as if" something remarkable is possible. I wonder . . . perhaps I might look for places in my life in which I could so act. Perhaps even I might sheepishly take one small step in that direction, and then watch with awe!

Prayer/Response

Chapter 7
VERSES 49–50

*T*he sixth step of humility is for a monk to be content with the most common and worst of everything, and in all that is required of him to esteem himself a bad and worthless laborer, saying with the prophet: *I have been brought to nothing, and I did not know it; I have become like a beast before you, yet I am always with you (Ps 73:22–23).*

Comment

Often we forget the connection between humility and humiliation. Benedict's language here is closer to humiliation—the consciousness that we are totally out of place, clothed with tatters in a place of great elegance, an embarrassment even to ourselves, utterly without dignity. There is no pride left to hold onto. What images evoke this condition for us? A modern science fiction novel imagines a meeting between earthlings and a superior race:

> [W]e are too poor ever to go there, even the richest of us. Anyway, we know they don't want us. . . . And now along comes an invitation (for five of us) . . . to escape our shabby village. And what do you think will happen when we get there? . . . We will gawk at the big city and they will laugh at us behind their hands. They will exhibit us to the curious. . . . Have pity on their provincials. . . .[45]

The point is to capture an image of deserved humiliation: that startling, momentary glimpse of the truth that one is profoundly inferior in the most fundamental sense. Occasionally in our lives, most of us get a glimpse of this reality for just a second—but we quickly turn away, for it is too painful to live with. But Benedict invites us to learn to live in it, accepting contentedly this recognition of what it really means to be created.

But (and this is an important "but") such a recognition is both more painful and ultimately totally eased by the simultaneous realization that we are always in the presence of the One whose glory is so great that our poor grayness is made even more colorless by comparison. Even in our humiliation, God chooses us as friends!

Reflection

Here's one of those tasks of the consecrated life that I would prefer to ignore altogether. To allow myself to be stripped of pride, to give up my entitlement to the extent that I release my right even to personal dignity. Oh, what a wound! Is it as hard as losing a loved one? Perhaps it is not so very different, in that both are felt as death.

Oddly enough, this insight of my true condition comes to me most often from my enemies, or from my "friends" when they strike out in anger. Suddenly a barb will be hurled at me with enough of the truth in it that I really see myself, as it were from the hidden back side as well as from the "presentable front." And I feel both angry and crippled.

It is hard for me to allow myself to embrace such a bitter insight into my humble self. But to do that and at the same time be aware that I am deeply, intimately, and overwhelmingly loved! It seems impossible. And yet, even the human ones who really love me have known all along about this awful, newly "discovered" secret about who I am.

Prayer/Response

Chapter 7
VERSES 51–54

*T*he seventh step of humility is that he should not only call himself with his tongue inferior and more common than all, but also believe himself in the depth of his heart to be so, humbling himself, and saying with the prophet: I am a worm and no man, the shame of all and the outcast of the people (Ps 22:6). I have been exalted, and then cast down and confounded (Ps 88:16). And again: It is good for me that you have humbled me, that I may learn your commandments (Ps 119:71,73).

Comment

Again, if we carefully trace the scriptural passages that Benedict has chosen, we are able to draw out a line of thought something like this: "I am a worm and no man" is a passage from Psalm 22, that heart-wrenching psalm beginning with the phrase Jesus cries out from the cross: "My God, my God, why have you deserted me?" and leading finally to a conviction of God's ultimate triumph. Throughout, the theme of the psalm is that the only true strength, the only true goodness, is God's. If even God's son must consent to depend utterly on God's mercy, then how much more so must we. The wisdom of humility is to teach us where the good truly lies.

The second scripture paraphrase, "I have been exalted, and then cast down," points out in context the importance of those moments in the spiritual life now popularly called "the dark night."[46] While this psalm seems to focus on these periods in one's life that seem full of darkness and lack of understanding, indirectly the psalmist is also acknowledging that the human mind and heart do not have the capacity to put boundaries around God by which to harness and possess God. Thus, there will always be some "darkness" of understanding in this life.

Finally, Psalm 119 seems to suggest that if we are to follow in God's way, it is good for us to be afflicted and humbled. This last section of that long psalm directly concerns the subject that is the underlying theme of Benedict's chapter on humility: the danger of pride. The parallel is extended in the reference to humility in one's heart; Psalm 119 reminds us that the hearts of the proud are "gross and fat," so that they cannot "learn your statutes with delight."

We notice too that here humility is not simply an abstract concept, but is discussed in relation to other people we encounter daily.

Reflection

There is a point at which I simply rebel. Part of me cries out, "Oh no, not this humility stuff again! Some humility is okay, but must we root out every last bit of pride?" Undoubtedly that simply shows how firmly rooted pride is in me, perfectly willing to be dormant for a while if need be, but fully expecting to blossom forth again next spring, like a hardy old weed.

So, in my heart (that deepest place, that center) I am to be humble. How do I do that? I suppose I accept the opportunities life naturally offers me to accept dependence, when I need others. Perhaps I might also consider acknowledging and even welcoming differences in others, recognizing that the body of Christ needs strengths the "great I" cannot give. In a sense, I can practice my dependence on God by being aware of my dependence on my brothers and sisters.

If humiliations are opportunities for humility, I imagine the best opportunities I get are the regular reminders of my limitations and my weaknesses. Recently I have noticed how angry I become when I discover that I cannot do something. For example, any period of brief sickness is sure to trigger depression in me, because it compels me to acknowledge my limits. Yet Benedict invites me to see these limitations as friends, reminding me who I really am, and putting me back in right relationship with God and my neighbor.

Prayer/Response

Summary of Chapter 7
VERSES 1–54 (TO DATE)

Let us pause to summarize the first seven steps of humility. The ladder begins with the internal cultivation of humility, the development of that interior purity of heart that is the essence of prayer and the fundamental disposition of the one who seeks Christ above all. These are the components:

1. Always be aware that I am in the presence of the Holy One. Know that God is doing the work in me, and I participate chiefly by allowing God to purify my desires until my will becomes more and more congruent with God's will for me.
2. Love not my own will, but day by day release it.
3. Submit obediently to my human superiors.
4. Accept obedience even in unjust conditions, trusting that is the surest method for me to share the death and resurrection of Christ.
5. Confess temptations to a human person, and accept the forgiveness received.
6. Be content with the humiliation of my (true) created condition.
7. Believe in my heart that I am inferior.

These steps are based on the words of our Lord that whoever is humble shall be exalted, and the implicit corollary that humility in our hearts is the condition for entrance into heaven.

Comment

The language above does not appear in the Rule, but it seems like a good idea to take a brief moment in the midst of this important chapter to look for a moment at the territory we have climbed. There is so much richness here that one is almost struck dumb in the face of such power. Perhaps that is why Benedict valued silence so greatly and was himself so laconic.

Obviously, the most effective thing to do with the above list is to pray it, slowly, at length, and over and over. The reason for its power is, of course, that we do not naturally have humility in our hearts. Our wills tend to be governed by our egos and by our self-pride. This ladder of humility is a concrete and practical way to train our wills toward a different foundational disposition—toward the basic orientation of choosing God in everything.

Reflection

As I become aware of the disposition of my deepest self, my will, I am appalled at how petty and self-serving I am. During the day, many moments creep up on me in which my spontaneous response reveals how self-satisfied I am. I find myself "complimenting" someone, in a way that lets him or her know that I have long experienced what I am pleased to see they are just learning. Or perhaps my tone of voice conveys the opposite of my words, so that effectively I let another know that he is infringing on my precious time. (And then I wonder why my husband gets angry, when "all" I said was something very innocent!) Yet again, I find myself eagerly trying to "manage" the interaction of those around me so that I will control the outcome, rather than let it be the product of the organic contributions of everyone. And all this in only one day! What a long journey I have before me.

Prayer/Response

Chapter 7
VERSE 55

*T*he eighth step of humility is for a monk to do nothing except what is authorized by the common Rule of the monastery, or the example of the seniors.

Comment

Benedict is moving from a discussion of humility as a matter of disposition of the heart to humility as expressed in daily actions. The very first things he mentions are the rules that govern the life of the faith community. For Benedict, the Christian life is most fruitfully lived in community. We do not have to live in a monastery to benefit from this insight.

Functioning as an integral part of a community of faith is essential for one committed to Christ. Fundamentally, this is a living out of the truth that as a Christian, one is a member of the body of which Christ is the head. This biblical image often seems obscure or irrelevant, but it must mean something like: there is no such thing as an individual Christian any more than there is a living set of lungs or little finger, apart from the living creature's body. To be a part of a community of faith means, on the one hand, to share in the liturgical enactment of the redemptive events of Christ's life through regular community worship. On the other hand, it also means to share some daily events of ordinary life with our community.

This insight is foundational to the Rule. But its placement here suggests that Benedict recognizes that resistance to the truth that we are mutually the body of Christ stems in part from personal pride. It is the work of humility to accept and live out one's place as a member of the body.

Reflection

Often I ponder how seldom I have actually experienced myself as a member of the body of Christ. How rare it is for me to be a part of a community (even a small group) where gifts and differences are recognized and celebrated, where each rejoices in the strength of all, where each accepts his or her own limitations and is glad to receive the help of a stranger to complete what is needed. Often I have longed for such a place.

And Benedict invites me to consider that maybe I don't long for it quite as much as I think. Maybe my own reluctance to need others, to welcome strangers, to rejoice in another's strength, or to enjoy what is different (in short, maybe my own pride) prevent me from receiving what otherwise might have been there for the sharing!

Prayer/Response

Chapter 7

VERSES 56–58

*T*he ninth step of humility is that a monk restrain his tongue from speaking, keeping silence until a question is asked him, as the Scripture shows: In much talking you will not avoid sin (Prov 10:19); and, The talkative one goes without direction upon the earth (Ps 140:12).

Comment

In commending silence here, Benedict is primarily condemning loose, easy talk or speech that is not "watchful." But here and elsewhere, he does actively encourage silence, so we must take him to mean not merely that loose talk is to be avoided, but that silence itself is meritorious. He seems to suggest two principal objections to wordiness: l) talking seems inevitably to go along with sinning, and 2) talking prevents us from discovering our authentic human roots in God. How can we relate these two concerns to the matter at hand, humility?

The Proverbs passage from which Benedict quotes is concerned with contrasting the behavior of one who is wise with that of one who is foolish. Interchangeably, the contrast is between one who is righteous and one who is wicked. To be wise is to be righteous; to be foolish is to be wicked. This is not merely a redundancy, but is rather a symbol, intended to point to the truth of a deeper reality. In the context of humility, we see that silence reveals much about our usual motives for speech: to feel important by displaying superior knowledge, to control outcomes, to distract and entertain others, and generally to express our willfulness and pride. The impulse to speak rarely stems from humility, wisdom, or righteousness. Thus, speaking is often not merely foolish, but also wicked.

The long practice of silence begins to nurture in us the humble word—the word of praise or compassion. Without silence, it is difficult to learn how to speak truly; without silence in our lives we hide from ourselves (in noise) the truth of who we really are and what our authentic place is in the universe. In other words, silence roots us. Silence helps us become established in God. Words generally carry us in the other direction, so that we drift like gyrovagues, slaves to our own wills (RB 1:10–11).

Thus, the practice of silence is an essential outward expression of humility.

Reflection

Silence is a gift seldom offered to us nowadays. Often I feel I must "fight" for it, and then, when I do get exterior silence, I realize with shock that I have become so habituated to noise that interiorly I create numerous words to overcome the silence.

I am aware, too, of how often I rush into the silence between another and myself because I am uncomfortable with the intimacy of the silence. I frequently use words to organize the shape of reality, rather than giving myself to the flow of it. Isn't it odd? I would have said that I don't have any sense of silence as a positive element, and yet in these two sentences I reveal to myself that I have indeed experienced the creative power of silence as an invitation. Perhaps that is just how silence works.

Prayer/Response

Chapter 7
VERSE 59

*T*he tenth step of humility is that he be not easily moved and prompt to laughter; because it is written: The fool lifts up his voice in laughter (Sir 21:23).

Comment

Like the verses from Proverbs cited in the last *lectio*, Sirach and much of the so-called "Wisdom literature" of the Bible are devoted to the question of what constitutes the wise life, practically and concretely. In these contexts, wisdom has a deeper meaning than simple knowing, and foolishness a deeper meaning than ignorance or playfulness.

Thus, the question revealed by the quotation, the one on Benedict's mind here, is: How does one live the centered life, the life grounded in the real and the important? Or we might say: What gives a life richness, quality, full-bodied-ness? And the related and immediate issue for us here is: Why is ready laughter not part of such a life?

First, what provokes or evokes laughter? Certainly, the response to this question must involve a long continuum, for in one important sense, laughter is uniquely human, almost a sign of what it is to be human, an expression of joy and compassion. But in another equally important sense, laughter is an acute method of focusing hostility and embodying separateness. Quite frequently we use laughter to criticize superiors (mothers-in-law no less than abbots), "put down" those deemed inferior (Polish and Italian jokes), or enjoy the awkward position of another (when someone slips on a banana peel). Laughter can be almost a lightning rod for the kind of pettiness that has as its purpose the nourishment of self-importance and pridefulness.

Second, what does it mean to be "prompt" to laughter? The phrase suggests an awareness of where our attention lies. While it is true that the whole Benedictine spirit is to be present fully to what is given in this time and place, such presence is intended to have a sacramental quality. That is, we are always to be looking within what is given for God's presence. In contrast, there is a kind of presence to the material that is all external, a presence that has no vision for the mysterious and wonderful and upsetting inner and spiritual gift of the present. A person given to ready laughter is likely to be someone whose attention is focused on surface things, thus missing the true quality of the present moment. Such a person finds only separation and hierarchy, rather than union in humble community.

Reflection

How is my life touched by the question of fullness of life? What gives my life richness and quality? I'm not sure that I even ask those questions of my life . . . and yet I see that in some measure, these questions do lie underneath all my activity. As usual, I begin to see it first on the negative side. In the last few weeks, I have been away from home in a variety of different settings, and I have begun to sense the interconnection of all the elements of the Rule. I have been in strange settings with strange rhythms, so I have lost that sense of organic unity of the day that is possible in the habitual routines I have begun to adopt at home. I am also acutely aware of how little rooted I am in the present. There are so many new stimuli constantly bombarding me that I feel totally disoriented and unable to give real attention to any of them. I am lost in the pure materiality of things—like the one who laughs too much, right now I feel that my awareness is locked at the surface level; I'm not truly present to anything. There never seems to be time or space to be with anyone or anything long enough to know its truth, and thus discover the way in which I am part of it, and it a part of me.

In this temporary absence of some of the patterns I have been adopting from the Rule, I begin to sense their importance to the overall quality of my life. I sense that humility, presence, silence, daily rhythms—all are essential elements for me to live a life recollected in God.

Prayer/Response

Chapter 7
VERSES 60–61

*T**he eleventh step of humility is that when a monk speaks he does so gently and without laughter, humbly, gravely, with few and reasonable words, and that he is not noisy in his speech, as it is written: "A wise person is known through his few words."*

Comment

In this section of the chapter on external manifestations of humility, three of Benedict's five steps to humility relate to speech. Why, we might ask, is speech so important to humility?

Humility, as the fundamental monastic virtue, is intended to correct excessive pride, that human characteristic so destructive of intimacy with God. Pride and humility are also evident qualities in the ordinary interactions of human relations, and speech is the primary vehicle of these interactions. Without minimizing the importance of body language, nor of interior motivation (the subject matter of the first seven steps), we can still acknowledge that speech remains a basic way we interact with each other. Thus, speech is a remarkably good mechanism by which to practice and assess the growth (or lack) of humility in our spirits.

What does Benedict suggest we might look for in the speech of a humble person? First, restraint: not much talk, and the willingness to persevere in silence. Second, attention to central or important concerns and seriousness—not so much in the sense of gravity as in the sense of being centered in the vital issues of life. Third, reason: the person of prayer need not be illogical or otherworldly. Fourth, absence of force: not raising the voice; letting truth "speak for itself." Finally, gentleness: a quality of compassion so great that one will "not break the bruised reed nor quench the wavering flame" (Isa 42:3; RB 64:3).

So often today we are preoccupied with issues of power and authority, what constitutes them, and how they can be expressed. And, as is true so often in our culture, much "hype" surrounds these discussions, whether they focus on the church, politics, the economy, or the family. In contrast, the simplicity of Benedict's description of the speech of the humble is truly powerful. Here indeed is a vivid portrait of what authority looks like in the humble person, the person who lives near to God.

Reflection

Often I long to be able to speak like that—out of the center of my being, simply and with authority. But recently I have begun to recognize that when I do so, I risk invisibility. For while there are those who will be deeply moved by the power of humble speech, there are many more who will not, cannot, notice it at all. Our culture gives so much attention to noise, neon, and force, that many among us have lost sensitivity to certain ranges of human experience, notably the humble and gentle ones. And my ego wants to be noticed.

On the other hand, sometimes when people do notice humility in me, I feel shy and awkward because I don't know quite "how" to be one through whom God is visible. Humility, it seems to me, stands in the center of these two responses, as a discipline that directly helps me learn intimacy with God and living as a channel of Christ's own essence.

Prayer/Response

Chapter 7
VERSES 62–66

*T*he twelfth step of humility is that the monk, not only in his heart, but by means of his very body always shows his humility to all who see him: that is, in work, in the oratory, in the monastery, in the garden, on the road, in the field, or wherever he may be, whether sitting,

walking, or standing: with head always bent down and eyes fixed on
the earth, he always thinks of the guilt of his sins and imagines himself
already present before the terrible judgment seat of God, always saying
in his heart what the publican in the Gospel said with his eyes fixed
on the earth: Lord, I a sinner am not worthy to raise my eyes to heaven
(Luke 18:13). And again, with the prophet: I am bowed down and
humbled on every side (Ps 38:7–9; Ps 119:107).

Comment

Christian saints throughout the ages have talked about "recollection,"
that attitude of concentrated awareness in which we are continuously
attuned to the truth about who God is and who we are in light of that
relationship with God. The word means collected again—not fragmented, scattered, dispersed, and partial—but centered in the truth
that makes us whole.

Recollection is a learned behavior that takes years and years of
practice. Five minutes given to the practice of recollection is an excellent teacher. Part of the reason it is so difficult to stay recollected is
that its practice requires us to live into paradoxical truths: that we
are creatures (in fact created/made by the High and Lofty One who
inhabits eternity), and that God loves each one of us utterly. It is
hard to hold the truth of both of these ideas simultaneously in our
consciousness.

And yet that's just what Benedict is asking us to do here. Psalm
119 expresses the human confession that I am deeply troubled (in
sin, confusion, and alienation from my true self), but I trust that
you (God) will preserve me and make my life unified, as you have
promised. Benedict has freely blended the quotation from Luke
with Matthew 8:8, thus deepening our understanding of the publican's humility by including the confession of faith by the centurion
(which we now use at the center of our eucharistic celebration):
"Lord, I am not worthy to receive you, but only say the word and I
shall be healed."

Reflection

I was vividly impressed by an image of Jim Wallis's that the Christian spirit involves something like this: constantly keeping before
our eyes both the image of a child's suffering face in bombed

Hiroshima and the image of the deepest love and comfort we have ever known.[47] To hold both images at once is the challenge, since either one alone is incomplete. As I ponder that, I experience my own helplessness in attempting to contain such profound and opposite passions. Yet, I sense too that this helplessness throws me back into that dependence upon God in which I am silent and waiting.

Prayer/Response

Chapter 7
VERSES 67–70 (END)

Having, therefore, ascended all these steps of humility, the monk will soon arrive at that love of God which, being perfect, casts out fear (1 John 4:18): whereby he shall begin to keep without effort and as it were naturally and by custom, all those precepts which he had formerly observed not without fear; now no longer through dread of hell, but for the love of Christ, through a good disposition and delight in virtue. This God will grant to appear by the Holy Spirit in the laborer, now cleansed from vices and sin.

Comment

Benedict cites a rich passage in 1 John to draw this chapter to a close. God is love; when we love, we abide in God; love is possible thanks to the gift of the Spirit; as this love is perfected in us, we lose fear, for we come to know God as Lover.

Words are inadequate to express the great mystery that is the relationship between our discipline and God's grace, as we come more and more to be the persons we are called to be. Benedict's sentences are one beautiful expression; St. John's are another. The invitation is to find words of our own to express this mystery as we grow to experience it in our lives.

In this chapter, Benedict has shown that humility consists of both inner motive and exterior expression. We might say that humility is a growing disposition, as is daily action, and both are formed in prayer. Don't be fooled by the image of the ladder into thinking this is a progressive achievement of human perfection. Above all, humility is growth into a relationship of love.

At the heart of the whole process is a profound sense of our inability to undertake any of this work without the help of God. And that is coupled with an eager longing to undertake it for the love of God. Humility encompasses both inability and eager longing. And it does lead us to new life.

Reflection

Do I really believe in the possibility of new life? Is there a way to get from here (fearfulness) to there (perfect love)? Am I allowing the Spirit to work God's love in me? Probably yes and no. Some days, yes. Some days, no. And what I hope is that gradually there are more yes days.

If I reflect on the mystery of the work of God's love in my life, however, I do see a growing response in me to love. I act as best I can, and find my simple and hesitant steps greatly enhanced by love operating inside as well as outside me. And then, at some moment when I'm not looking, something fundamental shifts inside me, and I look back surprised, realizing I am forever changed. This inner shift expresses itself in outer actions. Then the whole process repeats itself.

Since each day I'm dealing with today's issues, I don't always notice these shifts except when I look back reflectively. But I do think that noticing is a form of cooperation with the Spirit. That's one of the main reasons I write in a journal and annually review my journal. It often astonishes me to see what God has accomplished in me!

Prayer/Response

Interlude III
A NOTE TO THE READER

How is the pace of this *lectio* for you?

At times perhaps it seems as if we are spending too long on a point you already have well integrated. At other times it may seem as if we are rushing too quickly through an area that would lend itself to a more lingering approach.

We do not know exactly how the Rule was crafted, but as we explore it, it seems to be the result of years of pondering both scripture and daily life in community. Sometimes we encounter perspectives that seem quite new or that suddenly evoke a fresh resonance in us. As we consider the consequences and implications of a new insight, it may be that we also feel drawn to take time with it.

Feel free to do just that. If a word or phrase or segment of the Rule is particularly powerful for you, there is nothing at all wrong with spending several days or weeks or even months with that one word or phrase. As long as it holds you and seems to be working creatively within you, stay with it.

One way to linger with a passage is simply to re-read it each morning, preferably out loud, letting your body become engaged with the passage via your lips and teeth and tongue. Repeat it several times softly to yourself, letting it sink to the level of your heart as well as your mind, taking root and setting fire there.

Then quietly ponder the passage. Review its fundamental meaning and then explore the feelings it evokes in you today. Consider its relation to your life as you understand it at this moment. What might God be asking of you or offering to you today with these words? Bring your needs and longings to God and offer them in response to your reading.

Finally, rest in peace. Give all your reflections back to God, for whatever God wishes to do with them in your life. Physically, even, release all your wonderments back to God with a big sigh. Then sit in silence for a few moments, waiting on God, enjoying God's presence. Receive the gift God offers you, most especially the gift of Godself.

Gently and thankfully, return to your day.

Continue this each day with the same passage until you are ready to go on to the next one.

The Divine Office

Chapter 8, The Divine
Office at Night
(ENTIRE)

*I*n winter time, that is, from the first of November until Easter, the brothers are to rise at what is reasonably calculated to be the eighth hour of the night, so that having rested until a little past midnight, they may arise with their food fully digested. The time that remains after Vigils should be spent in study by those who still have some part of the psalter or readings to learn.

From Easter to the aforementioned first of November the hour of Vigils should be so arranged that after a very short interval, during which the brethren may go out for the necessities of nature, Lauds (which are to begin at daybreak) may begin without delay.

Comment

Without preface, Benedict has jumped immediately into directions for celebration of the monastic "divine office" (often called today the "Daily Office" or the "liturgy of the hours"). The next twelve chapters spell out Benedict's explicit instructions about this central feature of cenobitic life. The desert hermits hoped to pray unceasingly, and thus minimized specific periods of prayer as a concession to human weakness. In contrast, the urban cathedral communities of the early centuries had regular daily periods of prayer, roughly corresponding to the ancient Jewish synagogue and temple customs, in which a few persons daily offered formal prayers on behalf of the whole community of the faithful.

Benedict takes the best of both these traditions, and adds his own insight that the liturgical and corporate prayer of the (whole) people of God leads the people through the cycle of Christ's life, reproducing in their own lives the life and passion of Christ in order that they may become his body.

The full Benedictine office will be set forth in Chapter 16. As we proceed, we will see what Benedict considers the essence of these times of community prayer. In introduction, however, it is important to point out that he places this section as close as possible to the first seven chapters of the Rule on the "spiritual theology" of monastic life and as the essential bridge to the "practical living" section. More than anything else, the divine office informs the quality of the entire monastic Christian life and forms the monk in the goal of preferring nothing to Christ.

Benedict builds this essential work of community prayer on natural human foundations: it is integrated with natural seasonal rhythms of day and night, and natural human rhythms of nourishment, digestion, elimination, and rest. All of life is regarded tenderly and viewed as consecrated for God.

Reflection

Much as I know better, I still find myself separating things that are worthy and holy from things that are unimportant and profane. I do not truly love and cherish my body, for example, and how much Benedict startles me when he sets forth instructions about prayer within a framework of adequate time to rest and go to the bathroom! In contrast, I find myself more within the dualistic tension represented in part by Becker's wry definition of humans as "gods with anuses."[48] My heart experiences with amazement the difference between the weary cynicism and despair implicit in the modern view of the body, and the Rule's consistent tenderness for the ordinary, the weak, and the creaturely (the person). Benedict unites the holy and the mundane, the body and the Spirit, in an attitude of utter simplicity. More than anything else, that attitude of Benedict's teaches me what God's love must be like.

Prayer/Response

Chapter 9, How Many Psalms Are Sung at the Night Hours
(ENTIRE)

In winter time Vigils begins with this verse, repeated three times: O Lord, open my lips; and my mouth shall declare your praise (Ps 51:16).[49] Then follows Psalm 3 with Glory be; then Psalm 95 with a refrain, or at least chanted. After that comes an Ambrosian hymn, then six psalms with refrains.

These being sung, a versicle is read and the abbot gives the blessing.
All being seated in their places, the brothers read in turn three lessons
from the book on the lectern; three responsories are sung between the
readings—two of them without the gloria, but after the third the cantor
is to sing the gloria, all the monks rising from their places out of honor
and reverence for the Holy Trinity. The divinely-inspired books of the Old
and New Testaments are to be read at Vigils, as well as commentaries
upon them by the most renowned and orthodox catholic Fathers.

After these three lessons with their responsories six more psalms follow
with a sung "alleluia." Then a lesson from the Apostle is said by heart
with a versicle and the petition of the Litany—that is "Lord, have mercy".
And thus the Vigils of the night come to an end.

Comment

The office of Vigils begins the day, and Benedict's version is an expression of honor for the mystery and wonder of God. An appropriate ending to the night's deep silence is that the monks' first speech is the prayer: "Lord, open our lips and our mouths shall declare your praise." Repeating this phrase not only sets the monk's mind and heart on God, but also unites the monk with the solemn worship of Jesus' time, when this verse was used to introduce the eighteen benedictions of the synagogue.[50]

Psalm 3 is a reminder that the Lord is our shield and our glory and our deliverer, and requests the Lord's blessing on the people this day. Psalm 95 emphasizes the central Benedictine theme of listening for God: he is our God and we are his people; this day, if each of us hears God's voice, we dare not harden our hearts!

Later we'll see that Benedict calls for all 150 psalms to be prayed during the divine office each week. Since early Jewish times, the psalms have been considered the prayer of God's people, expressing the full range of human longing, confession, confidence—in short, expressing complete relationship with God.

To join in the corporate prayer of the psalms is to claim our inheritance in a long tradition of faith in God. But it is more. In praying the psalms, we participate in that marvelous ongoing ambiguity of relationship with God concerning how prayer begins. Are the psalms God's words to us through scripture or are they our prayers as humans crying out to God—or both? This mutuality in the nature of the office is emphasized by the regular refrains/responses to the prayed and heard scripture. The refrain is a reminder of the immediate and personal communication between God and each/all of the beloved people. The stipulated responses of praise (alleluia), reverence (Glory be), and petition (Lord, have mercy) span the range of our engagement with God.

This office and the others prayed during the day are a recalling of who God is and who we are; they are also a celebration of the conviction that God calls each of us as the beloved. The "recollection" and repetition of the office lets these truths enter deeply into our beings and become our personal as well as corporate truth.

Reflection

I feel fortunate that the Daily Office is a gift of the church to me as a laywoman. The Anglican morning and evening prayer services are modeled very closely on Benedict's formula, so I too may begin the day by opening my lips in praise of God and being reminded of God's calling out to my heart. It seems to me that the prayers must be offered in community, but on those occasions when I pray them "alone," I am acutely aware of being part of those living and dead, in my "time zone" and elsewhere, who are praying with me.

At first, it seems odd to return to the same words each day, and to discover my mind resisting the sometimes blatantly offensive sentiments of the old psalms. The boredom and routine often seem a burden. Distractions are numerous, and the temptation is great to let it go.

Yet, oddly enough, I am growing to realize how much more profound and joyful an experience the office is after it has been faithfully and foolishly repeated hundreds of times. Some days I realize my heart is singing with the wonder of these great truths that belong not only to me but to all God's people of all time.

Prayer/Response

Chapter 10, How the Night Office
Is to Be Sung in Summer
(ENTIRE)

*F*rom Easter to the first of November, the same number of psalms is sung as described above; however no lessons are to be read since the nights are shorter. Instead of those three lessons, one from the Old Testament is said by heart, followed by a short responsory; the rest is as described above. In other words, there are never sung less than twelve psalms at Vigils, not counting Psalms 3 and 95.

Comment

The Daily Office consecrates and is consecrated by the whole of life. Not only is Benedict sensitive to the needs and rhythms of the human body; as he constructs the format for these times of community worship, he also weaves the prayer very intimately with the cycle of nature.

Today we are so accustomed to electricity and standard measurements of time, to central heating and air conditioning and the availability of year-round produce, that it may be difficult for us to imagine the more intimate relationship with nature in Benedict's time. There were then two basic divisions to each day: the period from sunup to sundown (day) and the period from sundown to sunup (night). Each of these periods was divided into twelve segments called *horae* (hours). But since sunup and sundown varied throughout the year, so did the length of an hour![51]

Thus Benedict, instead of following the modern tendency to force the natural rhythms to conform to his desire for completion of certain activities, bows generously to the natural rhythms by adjusting the requirements of the Rule. This shift reflects an understanding of the human as steward of nature, cooperating in harmony with earth toward an organic sense of wholeness. Here and in many other verses in the Rule, Benedict reverences and praises the work of God in creation as well as adoring the work of God in redemption.

Reflection

Again and again I am humbled by the realization of how profoundly Benedict loves God in all things. I see how deeply I am separated from natural and organic rhythms, how very inattentive I am to situations and movements with which I might work harmoniously. Instead, my first question is always more of a "managerial" one: What do I want to accomplish here? How can I proceed to get it?

For example, in nature there is a far better balance of work and rest than I normally follow in my day. There are seasons of great fruitfulness, and seasons when all lies fallow. I sense that much the same might be true in the rhythms of my social and spiritual life. Several years ago I noticed that even in my service to others, I normally started with what I thought ought to be done, and later found myself exhausted with very little to show for it. So instead I began to ask this question first: What is already beginning to bloom that needs nurture in order to continue its growth? Then I would seek to cooperate with what I noticed was already underway. Gradually I realized that I was finally asking: Where is the Holy Spirit already at work? And cooperating there with God.

Prayer/Response

Chapter 11, How Vigils Is Sung on Sunday
(ENTIRE)

*O*n Sundays the brethren are to arise earlier for Vigils, in which Vigils there must also be discretion with regard to quantity. When six psalms and a versicle have been sung (as already prescribed), and all are seated on benches in their proper order, four lessons with their responsories are to be read from the book as before: and only to the last responsory is the reader to add a "Glory be", all reverently rising as soon as he begins it.

After the lessons six more psalms follow, with their refrain and versicles as above; then four more lessons with their responsories are read in the same way as described. Next follow three canticles from the prophets, as the abbot appoints, the canticles being sung with an Alleluia. After the versicle and the abbot's blessing, four lessons from the New Testament are read as above. At the end of the fourth responsory, the abbot begins the hymn "We praise you, O God". After the hymn, he reads from the Gospel while all stand with awe and reverence. The Gospel being ended, all reply "Amen", and the abbot immediately begins the hymn "To you be praise"; after the blessing, Lauds begins.

This order for Vigils should always be followed on Sundays, summer and winter, unless (which God forbid) they arise too late. In this case, the readings or responsories should be somewhat shortened. All care should be taken that this does not happen; but if it does, the one through whose neglect it has come to pass must make fitting satisfaction for it to God in the oratory.

Comment

This office is obviously constructed with great care, because it is, of course, the first community prayer of the week. Yet what personal freedom Benedict expresses in his simple acknowledgement that sometimes the monks might oversleep, and then things would have to be shortened! This is particularly remarkable because, at this time, other monastic abbots required an all-night vigil/watch on Saturday night to welcome Sunday morning. Benedict's admonition for "discretion" is quite serious. Everything is ordered to God, in light of the limits set by human nature. He takes very much to heart the words of our Lord, "What I want is mercy, not sacrifice" (Matt 9:13).

Sunday begins the week because it is the day of the Lord, the central Christian feast, the wondrous acknowledgment of God's saving and loving work in Christ's death and resurrection. The monastic cycle of the weekly office begins with Sunday Vigils, always with Psalm 21 (RB 18:6), which rejoices in the strength and blessings of the Lord. We see this celebration of the day of resurrection particularly in the third segment of Sunday Vigils, which begins with the hymns/canticles, continues with the "alleluias" (since Jewish times, this word has expressed thanks for the saving might of God), the New Testament readings, the Gospel, and the hymns of praise. The format is similar to that developed in the Syrian Christian Church in the fourth century and known as the "resurrection vigil."[52]

The whole of the monastic vocation has been summarized in the word "paschalization": reproducing in one's own life the pattern drawn by Christ, so that one becomes like Christ to the glory of God.[53] This first office of the week invites the monastic to take to his/her own heart the present wonder and joy of Christ's resurrection.

Reflection

I think paschalization is a process not limited to monks, but offered to every Christian who is open to the ongoing call of God. In particular, I find my own experience of God in Christ greatly deepened by regular participation in the liturgy. To experience the seasons of the church year and week as moments of the life and death and resurrection of Christ deepens my appreciation of the ways those mysteries appear in my own life. I discover a different and more holistic way of interpreting my daily experience; I gain peacefulness about whatever happens and feel great thanksgiving in the midst of ordinary events. The words I have for it are very inadequate, but I know that I am being gradually transformed from the inside out.

Prayer/Response

Chapter 12, How the Office of Lauds Is to Be Sung
(ENTIRE)

*A*t Lauds on Sunday Psalm 67 is first sung straight through without a refrain. After this, Psalm 51 is sung with "Alleluia", and then Psalms 118 and 63 are sung. After this follows the Blessed are You [Canticle of the Three Young Men], the Praises [Psalms 148–150], a lesson from the Apocalypse said by heart, a responsory, an Ambrosian hymn, a versicle, a canticle from the Gospel, the litany; and thus it is concluded.

Comment

Let us look in detail at the composition of this important office, continuing the Sunday morning praise, which is prayed particularly in thanksgiving for and celebration of the power of God made known especially in the resurrection of our Lord. Every element of this service contributes to the fullness of this praise.[54]

Psalm 67 begins the day with a petition for God's blessing, always followed by the penitential petition of Psalm 51. On Sunday, this is set in the context of the "Alleluia" antiphon/refrain. Psalm 118 is a reminder that "This is Yaweh's doing . . . a day made memorable by Yahweh" (verse 24), and Psalm 63 is a re-centering in our fundamental longing for God.

The canticle and Psalms 148–150 are full of praise (indeed, they are sometimes simply known as "Blessed are You" and "the Praises"), and again the "Alleluia" theme recalls us especially to this day of resurrection. The lesson from the Apocalypse/Book of Revelation celebrates the victory of the Lamb, shared by the church. And here, in his usual gentle way, Benedict reminds us that this shout of triumph is best spoken from the heart, for this passage is not to be read but memorized, "said by heart."

The Ambrosian hymn reflects Benedict's awareness that this fullness of joy may seek expression more exuberantly than allowed by ordinary chant.

The gospel canticle is always the Song of Zechariah (Luke 1:68–79)—every morning at Lauds—and it recalls the ancient Jewish idea that morning is the time of deliverance: "[O]ur God who from on high will bring the rising sun to visit us, to give light to those who live in darkness" (verses 78–79). And the litany includes prayers for the church and for the world; past, present, and future, living and dead.

Benedict concludes with a phrase often translated "let it come to an end," which might equally well mean "let it be so with me."

Reflection

My desire in response to this hymn of praise as crafted by Benedict is to offer up many of the words and phrases that comprise it. They are words that belong to us all; I pray they will more and more become my own.

My own God, give me and my family in Christ, your blessing.

Have mercy on me: Create in me a clean heart and renew a right spirit within me.

Most of all, do not cast me away from your presence.

Alleluia, for you hear my prayer before I call.

You are good and your mercy endures forever.

You have acted this day, and I rejoice in it!

Eagerly do I seek you. My soul clings to you and your right hand holds me fast.

Blessed are you, Lord God of our ancestors! We will praise you and highly exalt you forever.

We rejoice in you our Creator, for you take pleasure in your people.

By right, O Christ, do you have splendor and honor. For not only are you our maker, but also our redeemer. Your deeds surpass our understanding, and we draw near to you to offer you our grateful thanks and praise.

Prayer/Response

Chapter 13, How Lauds Are Sung on Ordinary Weekdays
VERSES 1–11

*O*n ordinary weekdays, Lauds is to be sung as follows: Psalm 67 is sung without a refrain and somewhat slowly as on Sunday in order that all may be in time for Psalm 51, which is to be sung with a refrain. After this two more psalms are sung according to custom, that is: on Monday, Psalms 5 and 36; on Tuesday, Psalms 43 and 57; on Wednesday, Psalms 64 and 65; on Thursday, Psalms 88 and 90; on Friday, Psalms 76 and 92; on Saturday, Psalm 143 and the Canticle from Deuteronomy, which is to be divided with two glorias. But on other days Canticles from the Prophets are sung, according to the practice of the Roman Church. Then should follow the Praises [Psalms 148–150], a lesson from the Apostle said by heart, a responsory, an Ambrosian hymn, a versicle, the Canticle from the Gospel; and thus it is concluded.

Comment

To practice the offices is to repeat the words from scripture, the words of salvation and covenant and promise, not only as God's words to us, but also as our words to God. As we rehearse and remember these holy events, they are to become real, part of our own personal experience. We are to be drawn more and more into the life of God. Thus, in this first office after daybreak, Benedict selects psalms for each day designed to remind us of the essential ingredients of our primary relationship with God. These ingredients are well summarized in the canticle from Deuteronomy (Song of Moses, Deut 31:30–32:43), which contrasts God's faithfulness with

Israel's faithlessness and celebrates God's love for and ultimate victory on behalf of God's people.

Again, we note the gentle touch of Benedict's own loving-kindness: some will undoubtedly be late for the first psalm, so let it be sung slowly so that all at least will be present for the second one.

And so the day begins with God's praises on our lips and in our hearts.

Reflection

It almost seems like it would be good to take a week, simply beginning each day with the two psalms Benedict recommends, saying them slowly, and letting myself wonder about them during the day following. What, if anything, do these words have to do with me today? "The one who wishes life must fear God" (Ps 36: Monday); "My heart is fixed on God and I find myself singing" (Ps 57: Tuesday); and so on.

It feels a little foolish even to think of it, but why not regard it as a sort of experiment? Why not take the words of scripture and pray them as my own? And maybe I could even try it in community, that is, when I knew that a few other Christian friends would also be reading the same psalms that morning in their own homes. The idea "tempts" me greatly.

Prayer/Response

Chapter 13
VERSES 12–14 (END), AND
Chapter 14, How the Office of Vigils Is Sung on Saint's Days
(ENTIRE)

*M*ost certainly, the Offices of Lauds and Vespers should never conclude without the Lord's Prayer being sung aloud by the Superior so that all may hear it, because of the thorns of scandal which are likely to spring up: in this way the brothers are warned by the covenant which they make in that prayer: Forgive us as we forgive (Matt 6:12), they may cleanse themselves of this sort of vice. But at the other Offices, only the *last part of the prayer is sung aloud, so that all may answer: But deliver us from evil (Matt 6:13).*

[Chapter 14] On the feasts of saints, and indeed on all solemnities, the Office should be ordered as on Sundays, except that the psalms, refrains and readings suitable for that day are used. Otherwise the arrangements are the same as described above.

Comment

At the beginning and end of each day, the monks are to remember the words of the Lord's Prayer, the essential prayer of one seeking God. The attention here given to two petitions of this prayer emphasizes a purpose underlying all the prayers of the office: the fact that the Daily Office is intended to influence the daily life of the monks, particularly in their relations to each other. As we pray to be forgiven as we forgive, we are essentially making a commitment to be forgiving with those now praying with us. This doesn't sound like a radical idea, but as we look at the way we live with each other, we see how profound a conversion is involved each time we pray.

This instruction reflects a clear-eyed recognition that committed Christians are human, and thus we will indeed encounter thorns, contention, and evil in each day—not only outside ourselves, but inside as well. Each time we notice this yet again, we are reminded of the centrality of the "spiritual instrument": never despair of God's mercy (RB 4:74).

And then we continue on, to the next item of ordinary life and its shape, dealing as best we can with what is given to us in each moment. We weave our course between pride and despair, holding to the truth that God's name is hallowed, and God's will is to be done on earth, as we open ourselves humbly to God's Spirit and God's care.

Reflection

Lately I have been thinking hard about why the church often seems to be the least holy place I can imagine. There may be many reasons for it, but I am struck by Benedict's approach to the problem. He seems never to be surprised when anyone falls short, which makes me think he was well acquainted with his own shortcomings. But on the other hand, he always insists that we are called daily to greater intimacy with God.

In contrast, I usually tend either to wallow in my shortcomings or in those of others, depressed and fearful, convinced that I will never be released from the power of sin and death. Or else I ignore the possibility of shortcomings, only to be reminded with shame all too soon. How difficult it is to keep a balance between the two: remembering that this world is not yet fully free, and equally remembering that Christ has already won the final victory, and the darkness cannot overcome the Light. I struggle to hold that vision firmly and to live each day simply in accord with it.

Prayer/Response

Chapter 15, At What Times of the Year "Alleluia" Is Said
(ENTIRE)

*F*rom holy Easter until Pentecost, without interruption, "Alleluia" is said both with the psalms and the responsories. From Pentecost until the beginning of Lent, it is to be said every night at Vigils with the second six psalms only. On every Sunday except during Lent, the canticles, Vigils, Lauds, Prime, Terce, Sext and None are said with "Alleluia"; however a refrain is used at Vespers. The responsories are never to be said with "Alleluia", except from Easter to Pentecost.

Comment

The Jewish practice was to say *Hallel-Yah* (Praise Yahweh/God) at the beginning of the psalms. Christian custom adopted the term early, as a heartfelt expression of joy and gratitude at God's saving action, especially in Christ, in the paschal mystery of death and resurrection in which each Christian is also born to new life. This paschal theme is at the heart of Benedict's understanding of monastic life and is symbolized by the term "Alleluia" in the offices.[55]

The consecrated life of monasticism is a way of responding to the baptismal covenant of each Christian. In Baptism, each dies to the old life and is born to the new; each shares the work of Christ and benefits from its fruits. In Baptism, this dying and rising is given as a seal and a "first fruits." The full integration of this promise into our lives is the purpose of the life of consecration to God. Benedict's Rule intends to show how someone can be faithful to the promise of Baptism in the daily consecration of life.

One of his key ingredients is the centering of the life in the Daily Office and the liturgical calendar. "Alleluia," that small word of praise and thanksgiving, is a simple way to highlight and punctuate the shift of liturgical seasons. During Lent, a time of penitence and preparation for Easter, the Alleluia is suppressed altogether. During the Easter season, on the other hand, it is said with all the psalms and responsories. On all Sundays except in Lent, it is said with the psalms. And each night, as the monks rise for the first office and recollect themselves to the truth of things, the Alleluia is said with the psalms (again, except during Lent).

Here, too, Benedict's simplicity is evident. He is glad to make use of a small word to engage the body (the mouth, the ear) and thus to reach the mind and spirit and heart.

Reflection

One year a friend of mine from a nonliturgical church joined me for midweek worship during the seasons of Lent and Easter. During Easter week, she told me with tears in her eyes: "Now I see why the Alleluia was suppressed during Lent. On Easter I received it and the gift of the season with much joy!" I was profoundly moved by her words.

As I write now, it is Ash Wednesday, and the season of "darkness" begins. We prepare for the cross, and for those moments when God seems far away, when our minds cannot comprehend God's wisdom. We pray in repentance and in trust in God's mercy. And "Alleluia" is gone for a time.

Prayer/Response

Chapter 16, How the Work of God Is to Be Performed during the Day

As the Prophet says: Seven times a day I have given you praise (Ps 119:164). We will complete this sacred number of seven if at the times of Lauds, Prime, Terce, Sext, None, Vespers and Compline, we fulfill the duties of our office. For it was of these daytime hours that he said, Seven times a day have I given you praise (Ps 119:164); just as the same Prophet said concerning Vigils, At midnight I arose to give praise to you (Ps 119:62). At these times, therefore, we should sing the praises of our Creator for his just judgments: Lauds, Prime, Terce, Sext, None, Vespers and Compline; and at night let us arise to give him praise (Ps 119:164, 62).

Comment

Here Benedict sets forth the daily schedule for the divine office, the periods during which the monks come together for prayer.[56] By setting this schedule in the context of Psalm 119, Benedict implies several things about the purpose of the office.

First, it is to praise God. Prayer may be for many purposes and all are legitimate in the context of communication and communion with God. Yet, is it not the case that at the heart of all the other reasons is praise—the joyful overflow of a heart filled with gratitude and delight?

Traditionally, Psalm 119 is chosen to be recalled in the midst of ordinary routines, to recollect ourselves to the central realities of God's presence and governing power in all created things and movements. It is said at noon and on Wednesdays in the American Anglican cycle of prayer—exactly in the midst both of the day and of the week, to recall us to our center. There are those who regard it as a legalistic prayer, since each verse recites some application of God's law. And others interpret God's law as the essence of God's being— Love. In any case, it helps center our attention in the sacramental reality of the present moment: God is here! God is now!

And this is the purpose of punctuating the day with the office, to ground ourselves in God, to build habitual recollection of the I-Thou relation in our deepest spirit. Seven is a "sacred number" because it signifies perfection or completion,[57] and we might imagine that both Benedict and the psalmist envision recollection as embodying both the perfection of the person and the glory of God.

Reflection

Is praise a learned response, a spontaneous emotion, or both? Sometimes when I think about praise, I feel that I know nothing about it. What is praise, and how does one come to experience it? Sometimes, too, my heart "naturally" flows over, in what is partly love and gratitude, but partly also something more—nearer awe or wonder, or even respect. I've never thought of respect as a heartfelt emotion, yet I see that it may be so.

I do think that in some sense praise is learned, or at least practice deepens our capacity for it. And I see what a good setting the office (the community's prayer) is for the practice of praise. When I am together with others in worship, recalling the promises and actions of God in history as a reminder that God is present today, then I begin to apprehend how mighty and how loving is the God who was and is and will be. I realize how much I am in debt, and how deeply I am linked to an astonishingly rich world of creatures and created matter, and I glimpse how great must be the One in whom we all find our source and goal. All this is something that grows in me as I practice turning myself toward it. Or so it seems.

Prayer/Response

Chapter 17, How Many Psalms Are to Be Sung at these Hours
(ENTIRE)

We have already dealt with the order of psalmody for Vigils and Lauds. Let us proceed to arrange for the remaining hours.

At Prime three psalms are to be sung, separately and not under the same "Glory be". The hymn at this hour is to follow the opening versicle, O God, come to my assistance (Ps 70:2), before the psalms are begun. Then, at the end of the three psalms, one lesson is to be recited with a versicle, the Lord have mercy, and the dismissal.

At Terce, Sext, and None prayer is celebrated the same way: that is, the verse, the hymn proper to each hour, three psalms, the lesson and versicle, the Lord have mercy and the dismissal. If the community is somewhat large, the psalms are to be sung with refrains; if smaller, the psalms are sung straight through.

The Vespers Office is to consist of four psalms with refrains: after the psalms a lesson is to be recited; then the responsory, the Ambrosian hymn and versicle, the canticle from the Gospel, the litany, and, immediately before the dismissal, the Lord's Prayer.

Compline consists of the recitation of three psalms, to be said straight through without refrains; then the hymn for that hour, one lesson, the versicle, the Lord, have mercy, the blessing, and the concluding prayer.

Comment

Benedict is not, of course, creating this schedule of offices "from scratch"; he is calling upon many sources, and integrating them as seems best for his purposes. In the whole Rule, Benedict never seeks to be original, but rather to draw on the wisdom of tradition in light of the Gospel and his community's needs. His goal is to penetrate the truth of the Gospel deeply, to determine how it is best lived in the concrete setting he faces. Paradoxically, his attentiveness to the limitations of his setting results in guidance profoundly relevant to our own situatedness.

The quality in this overall structure of the offices is reminiscent of the Prologue's promise that there will be "nothing harsh or oppressive" (verse 46). Each office during the day is concise and succinct, a brief gathering to praise and to recollect oneself to God, but none is elaborate, lengthy, or strenuous.

The distinction made for practice between large and small communities suggests a desire that the office be participative, not entertainment for the many by the few, but assuring that every person joins in the worship of God.

Two ingredients in particular seem to tie all the offices together in continuity and unity. One is the hymn at each hour (is this because the hymn is a glorious natural way to express the fullness of praise?); the other is the versicles ("O God, come to my assistance"; and "Lord, have mercy"). These two short prayers were firmly established in the Christian community as key means of recollection, even by Benedict's time. They were understood to be prayers to be taken into all the moments of the day, in the mind and heart, in order to pray constantly, to deepen the habitual awareness of relationship with God.[58]

Reflection

I do not often leave worship or prayer taking with me what Francis de Sales calls a little "bouquet"[59]—a verse or phrase of prayer to sustain me during the hours of the day and night that follow. It seems a lovely idea. It comforts me just to think of it, and yet I seldom do it.

Perhaps I might try it for a week or two and discover what effect, if any, it has in my life and on my attitudes.

Prayer/Response

Chapter 18, In What Order
the Psalms Are to Be Sung
(ENTIRE)

At the beginning of the day hours this verse is always to be said: O God, come to my assistance; O Lord, make haste to help me (Ps 70:2) with the gloria, followed by the hymn proper to each hour. At Prime on Sunday, four parts of Psalm 119 are said. At the other hours, that is, Terce, Sext and None, three parts of this psalm are said. At Prime on Monday three psalms are said: Psalms 1, 2, and 6; and so in the same way every day until Sunday, three psalms are said at Prime in consecutive order up to Psalm 20. Psalms 9 and 17 are each divided into two glorias. And thus it shall be that that Vigils on Sunday always begins with Psalm 21.

At Terce, Sext and None on Monday, the nine remaining parts of Psalm 119 are said, three parts at each hour. This psalm having thus been completed in two days—Sunday and Monday—the nine psalms from 120 through 128 are said on Tuesday at each of the hours of Terce, Sext and None, three psalms per hour. These psalms are repeated at the same hours every day until Sunday. The arrangement of hymns, lessons and versicles remains the same for these days. Thus Psalm 119 is always to begin on Sunday.

Vespers is to be sung each day with four psalms, beginning with Psalm 110 and ending with Psalm 147, omitting those of their number already set apart for other hours, namely, Psalms 118 to 128, Psalm 134 and Psalm 143. All the rest are to be said at Vespers. And as this leaves three psalms too few, the aforementioned somewhat longer ones should be divided: namely, Psalms 139, 144, and 145. But because Psalm 117 is short, it should be joined to Psalm 116. The order of psalms for Vespers having been dealt with, the rest—that is the lesson, responsory, hymn, versicle and canticle—are arranged as above.

At Compline the same psalms, that is 4, 91, and 134, are said each day.

The order for psalmody at the day hours now being arranged, all the remaining psalms are to be equally distributed among the seven nocturnal Vigils by dividing the longer psalms into two, and assigning twelve to each night.

Above all we recommend that if this arrangement of the psalms is displeasing to anyone, he should, if he thinks fit, arrange it otherwise; taking care especially that the whole psalter of 150 psalms is recited every week and always begins anew at Vigils of Sunday. For those monks show themselves lacking in devotion for their service who say less than the entire psalter in the course of a week with the usual canticles. For we read that our holy Fathers resolutely performed in a single day what we, lukewarm as we are, may achieve in a whole week.

Comment

Is there a theological reason for the distribution of the psalms, with certain themes recurring on certain days and hours? Some commentators think so, and perhaps indeed, Benedict had that in mind. In any case, he has clearly given careful thought to the distribution of the psalms among the offices, obviously taking into account those usual matters of his concern, such as length and uniformity and ease in the Daily Offices.

A question that may occur to you is: Why the psalter at all? Many have wondered at the devotional significance of the Psalms for Christians. As indicated previously in this segment of reflections, the richness of the psalter as a devotional framework seems to emerge over time spent praying it. The Psalms are a précis of the Old Testament: they give Christian faith its roots in the history of God's covenant relationship with the beloved people. And they are written in utterly human and personal terms, revealing the intense range of emotion involved in this intimate relationship. When prayed, they draw the worshiper into God's own life of loving communion. Regularly praying the psalms helps us grow toward humility and allows Benedict to say of his careful crafting here: let one who sees a better way freely choose that option!

The Psalms are both God's word to the people and the people's prayer to God. And notice, here Benedict calls the Psalms the monk's zealous service to the Holy One: "This is the work of God, to which nothing is to be preferred" (RB 43:3).

Reflection

I am aware that this detailed instruction is not obsolete advice, merely of academic interest, for my own prayer book lists the daily evening psalms for Compline as 4, 91, and 134! It often occurs to me that not only we Christians daily pray in the Psalms—so did Jesus in his life at Nazareth and his Jewish disciples for their whole lives. The Psalms were so deeply ingrained in Jesus' own human consciousness that he found in them the language of his own temptations in the desert (Luke 4:10–11, Psalm 91) and the language of his own despair/comfort on the cross (Matt 27:46, Psalm 22). These prayers make me feel so connected to God and to God's people!

Prayer/Response

Chapter 19, The Discipline of Singing Psalms
(ENTIRE)

*W*e believe that the Divine Presence is everywhere, and that the eyes of the Lord behold the good and the evil in every place (Prov 15:3). Especially do we believe this, without any doubt, when we are assisting at the Divine Office.

Let us, then, ever remember what the prophet says: Serve the Lord in fear (Ps 2:11), and again, Sing wisely (Ps 47:8); and, In the presence of the angels I will sing praise to you (Ps 138:1). Therefore let us consider how we ought to behave in the presence of God and of His angels, and so assist at the Divine Office that mind and voice be in harmony.

Comment

This simple chapter may well be the most important one in the Rule: certainly it is a keystone to all the rest, for here Benedict deals explicitly with the key disposition of the Christian life, which monastic practice is designed to develop and deepen. "God's omnipresence is not just an idea: it is a habit that calls for cultivation."[60] The habitual awareness of and responsiveness to God's presence is a very deep attitude of mind and heart, a disposition, which might be described as a vivid, integrated knowing of who God is and who we are in relation to God in this moment. The word "discipline" in the title of the chapter is a clear call to cultivate this particular habit or disposition.[61]

Very likely, this chapter and the next are meant to be read in tandem as a supplement or summary to the ordering of offices presented in the preceding chapters. "Singing Psalms" (Chapter 19) is about listening to the word of God in scripture and the psalms; "Prayer" (Chapter 20) is about the subsequent silence in which the word percolates into the heart. All this liturgical code intends that each office contain the rhythm of psalmody and prayer, of listening and silent response. Of course, such an inherent rhythm is typical not only of the ancient monastic office, but also of the entire art of *lectio*, which we are imitating in our process with this text.

In this chapter, it is no accident that the flow of ideas are directly parallel to those in the first degree of humility (RB Chapter 7, verse 10–30).[62] The Christian's essential awareness begins with the fear of God, an awed silence in the face of power and mystery utterly beyond comprehension. Gradually this awareness permeates into every segment of his or her being—and astonishingly enough, bears fruit in praise. This is fundamental not only to the divine office, but also to the whole of the Christian life.

Reflection

The phrase that touches me is "let us consider how we ought to behave in the presence of God." What an astonishing idea. I hardly know how to begin.

To start with, I believe that in fact God is with me here and now. Certainly I believe that when I pray, or I wouldn't be praying. But the question is, does it make any difference to my behavior that I think God is here? Well, yes; but on the other hand, no. The truth is, I guess, that I forget. I forget that God is here. But even worse, I forget who God is. Occasionally, I am overwhelmed by an acute sense of who God is—when I take time to breathe in a sunset, or when I ponder the astonishing world of the stars or the microbes. And even less occasionally, I think about who I am in relation to One who

could be Creator of all that. It is sometimes humiliating and sometimes comforting; in comparison to that One, I might as well be an
ant. Yet everything in the tradition invites me to be aware that I am
a beloved ant!

The Psalms are wonderful grist for this mill of reflection. They
emphasize over and over (in the language of their times) who God
is and what the human is by comparison. And they never forget that
there is an essential relation between us. The daily morning psalm
(95) is one of the best reminders for that.

Generally, I only glimpse this mystery, and then I back away, for
it is well beyond my ability to conceive it in its fullness. Yet, as I
pray the prayers of God's people, over and over in daily sequence,
my heart begins to understand and rejoice in the truth of that relationship, that loving, which comes against all probability to the
"odd couple" of God and me.

Prayer/Response

Chapter 20, On Reverence in Prayer
(ENTIRE)

*If, when we wish to make any request to those in power, we pre-
sume not to do so except with humility and reverence; how much
more ought we with all humility and purity of devotion to offer our sup-
plications to the Lord God of all things? And let us remember that we
shall be heard, not for our much speaking, but for our purity of heart and
tears of compunction. Therefore prayer ought to be short and pure, except
when it is occasionally prolonged by the inspiration of divine grace. But
let prayer made in common always be short: and at the signal given by
the superior, let all rise together.*

Comment

This is one of two chapters in the Rule explicitly devoted to the subject of personal prayer (Chapter 52 is the other), and these two provide the only direct comments Benedict makes on the matter. As
might be expected, elaborate discussions have arisen on the mean-

ing of these few short verses. One common argument is that Benedict does not really "approve" of personal prayer apart from the office, since this chapter is clearly connected with the liturgical code. Others argue about whether these comments are simply appeals to common sense, or instead are specific technical terminology based on Cassian's work.[63]

Several points seem central. The desire to make distinctions (like those raised here) is a modern Western phenomenon that would have seemed quite foreign to Benedict's thought. Of course, there exist both corporate and personal prayer in the monastic community; how could one exist without the supplement of the other? Of course, this language is both technical, as used by Cassian and others, and common sense; after all, is not the deepest wisdom of the truly prayerful grounded in common sense?

The fear of presumption is also an idea that eludes the modern mind. In ordinary twenty-first-century America, "our basic rights" are so fundamentally ingrained that we tend to ask favors assertively, as if we deserved them, and had been robbed of them by cruel and unjust oppressors. This is, no doubt, one of the main reasons why our prayers are seldom accompanied by tears; tears suggest not only that we do not deserve that for which we long, but also that it has been given abundantly!

As Benedict understands it, purity of heart is the essential characteristic of prayer. Of course, no human heart is truly pure, but that is our goal. A good synonym for purity of heart is singleness of eye, that is, focus on the one thing necessary. Pure prayer is directed toward God, undistracted by competing claims. Indeed, such prayer belongs to God, because it is made possible by the inspiration of divine grace. This brief, pure moment of prayer is what the long hours of waiting, preparation, and listening (which we call prayer) are attuned toward—the moment of exchange from God's heart to ours, comforting, inspiring, and enabling.[64]

Reflection

The more I feel myself drawn to prayer, the less I understand what prayer is. How well I know the dangers of self-righteousness, simply because my need for prayer grows stronger! How well I know the dangers of presumption, simply because God's nearness to me sometimes blurs my awareness of what Utter Being is! But—praise God—beyond and through all that do, I know primarily the song of my soul: that God claims me, and teaches me who I am.

Prayer/Response

Interlude IV
A NOTE TO THE READER

Are you feeling more at ease with your pattern of daily *lectio?*

Perhaps it goes in fits and starts, some days easily, some days with great difficulty, if at all. Perhaps it goes fine when you can get to it, but you're finding it hard to make the time. Perhaps even when you do sit down, your mind races and you are unable to release the many things you are trying to juggle.

Here are a few practical tips that are a great help to effective *lectio.* They have to do with "stopping." Let me start with an analogy. Here in southern California, we are very much oriented toward the freeways. When we come on to the freeway from an on-ramp, we are gaining speed on the on-ramp so that we can merge into the stream of freeway traffic at its full speed of 55 mph. It was quite a revelation to me to try driving the expressways on the East Coast, where the pattern is to come to a full stop at the entrances, look carefully for traffic, and only then pull out slowly onto the expressway lane.

That image provides a helpful analogy to any process of meditation, reflection, or prayer. Often we busy moderns think that we can enter a time of meditation just like southern Californians enter the freeway—at full speed, without any real period of transition. The truth is that in meditation such nonstop momentum is counterproductive.

Because what we are hoping for in *lectio* is true dialogue with the Word, an essential component is relaxed waiting for the Other. There must be a transition from busyness, a fundamental shift in the mode of our presence. That's why the simple instructions we all know are so important to follow.

Find a quiet place at a time when you won't be interrupted for fifteen minutes to an hour, depending on your preference. Sit comfortably but be alert; shake out any tension or discomfort in your body. Breathe deeply about three times. Give yourself permission to release any preoccupations or worries for this few minutes, coming back to them later if you need to, but giving them up for now. Be consciously aware if you can that you are not alone but are in the presence of the living God. Then turn to your *lectio*. And when you are finished, take some time to make the transition back.

As Christians, we inherit the astonishing tradition of the Sabbath: a time to withdraw, to rest, to marvel, and to praise. At the heart of Sabbath is the concept that we can leave our important work to God, at least for a few moments, in order simply to be with God for worship and refreshment. This is, of course, what the Benedictines are doing in the Daily Office. This is, of course, what we are doing in our *lectio*.

Disciplines of Community

Chapter 21, The Deans
of the Monastery
(ENTIRE)

If the community is large, let there be chosen from it certain brethren of good repute and holy life to be appointed deans. Let them carefully direct their deaneries in all things according to the commandments of God and the orders of their abbot. And let such persons be chosen deans as the abbot may safely trust to share his burdens: let them not be chosen according to order, but for the merit of their lives, for their learning and wisdom.

And should any one of them, being puffed up with pride, be found worthy of blame, and after being thrice corrected, refuse to amend, let him be deposed and one put in his place who is worthy. And we order the same to be done in the case of the Prior.

Comment

A strategy for small groups in the time of Benedict! Should that surprise us really? For someone as concerned as Benedict with integration of the life of faith and as sensitive to human development, it must have been clear that individual monks were far more likely to develop fruitfully if they had a keen sense of belonging and a fellowship in which they were specially valued.

The word "dean" literally means one in charge of a group of ten (*decanus* = dean/*decania* = group of ten). The idea is rooted in Moses' decision to establish the smallest units of ten persons for the Israelites wandering in the desert (Exod 18:13–17; Deut 1:9–18), as well as in the early Christian church's decision to have special servants of the people (Acts 6:3). This deanery group was a common practice in early monasteries.[65] As the scriptural sources suggest, the deans are both responsible for the care of those in their group and for obedience to the abbot, as God's representative.

The dean's own life must be an example of the monastic ideal: the language Benedict uses for "holy life" is *sanctae conversationis*. *Conversatione* is the third monastic vow, which we can approximately translate "ongoing conversion of heart," the monastic life in a nutshell. The reason why pride is such a grave failing in a dean is that it reveals him to be centered in his ego rather than in Christ. And yet Benedict is well aware that promotion is a frequent stimulus of pride.

Why is this chapter here? The section on the Daily Office was offered as a bridge between the theological framework and the concrete realities of daily life in the monastery. This unit begins the daily life section with discussions about the discipline of living together with others. Living together, community life, is for Benedict a fundamental aspect of Christian formation. It is both rigorous and fruitful for our spiritual maturation—if we allow it to be so. The asceticism of community is a marvelous harness on pride. Community speaks of membership in one another; pride speaks of being separate. Community speaks of the importance of participation; pride of the importance of self-sufficiency. Community speaks of the way in which our weaknesses can be remedied by the strengths of others, even as we offer our strengths toward others' care; pride speaks of "flying" alone. We shall see that the principal punishment of the Rule is to subject a monk to the absence of community: excommunication.

Reflection

How do we move from longing to be faithful to God, through prayer, to living a virtuous life? My own experience certainly confirms what I believe to be Benedict's hunch: I more readily make that transition as I belong to and have the support of and accountability to a few other Christians who really care about me. For the last few years I have been meeting regularly with a very small group of friends, and we are helping each other to clarify concretely: What is Christ asking me to do in my life circumstances today? We love each other and pray for each other, and we also are risking ourselves by helping each other think about and respond to the opportunities our lives hold for us to be more faithful Christians. I have found blind spots in my own perceptions revealed. I am called to account for my own life in a way I never experienced before. Occasionally I am willing to take a step toward Christ in a specific situation that I don't think I would have had the wisdom or courage to do without them. And remarkable fruits blossom.

Prayer/Response

Chapter 22, How the Monks Are to Sleep

*L*et them sleep each one in a separate bed, receiving bedding suitable to their manner of life, as the abbot shall appoint. If it is possible, let all sleep in one place; but if their number does not permit this, let them sleep by tens or twenties with the seniors who have charge of them. Let a candle burn constantly in the room until morning.

Let them sleep clothed, and girded with belts or cords (but not with knives at their sides, lest perchance they wound themselves in their sleep) and thus be always ready; so that when the signal is given they rise without delay, and compete with each to the other in hastening to the Work of God, yet with all gravity and modesty. The younger brethren should not have their beds by themselves, but among those of the seniors. And when they rise for the Work of God let them gently encourage one another, on account of the excuses which the drowsy tend to make.

Comment

This subject matter seems more suited to "domestic arrangements" than to community disciplines. In fact, this chapter is a kind of disciplinary measure, although Benedict treats it with great tenderness, in part by juxtaposing it to a reminder of the great vocation to which we are called by our liturgical prayer. Indeed, the office is explicitly mentioned here twice, because the monks arise from sleep about 2:00 A.M. to go directly to the office.

What is the discipline here? For the fourth-century Egyptian monks, the private cell was the principal place of prayer, a sort of private oratory. And by the twelfth century, the monastic cell had been reintroduced. However, in the beginning of the sixth century, the private cell was abolished in favor of the dormitory as the norm, as a move to remedy the abuses of the private cell. Benedict adopted the practice current in his time, that of the dormitory. The discipline of the dormitory is designed to forestall occasional temptations to abuse of a private space. No doubt the special practices Benedict introduces, such as the watch of the seniors and the burning candle, are also instituted to insure "elementary good morals."[66]

Yet there is a wonderful integration of motives in these disciplinary measures. It is clear from the tone that even here Benedict holds the greatest tenderness toward his monks. His tenderness reminds us that the night is a time of great danger from which we still pray daily for deliverance from the "shadow of death."[67] Night carries with it many temptations and the power of the evil one; night is the symbol of death, and daybreak always brings the renewed joy of resurrection. All these arrangements of discipline are thus also arrangements in caregiving, just as with God. The living power of the paschal mystery becomes nightly present to each monk, as the community together embarks upon the trust of sleep.

Reflection

Tenderness is so difficult for me to accept and live out, especially when it is juxtaposed with danger and fear, not to mention when it is juxtaposed with "backsliding"! What a model Benedict is for me in his constant, loving care for souls. He is so "at home" with human weakness, just as he is with the call to each person to share the divine life. He really never loses hope in God's mercy or in God's power to transform.

So often I have considered people who always see the good, the redemptive, as innocent and unrealistic. Yet Benedict helps me see that is a "put-down"—not only of them, but also of myself. Benedict is a realist (in many ways, he is "unshockable"); yet that only deepens his faith and conviction in the living and active power of God to bring forth good.

Prayer/Response

Chapter 23,
Excommunication for Faults
(ENTIRE)

If any brother shall be found obstinate, or disobedient, or proud, or a murmurer, or in any way despises the Holy Rule and the orders of his seniors, let him, according to Our Lord's commandment, be once or twice privately admonished by his seniors (Matt 18:15–16). If he does not amend, let him be rebuked in public before all. But if even then he does not correct himself, let him be subjected to excommunica-

tion, provided that he understand the nature of the punishment. Should he, however, prove unable to understand it, let him undergo corporal chastisement.

Comment

The so-called "Penal Code" of Benedict comprises Chapters 23 to 30 and 43 to 46 of the Rule, and there is some controversy in modern scholarly circles about whether it has much "spiritual profit" for the contemporary reader, particularly because it specifies corporal punishment.[68] So we must give careful attention to these chapters to inquire what they offer us.

These chapters are placed within my category "Disciplines of Community," because, as previously suggested, the fundamental punishment is exclusion from the community. This chapter emphasizes three elements of the discipline of community, and we'll see more of them as we continue. First, the title. Second, a listing of behavior viewed as "faults." And third, a graded series of punishments.

The title of the chapter calls our attention to excommunication, that is, separation from the community, as the key to the Rule's punishments. The motives for this seem to include both the practical and the spiritual. Practically, some order and common behavior must be enforced if the monastic community is to preserve itself from dissolution.[69] Spiritually, the model of Christian life undergirding the monastery is the community described in the Acts of the Apostles.[70]

Benedict's community is rooted in the conviction that we learn to be Christians precisely in the normal daily interactions that constitute the community. Thus, his list of faults, which includes utterly ordinary behaviors—obstinacy, murmuring, and pride—suggests that a fault is not simply an offense against others, but also a serious impediment to one's own spiritual growth. The two aspects are merely different sides of the same issue. And the penalty of excommunication is simply an enforcement of the separation that the monk has already caused by his or her behavior.

The range of punishments is provided to enable monks to understand and take responsibility for their actions, repent, and return to health. Benedict realizes not only that it takes maturity to recognize the seriousness of faults against the community, but also that we do not always act on what we know. Thus, various punishments are to be applied depending on appropriateness and need, centered in the Matthean gospel warning of wrath and promise of forgiveness (Matt 18:7–9, 21–22).

Reflection

During Lent this year, I asked my pastor to help me forgive the wound administered by a "friend" for whom I felt only anger. Fortunately, he is a wise and compassionate man who helped me look at why I needed to hold on to my anger. Thus began a somewhat painful but gradually liberating journey. I discovered that beneath the anger, indeed, beneath the wound, was the truth that I was insisting on being "my own person." My pride was a way of hiding from myself, no less than from others, my active need to be held in another's caring love. What I could not do for myself, I refused to admit I needed. And the natural consequence of that pride was to exclude me from experiences of deep friendship. Pride does prevent me from being open to love. Thus, indirectly, the wound was the gift of a merciful God who aches for me to know more fully how much I am loved—a reality obscured by my preference for self-sufficiency.

Prayer/Response

Chapter 24, On the Degrees of Excommunication
(ENTIRE)

*T*he measure of excommunication or chastisement should correspond to the gravity of the offence, the estimation of which shall be left to the judgment of the abbot. If any brother be found guilty of lighter faults let him be excluded only from the common table.

And this shall be the rule for one deprived of the fellowship of the table: he shall intone neither psalm nor antiphon in the oratory, nor shall he read a lesson, until he has made satisfaction. Let him take his meals alone, after those of the brethren, in the measure and at the time that the abbot shall think best for him. Thus, for example, if the brethren eat at the sixth hour, let him eat at the ninth; if they eat at the ninth, let him eat in the evening, until by proper satisfaction he obtains pardon.

Comment

It is evident that Benedict has carefully sought to let the punishment correspond to the fault—not only in amount, but also in kind. As noted before, the offender who has in essence rejected the community life by violating its rules is propelled further in the direction of his own willfulness, that he might see its natural consequences; that is, he is excluded from the community life even more.

Perhaps at first we are surprised that Benedict speaks of faults in prayer in the same breath as faults at meals. Obviously, Benedict highly values the shared mealtime. The physical meal that the monks share is a common symbol of the life of Christ, shared mystically in the Eucharist and ordinarily in all the common events of the day. Thus, it is natural that someone who does not participate fully in the mealtime also does not participate fully in the prayer time. Notice carefully: it is the community life from which the offender is removed, not from the food. He does eat and is not required to fast from physical nourishment. He is removed from human warmth, the nourishment given in the *koinonia* (community).

Reflection

I am seldom attentive to the nourishment I actually receive from being with those with whom I am obliged to interact each day. I may enjoy or not any specific interaction—feel it as pleasurable or useful or not. But rarely do I acknowledge that I am fed by it, made whole and given vitality by it.

How often does my self-will see others as feeding me insofar as they cooperate with or at least do not interfere with my plans and hopes? Insofar as I can possess or manage others, I see them as contributors to my self-enhancement. But to appreciate and to be grateful for their gift to my being simply because they are—when they are complete strangers, or opponents, or indifferent—simply because they exist and have been given to me and I to them,

> to recognize that they are ear and I am nose; both of us essential to the body of Christ,

> to see that I am complete and whole only in the presence of the fullness of their being,

> to allow myself to be changed by others in ways I do not expect—

what a challenge. And what an awesome possibility!

Prayer/Response

Chapter 25, Serious Faults
(ENTIRE); AND
Chapter 26, Those Who, Without Permission, Associate with the Excommunicated
(ENTIRE)

*L*et that brother who is found guilty of a more grievous offence be excluded both from the table and from the oratory. Let none of the brethren associate with him or speak to him. Let him be alone at the work enjoined him, and continue in sorrow of penance, remembering that dreadful sentence of the Apostle: That such a one is delivered over to Satan for the destruction of the flesh, that his spirit may be saved in the day of the Lord (1 Cor 5:5). Let him take his portion of food alone, in the measure and at the time that the abbot shall think best for him. Let none of those who pass by bless him, nor let the food that is given him be blessed.

[Chapter 26] If any brother presumes without the abbot's permission to associate with an excommunicated brother, or to speak with him, or to send him a message, let him incur the same punishment of excommunication.

Comment

The one who defaults on his or her commitment to the community is reduced to being alone. He or she is allowed fully to enter this separation, to endure it, and to drink it to the full. Perhaps Benedict is echoing Psalm 129 here, which also presents a refusal even to be blessed by those who pass by, set in the context of the ascent to Jerusalem and the folly of refusal to fear God.

If we ponder deeply the quotation from Corinthians and other such statements of St. Paul, as Benedict clearly has done,[71] what do we make of it? There is a profound concern for lack of faithfulness in the context of God's proffered covenant of love. It is not lack of "belief"; rather, it is behavior inconsistent with belief: an assertion of self-will against that of God and God's community. Such behavior by its nature keeps one away from salvation. There are clear echoes here from the Sermon on the Mount: better to tear out and throw away the offending part, be it the person's body, or the person from the body, if it comes to that (Matt 5:29–30).

Benedict believes that the choice for or against salvation is real, and that it is made in the context of behaviors for or against membership in the community of faith. The danger of choosing "against" is very great; it is like a viral attack that is very infectious. The offending and diseased part must be burned and cast out. But only for the sake of healing and ultimate wholeness.[72]

Reflection

It is hard for me to take this seriously. So much of my cultural upbringing not only finds self-will a fairly innocent disease; it actually often applauds it. A deadly virus that will keep me dead for all eternity? It's difficult to believe.

And that is true not only for myself but for others. When someone is suffering the consequences of self-will, instead of letting him or her taste them in full, I am always tempted to intervene and offer "comfort." Tough love is a hard learning, as all of us who have lived with alcoholics and other compulsives have discovered.

But, there is a part of me that experiences the truth of Benedict's conviction. Just yesterday, I was talking with a friend about those moments when I see clearly that God is calling out to me with love, and I am deliberately slamming doors in God's face, so to speak. I can feel when I am resisting the divine invitation with all my aggressive energy. Who knows why I do it? For fear I will lose control or be asked to do something I don't like? For fear of becoming too close to that "refining fire" that is God's love and having to give up some identity I feel is essential to me? Whatever it is, it is an assertion of self-will, and there are moments when I weep for my own hardness of heart.

Prayer/Response

Chapter 27, The Abbot's Care for the Excommunicated
(ENTIRE)

*L*et the abbot with all tenderness take care of offending brethren, *for those who are healthy do not need a physician, but those who are sick (Matt 9:12). To this end he ought to behave in every way as a wise physician, sending* senpectae *to sympathize with him. That is to say, some brethren of mature years and wisdom may, as it were secretly,*

console the wavering brother, induce him to make humble satisfaction,
and comfort him, that he not be overwhelmed by excessive sorrow
(2 Cor 2:7); rather, as the Apostle says, Let love be strengthened
towards him (2 Cor 2:8), and let all pray for him

For the abbot is bound to use the greatest care with erring brethren,
and to strive with all possible prudence and zeal not to lose any one of the
sheep committed to him. He must know that he has undertaken responsi-
bility for weak souls, not tyranny over the strong; and let him fear the
warning of the prophet, where God says: What you saw to be fat you took
yourselves, and what was diseased you cast away (Ezek 34:3–4). Let him
imitate the loving example of the Good Shepherd, who, leaving the ninety-
nine sheep on the mountains, went to seek one which had gone astray; on
whose weakness He had such compassion that He chose to lay it on His
own sacred shoulders and thus bring it back to the flock (Luke 15:5).

Comment

Physician and shepherd! Here as in Chapter 2, Benedict uses these
key metaphors to describe the quality of governance essential for
Christian community.

It is important to consider the tone of this chapter in relation to
the concerns of the previous two chapters. There, Benedict turns our
attention to the virulent disease of sin and the attacks of Satan that
confront Christians as they live out their journey. Even in this chapter,
that reality appears as a factor in the abbot's life (Ezekiel quotation).

But Benedict does not use this awareness as an excuse to become
hysterical or rigid. Indeed, he sees it as the sure sign of the necessity
for even greater loving-kindness, openness, and humble dependence upon God's Spirit. We noted previously that the twin temptations of the consecrated life are pride and despair.[73] In this chapter
Benedict assures that the abbot will be sensitive to both types of
temptations, as well as discerning in his application of remedies.
The attitude of the abbot is always to be that of "a good shepherd or
physician, who is not shocked or dismayed by sickness, but challenged by it."[74]

The words care, compassion, and love infuse this chapter. They
suggest a whole way of being that involves gentle firmness and
health-giving care. In the Latin, the prose possesses the rhythmic

and beautiful cadences typical of the liturgical formulas of the Roman office.[75] In this chapter as in Chapter 20, Benedict's deep prayer informs and infuses the word as well as the spirit of the Rule, because the task of disciplinary health-giving is one above all in which the abbot is dependent upon co-creative grace. Therefore, "let all pray."

Reflection

I believe this model of care could fruitfully be applied to my peer relationships with others as well as to my attitude to my own "sickness." I suspect I am least gentle to myself, least accepting of my own limitations and sinfulness. Yet to accept them in a way that involves hope and wholeness is the "trick."

One of the regular matters I ponder is how reconciliation comes about in our world. Our catechism states that the baptized Christian's main ministry is to join Christ's work of reconciliation in the world, and I remember being utterly dumbfounded when I once heard someone say that reconciliation is needed only where there is brokenness. I always thought of reconciliation as the "after" state, rather than as the "potential" state. So, brokenness, weakness, and sin are actually boundless opportunities for reconciliation. I think this is how Benedict sees "waywardness"—as a special opportunity to work toward wholeness.

Sometimes I try to remind myself in moments or circumstances of brokenness that Christ is present, longing to be released by a cry for help. One time in the frantic setting at the Los Angeles airport, when my husband Doug and I were both very anxious and angry, it suddenly occurred to me that this was a place badly in need of reconciliation. So I slipped over to Doug and whispered, "Breathe!" He looked at me, we both laughed, and the next half hour was easier to bear!

Prayer/Response

Chapter 28, Those Who Do Not Amend
after Frequent Correction
(ENTIRE)

*I*f any brother who has been frequently corrected for some fault, or even excommunicated, does not amend, let a more severe chastisement be applied: that is, let the punishment of the rod be administered to him. But if even then he does not correct himself, or perchance (which God forbid!), puffed up with pride, he even wishes to defend his deeds, then let the abbot act like a wise physician. If he has applied bandages and the ointment of his admonitions, the medicine of the Holy Scriptures, and at last the cautery of excommunication or corporal chastisement, and if he see that his labors are of no avail, let him add what is still more powerful—his own prayers and those of all the brethren for him, that God who can do all things may accomplish the cure of the sick brother. But if he is not healed even by this means, then the abbot may ultimately use the sword of separation, as the Apostle says: Put away the evil one from you (1 Cor 5:13). And again: If the faithless one depart, let him depart (1 Cor 7:15), lest one diseased sheep should infect the whole flock.

Comment

One is reminded here of John 6:60: "This is intolerable language. How could anyone accept it?" It is one of Benedict's strengths that he can look intently at the day of judgment and speak gently but firmly of its requirements. Here again, he joins St. Paul in asking difficult questions about the relationship of faith and behavior: How real is our faith when tested against how we actually live?

In Latin, the close relationship of the words health *(salus)* and salvation *(salutare)* is more evident than in English. Benedict's "Penal Code" is utterly oriented toward salvation; it has none of the vindictiveness and formalism often found in other Rules of the period.[76] His foremost concern is to establish measures that will draw the offender into repentance and thus into health and salvation. He is not interested in measures that induce defensiveness, pride, or a spirit of rebellion.

This is why his penultimate remedy is simply the power of prayer. The phrase in verse 5, "God who can do all things," is probably a reference to Matthew 18:26, where the servant who cannot pay is forgiven his debt.[77] Again and again, Benedict relies on his keen awareness that salvation is not possible to anyone unless we trust in the mercy of God (RB 4:74).

But finally, it is the choice of each one whether he or she will accept being indebted to this mercy. Those who persistently refuse must at last be separated, as they continue to insist they already are.

Reflection

To refuse the divine invitation . . . at first, it seems totally improbable that anyone would choose to do so. Yet, upon deeper reflection, which Benedict invites in this section, I realize the many ways in which I refuse God's invitation each day. I feel that Benedict has invited me to ponder on those specifics and offer them up to God as fully as I can. But I am also aware of another underlying dimension of refusal implicit here: I can refuse God by refusing my sisters and brothers. That is, it is not just a question of allowing my life to be interpenetrated by God's life. It is also a matter of allowing my life to belong to the community of persons I am given. I learn about and receive God in the here and now.

Both are so hard for me. How deeply ingrained in me is the desire to "be my own person," to work out my own salvation! I also deeply desire to belong, but it takes training and practice for me to learn how to live that out. I see that the community is a place to be trained and to practice this way of belonging. The community provides rules and boundaries against which I can break off some of my sharp edges (or they are broken off!). And it provides authentic models, which is one of the best gifts Benedict gives me. It's hard work, but, I think, good work. I feel better, more whole, when I give myself to it.

Prayer/Response

Chapter 29, Whether Those Who Leave the Monastery May Be Readmitted

If any brother, who through his own fault departs or is cast out of the monastery, is willing to return, let him first promise complete amendment of the fault for which he left. Then let him be received back into the lowest place, so that his humility may thus be tried. Should he again depart, let him be taken back up to the third time. But let him know that after this all way of return is denied him.

Comment

There is a quality to this paragraph much like that of Jesus' instruction about how many times one must forgive another (Matt 18:21–2). Again and again the community is to welcome back the one who has rejected it by turning away. (This is also characteristic of a family, is it not?) True, the one returning must make amends and show willingness to grow in humility, but these are prudent safeguards to ensure the authentic repentance of the returnee. The essential matter is that the monk is to be forgiven and welcomed home in all charity.

This requirement is surely a practical consequence of Benedict's conviction about the nature of the kingdom of God. It suggests that 1) God is a wildly extravagant lover; 2) our response to that love is the matter of eternal salvation, the essential matter of our lives; and 3) individual response is most fully lived out in the context of Christian community. True community exists always and only within this matrix of salvation and forgiveness/mercy.

Reflection

Today my emotional response to this passage is centered on the costliness for the community of the required openness. (On other days, it might be more along the lines of the grief and joy of the one who finds him- or herself blessedly reunited.) When I live with someone, whether I "like" the person or not, part of me inevitably grows in intimacy with him or her. Thus, when and if the person is pulled away from me, I feel an enormous, wrenching pain, especially so if the person deliberately turned his or her back on my values and chose a different path. Even when I can accept the situation intellectually, my heart throbs. To welcome such a person home willingly and fully involves opening myself to vulnerability, risking restoration of the lost intimacy. I may be able to do that once, but again and again? I do not have the necessary resources.

This situation occurs with acting-out children, stubborn parents, and unfaithful spouses. We are repeatedly given the opportunity to risk this restoration throughout our lives. As someone who has been hurt in this way, I am aware that the risk involves not only my current relationship, but also my next one. Will I ever trust anyone again with my most tender feelings? The problem arises even in a good relationship: Dare I continue to trust/love this person one bit more?

As I understand it, Benedict's insistence on this welcome (this openness where there has been a wound, this risk where there is vulnerability) is a profound affirmation of the power of love. I may not have the necessary resources, but God does, offering them to me generously for my use and in my need.

Prayer/Response

Chapter 30, The Manner of Reproving Children
(ENTIRE)

Every age and understanding should receive what is appropriate to it. As often, therefore, as boys, or those under age, or those who cannot fully understand the greatness of the penalty of excommunication, commit faults, let them be punished by severe fasting or sharp strokes, in order that they may be cured.

Comment

Chapter 59 of the Rule (below) makes clear that boys may be offered "to God in the monastery" by their parents, and that this was a binding way of entering monastic life in Benedict's time.

In this chapter, Benedict is concerned about how to discipline these and other members of the monastic community whose maturity is insufficient for reasoned communication to bring their souls to repentance. As always, the goal is health and salvation. Reproof in the Christian community is always to lead to that goal. Thus, it is to be "appropriate"; that is, specially designed to produce positive response in the one receiving the rebuke (not simply the habitual temperamental preference of the one administering it).

Benedict acknowledges that the developmental stage of some persons is such that physical punishment is the most effective remedy.[78] Even so, he stops short of actions called for by other rules in his time, such as whipping and severe beating.[79] And his goal in this entire section is the gradual drawing of every member of the community into that keen awareness of deepest regard for this ordinary Christian gathering as Christ's body.

Reflection

Some time ago, a professor of mine asked the members of a class whether we would prefer to be physically ill or mentally ill, if we had to choose. By far the majority of us, myself included, chose physical illness. And yet, both he and we understood at once that most of us moderns "go overboard" to care for our physical health, but are very lazy, independent, and undisciplined about our mental health. And, of course, if we add our soul's health to the comparison, it probably would come in last in terms of actual disciplined care and attention.

What am I prepared to do for a healthy soul in this life and in the next? How seriously am I willing to discipline my body, mind, and spirit when I know it would be helpful for my maturity in Christ? How fully do I understand such concerns to be lived out in the traditions and daily practices of my community of faith? And how can I help those around me to learn to appreciate these life-giving practices? Benedict's guidance on community discipline forces me to wonder about all this, as I live into it day by day.

Prayer/Response

Interlude V
A NOTE TO THE READER

Are you sometimes feeling "stuck" during your *lectio*?

Perhaps you occasionally feel like a dog chasing its tail: you seem to go around and around the same issues, not getting anywhere. Perhaps once in a while you wonder if you're not walking through quicksand: you've raised a lot of sticky stuff, but you're not sure whether it's got you, or you've got it. Or perhaps you just wonder if you're on the right track, and would like some feedback.

You have undertaken a regular process of reflection on your life experience in light of the Gospel (via the Rule). It is a powerful process and it's not unusual to feel the need to share it with someone else—for feedback and maybe for new insight. To ask: Am I being honest with myself? Am I dwelling on one issue for too long or not taking enough time with something else? Am I really being faithful to God in all this? How can I know?

A spiritual director is a friend who is committed to help you listen carefully for God's voice in your experience. Usually, the director is a person acquainted with the Christian traditions of prayer and discernment who has some feel for the normal patterns in an evolving relationship with God, and who can help you assess your present situation in that context.

We often think that a director will help us primarily with accountability. It seems so easy to delude ourselves about our motives and our behavior that we seek a director to "keep us honest." But in my experience, the director's role is more often to remind me of how greatly I am loved. I am far more likely to forget my value than my sins.

How do you find a director? We may neglect the obvious first step: be a part of a Christian community, a place where like-minded people come together in worship, praise, and thanksgiving. Many cities have special spiritual centers or retreat houses you might contact.* Having taken such steps, keep your eyes open. Let God know you desire a guide, and watch with expectancy. Keep praying. When you discover someone you respect, tell him or her what you seek, and ask if he or she will join you in listening for the Spirit in your life.

What do you say to a director? You talk about your life, your experiences, your reflections, your longings. You talk about who God is for you, and who you are for God, much as you and I are doing in these daily *lectio* meditations. And then you and your director listen together. When two are gathered in Christ's name, the Spirit is in their midst.

---

*You may also wish to contact Spiritual Directors International at www.sdiworld.org.

Domestic
Arrangements

Chapter 31, The Qualities
of the Monastery Cellarer
VERSES 1–9

*L*et there be chosen from the community as cellarer of the monastery,
one who is wise and of mature character, temperate, not a great
eater, not haughty, nor headstrong, nor offensive, not dilatory, nor
wasteful, but God-fearing; one who may be like a parent to the whole
community. Let him have charge of everything, but do nothing without
permission of the abbot. Let him take heed to what is commanded him.

Let him not sadden his brethren. If a brother ask him for anything
unreasonably, let (the cellarer) not treat him with contempt and so
grieve him, but reasonably and with all humility refuse what he unreasonably asks for. Let him be watchful over his own soul, remembering
always that saying of the Apostle: he who has ministered well purchases
for himself a good standing (1 Tim 3:13).

Let him have particular concern for the sick, for children, for guests,
and for the poor, knowing without doubt that he will have to render an
account of all these on the day of judgment.

Comment

Now begins that section of the Rule here termed "Domestic Arrangements," and elsewhere called "offices of service to the community".[80]
"cellarer" is a specifically monastic term, referring to the one responsible for the storeroom *(cellarium)*. The job of cellarer includes a
wide range of responsibilities we might call business management,
meaning both the accounting and treasury functions as well as the
management and distribution of needed goods.

The overall tone of this chapter is one of care, or stewardship. In
a sense, here Benedict guides all those who deal with things, especially when they are in a position of authority. Such people are to be
God-fearing, above all, remembering that all goods are God's gifts.
In the interactions by which goods are shared (again!) lies the matter of salvation. The cellarer is especially to care tenderly for the
weak and vulnerable, whenever possible seeing Christ in those who
come to him in their need, and treating them as if they themselves—

the supplicants—are precious gifts of God, even when their requests are unreasonable.

All those in the monastic community who carry authority of any kind are to be persons of the most profound humility and devotion. This is indeed the mark of true authority. Good service, charity, and tender loving care: these are the signs that we are Jesus' disciples (Matt 20:25–28). In Benedict's usual practical way, he shows that the best opportunity to practice these virtues is with an irate customer.

Reflection

I am struck by the interchangeability of the terms "domestic tasks," "business management," and "good service." One of Benedict's qualities that often shocks me awake like a dousing of cold water is his continual insistence on the opportunity we have to serve God right in the midst of our daily annoyances and interruptions. Sometimes it seems like it would be ever so much simpler to give my life as a martyr than to be sweet-tempered when my cat gets under my feet (again!) at just the moment everything on the stove is ready to be served up! On the other hand, as I begin to consider seriously the possibility that salvation can be found in such ordinary service, I glimpse a breathtaking harmony and wholeness in the very details of my life.

Prayer/Response

Chapter 31
VERSES 10–19 (END)

*T*he cellarer should look upon all the vessels and goods of the *monastery as though they were the consecrated vessels of the altar. Let him not think that he may neglect anything: let him not be given to greed, nor wastefulness, nor be a squanderer of the goods of the monastery; but let him do all things in proper measure, and according to the bidding of the abbot. Let him above all things have humility; and to the one on whom he has nothing else to bestow, let him give at least a kind word, as it is written: A kind word is above the best gift (Sir 18:17).*

Let him have under his care all that the abbot has entrusted to him, and not presume to meddle with what is forbidden him. Let him distribute to the brethren their appointed allowance of food, without arrogance or delay, that they may not be scandalized: mindful of what the Word of God declares he deserves who scandalizes one of these little ones (Matt 18:6).

If the community is large, let helpers be given to him, by whose aid he may with peace of mind discharge the office committed to him. Let necessary things be given and asked for at appropriate times, that no one may be troubled or grieved in the house of God.

Comment

Benedict is concerned here with stewardship, or how to serve God in caring for the material goods entrusted to us. Key phrases for this lesson are presented in the first and last sentences of this *lectio:* "consecrated vessels" and "house of God." Essentially, Benedict views these material goods as gifts from God that have the potential for revealing God's glory. Like Zechariah, he proclaims that even the "horsebells will be inscribed with the words 'sacred to Yahweh'" (Zech 14:20–1). For one who learns to see the created order in this way, humility, tenderness, and wonder arise naturally and inform all interactions.

And this vision is intended not only for inanimate objects, but also for humans. Even the brothers are sacraments of God, to be treated tenderly and with respect, as "little ones" precious to God and somehow revealing of God's nature. Notice that not only is each monk accountable for his own deepening humility but is also responsible not to stimulate or arouse the pride of a brother or sister. Their life together is God's household, where all are to support and encourage the deepening holiness of each.

One especially valuable idea here is that enough people are to be assigned to do the necessary work so that no one need be frantic or distressed. Good stewardship calls for care of our own body and spirit, and habitual recollection toward God's presence in the ordinary flourishes best in a peaceful and spacious setting.

Reflection

I am touched by the contrast between Benedict's spirit and the spirit of the environment in which I normally find myself. In my environment, there is not much authentic mutual support and not much peace. But I wonder if that is always due to forces I cannot control. It is within my power to begin to behave in those ways myself, wherever I am placed, and to pray for the Spirit's strength and guidance as I do so. There is at least the possibility that such action would positively influence my current environment, which is, after all, God's gift to me.

It is also within my power to be more realistic about what actually does need to be done today, and to value more the contributions that come from my colleagues. These seem almost foolishly simple things to try, but why not?

Prayer/Response

Chapter 32, The Tools and Possessions of the Monastery
(ENTIRE)

*T*he abbot should appoint brethren on whose manner of life and character he can rely on to be responsible for the tools, clothes, and other possessions of the monastery; and let him consign the various things to their care as he shall think fit, to be kept and to be collected after use. Of these let the abbot keep a list, so that as the brethren are reassigned to different tasks, he may know what he gives out and what he receives back.

If anyone treats the possessions of the monastery in a slovenly or negligent manner, let him be corrected; and if he does not amend, let him be subjected to the discipline of the Rule.

Comment

One of the most remarkable qualities of the Rule is the ease with which Benedict shifts from the sacred to the mundane, which clearly for him form an integrated unity. In the previous chapter, we noticed his perspective that all material things are sacraments, transparent to the divine. Here there is no weakening of that theme (i.e., verse 2: "to be kept"; verse 4: "[not to] treat the possessions in a slovenly or negligent manner"), but it is juxtaposed firmly with the awareness of the temptation to greed that "things" often present. Here Benedict requires the keeping of careful records and appropriate locks, in much the same way we might say: "Don't leave money clearly visible in an open and vacant car, lest you unnecessarily tempt someone."

Probably Benedict is drawing on Sirach 42, which contains a very similar juxtaposition of prudent calculation and wonder at the glory of creation. Yet again, this passage suggests the resonance of Benedict's own spirit, his capacity not to be shocked or dismayed by human sinfulness and not allowing it to be a diversion from divine goodness, eternally offered even and especially to the sinner.

In this context, the last two sentences are an indication of one of the "faults" for which monks become subject to the Rule's discipline, giving insight into the fundamental basis for the disciplines of the Rule: to provide a framework in which to practice the presence of the sacred so that eventually it becomes a deep inner disposition.

Reflection

Learning this disposition to respond to the sacramental in all things is not easy. I tend to alternate abruptly between carelessness and excessive care, forgetfulness and pride. The difficulty and the challenge is to practice a calm and patient willingness simultaneously to see both responses in myself, set within the context of God's constant presence. It is never easy for me to see that all belongs to God, whatever its condition or character.

I think it helps to have models. And isn't it interesting that when I notice someone treating something especially gently or lovingly, it is as if they suddenly bring me back "into myself"? I mean that I am awakened to the presence of the sacred in that moment and in everything I see. And for a short time, I, too, live in the pleasure of the sacred.

Prayer/Response

Chapter 33, Whether Monks Ought to Own Anything
(ENTIRE)

A bove all let the vice of private ownership be cut out of the monastery by the roots. Let no one presume to give or receive anything without leave of the abbot, or to keep anything as their own, either book or writing-tablet or pen, or anything at all; since they are permitted to have neither body nor will in their own power. Rather, let them trust that they will receive all that is necessary from the father of the monastery. Nor are they allowed to keep anything which the abbot has not given or permitted. Let all things be common to all, as it is writ-ten, nor let anyone say or assume that anything is his own (Acts 4:32).

But if anyone is found who indulges in this most corrupt vice, and after one or two admonitions does not amend, let him be subjected to correction.

Comment

In a world as acquisition-oriented as ours, the language of this chapter seems very strong. Nowhere else is Benedict as adamant. Here our guide, who is ordinarily flexible and "realistic," is uncompromising: private ownership is to be pulled out at the roots in the Christian community.

It is fascinating to compare this with the two prior chapters concerning the importance of care for material goods. It is considered a truism in the real estate business today that where there is no ownership, there is no care. It is "common knowledge" in the city planning profession that housing development areas designated for "common use" are the trashiest, since no one takes responsibility for them. If it "belongs" to everyone, it belongs to no one. Or so we believe.

And yet Benedict insists that no one can own what actually belongs to all. (Not even a pencil!) He insists that true care— human stewardship of God's gifts—comes only when we recognize that we do not possess anything. And this is perhaps the key: sacramental awareness is to involve not only awareness and appreciation but also stewardship or co-participation with God in the ongoing creation of the world. When we see the world in this light, we recognize at once that we cannot do it alone. Even and especially stewardship must involve the integration of gifts brought by many loving hands.

Observe also that the model Benedict is using is the Christ-empowered, post-Pentecost community of Acts (Benedict says more about this later), and that the "punishment" here as elsewhere is separation from the community.

Reflection

I can't imagine it! Not even a pencil to call my own! Quite apart from things I buy, I think of several key items as "mine" because of use. For example, there is my favorite chair in the living room; whenever anyone else sits in it, I feel slightly offended.

I've been reflecting recently on the situations or events that stimulate me to use the word "my" or "mine." One telling example is how I say "my" when speaking of my children. The odd thing is that not only does such language leave out my spouse (the other parent), it suggests that perhaps my children belong to me more than to themselves. A child is, of course, a gift from God, for which we have stewardship only for a time. How can I learn not to "possess" the persons to whom I give so much—my deep, loving, caring energy? There it is again, "my" energy!

Prayer/Response

Chapter 34, Distribution of Necessities according to Need
(ENTIRE)

*I*t is written: Distribution was made to each, according to his need *(Acts 4:35). By this we do not mean that there should be partiality concerning individuals (God forbid!) but rather consideration for infirmities. Let the one, therefore, who needs less thank God and be not distressed; and let one who requires more be humbled because of his infirmity and not puffed up by the mercy that is shown to him: thus all the members shall be in peace. Above all, the scourge of murmuring must not be manifested, for any reason or by any word or sign. If anyone is found guilty of this let him be subjected to the most severe punishment.*

Comment

This chapter is almost a culmination of several preceding ones, a rising to a peak of what feels like praise. Read thoughtfully, it illumines a concept of the monastic community that is a celebration of God's goodness and glory. Each member is special, unique, and precious. Each has been gifted with needs and with a capacity to give, all of which, taken together in harmony, unfold in the most glorious symphony. The passage cited from Acts is a very crucial one in Benedict's own prayerful reflection; he not only cites it here and in the previous chapter, but also in Chapter 55:20.[81] Clearly, he has pondered at length the shape and experience of that first Spirit-filled Christian community, and it is his model for the monastic family.[82] Here he expresses his joy at the wonder of an empowered human gathering in which there is kindness. (In English, kindness is a pun on the meaning "belonging to one kind"; in Latin, it clearly expresses an imitation of God's womb-like mercy.) Indeed, such a community contains the fullness of peace.

Again, realism is always a part of Benedict's vision of peace. Benedict recognizes that participation in such a community is learned, and the seniors must guide and discipline and model behavior for the juniors. The goal is mutual uncovering of ways not to block the experience of God's wondrous gifts. Grumbling, that assertion of ego, is a serious refusal of this vision of uniqueness-within-community that Benedict is building. Thus, it is to be immediately curbed when it appears.

Reflection

I flatly dislike my limitations. Very little else can so quickly stimulate my grumbling behavior. Indeed, I strenuously seek to avoid any experience of my own inadequacy, my fatigue, or my failure. As a result, I would very much rather give than receive.

So, I have a hard time being a real participant in a giving community. It is difficult for me simply to receive help with thanks. I know others gladly give what is necessary to strengthen and support me, but I hate to need it. Recently someone promised to pray for me, and for a moment, I was actually alarmed, wondering if I had somehow signaled that I needed prayers. And then I laughed at myself.

Prayer/Response

Chapter 35, Weekly Servers in the Kitchen
VERSES 1–9

*L*et the brothers serve each other in turn, so that no one is excused from the work of the kitchen except on account of health or because one is engaged in some matter of great importance. For in this way greater reward is obtained and love is acquired. Let the weaker brethren, however, be helped so that they do not work in sadness: and let all generally have assistance according to the size of the community and the circumstances of the place. If the community is large the cellarer should be excused from kitchen service, as well as any others who are engaged (as we have said) in matters of greater importance. But let the rest serve one another in love.

Let him who is ending his week's service clean up everything on Saturday. He must wash the towels with which the brethren wipe their hands and feet; and both the one who is finishing his service and the one who is beginning it are to wash the feet of all.

Comment

The discussions of the sacramental quality of things and of the Spirit-filled life of gathered Christians serve as prelude to what now becomes a review of the mundane matters of monastery life. Many regard these details as being of no interest to the spiritual life and as having only passing relevance to contemporary monastic communities. We do not need to argue that each detail must be adhered to precisely to observe that there is much here of profound contemporary interest, even for those of us who have no vocation to the specifically monastic life.

At issue in this chapter is what it means to be a creature. Our bodies are nourished by food, which we intake, assimilate, and excrete. Our bodies interact with the natural environment in such a way that they become dirty, smelly, and calloused. Engaged in our "god-project," we like to pretend that we can and do "rise above" these natural phenomena. Preparation of food and removal and cleansing of waste are ordinarily considered menial tasks, to be assigned to those who "cannot do anything of value."[83] Soaps, deodorants, perfumes, and fancy clothing are among a few of the responses we use to hide our creatureliness even from ourselves.

So the shared service of one another described here is yet another example of Benedict's intention to practice a crucial shift in disposition. Instead of disdaining the creaturely, we learn to honor it and treat it with reverence, as appropriate to God's good creation. This service is a way of accepting our own true place in the scheme of things: being willing to be creatures of God. This acceptance, this willingness, is the first step in learning to notice God as sacramentally present even in the frailest and "dirtiest" of our beings.

Reflection

There is so much to think about here! Today, I think of the necessary relation between charity and the creaturely. Is it perhaps the case that I can only fully experience charity in and through acceptance of my body? When I consider St. Francis kissing the leper, or Mother Teresa cradling a broken and maimed beggar, it occurs to me that their outpouring love must involve such acceptance of the creaturely. What is necessary not to be repelled by such disfigurement? Among other things, it requires an ease with our own bodily functions, a profound sense of our place in creation.

Recently my grandmother anticipated a severe worsening of her health. Many years ago, she had a colostomy, which she personally has cared for and cleansed each day. Anticipating her decline, she described to me the necessary procedures, willing to turn them over to me should circumstances require. There was a profound intimacy in the conversation, and I was humbled and uplifted. I became aware that I was praying for the ability to serve her with openhearted and easy grace and in deep thanksgiving for her trust.

Prayer/Response

Chapter 35
VERSES 10–18 (END)

*L**et the server hand over to the cellarer the vessels used in his work, clean and in sound condition; and let the cellarer hand them to the one beginning his service, so that he may know what he gives out and what he receives back. An hour before the meal these weekly servers shall receive, over and above the appointed allowance, a drink and a piece of* *bread, so that they may serve the brethren at meal time without murmuring or excessive fatigue. On solemn days, however, let them wait until after Mass.*

On Sunday, as soon as Lauds has ended, both the incoming and outgoing servers for the week shall bow deeply in the presence of all and ask their prayers. Let the one who is ending his week say this verse: Blessed are you, O Lord God, who have helped and consoled me (Dan 3:52; Ps 86:17); and when this has been said three times let him receive the blessing. The one who is beginning service shall then follow and say: O God, come to my assistance; O Lord, make haste to help me (Ps 70:2). Let this also be repeated three times; and having received the blessing let him begin his service.

Comment

Every action is undertaken in the sight of God: this is a fundamental precept of the Christian life for Benedict. Again, it doesn't sound radical, but actually to practice it is a remarkable idea. The kitchen service is officially to be set within the framework of prayer. Benedict does this in two ways. The servers are to receive a little extra food after mass in order to keep up their strength as they prepare and serve the one meal, in late afternoon. The physical nourishment of bread and wine is a prayerful action.

And second, the actual service in the kitchen itself is set within the context of the daily office, with time taken each week in Sunday Lauds to give thanks for help received and to ask for grace to come. The phrase from Psalm 70 is also the one used to begin each of the midday offices, and is the unceasing prayer of the desert fathers.[84]

Reflection

It occurs to me that this routine on the one hand ritualizes and thus provides opportunity for sacramental integration of the truth that God assists all work. But it also carries the danger of any ritual—that is, it might become "routinized," become a rote performance carried out automatically, without inner meaning. Our modern world has discarded most rituals because of that danger, but what have we lost?

At Eucharist, for example, I am aware that repetitive actions do sometimes become routine, not carried in my heart nor felt with any personal engagement. But even so, there is a sense in which the participation of my body and my will allow me to carry around some possibilities that any moment may blossom into a fresh consciousness of God's presence. And, particularly when the routines are shared ones, sometimes I am sustained by the engagement of others, even when my own engagement is weak.

Prayer/Response

Chapter 36, The Sick
(ENTIRE)

*B*efore all things and above all things, care must be taken of the sick, so that they may be truly served as Christ Himself, for He has said: I was sick and you visited me (Matt 25:36) and, Whatever you did to one of these, my least brethren, you did to me (Matt 25:40). But let the sick themselves consider that they are served for the honor of God, and not grieve their brethren who serve them by their demands. Yet they must be patiently borne with, because from such as these is gained more abundant reward. Therefore the abbot shall take the greatest care that they do not suffer neglect.

Let a room be set apart by itself for the sick brethren, and an attendant be appointed who is God-fearing, prompt, and painstaking. Let the use of baths be granted to the sick as often as it is appropriate; but to those who are well, and especially to the young, baths shall be seldom permitted. The use of meat, too, shall be permitted to the sick and to the very weak, that they may recover their strength; but when they are restored to health, let all abstain from meat in the accustomed manner.

The abbot must take all possible care that the sick are not neglected by the cellarers or their attendants; because he is responsible for whatever is done amiss by his disciples.

Comment

Benedict cites this passage from Matthew 25 in several places.[85] While he is not minimizing its reference to the day of judgment, in his usual affirming way, he uses it primarily to remind us that we can meet Christ within our daily context of simple and mundane service for one another!

In this chapter we also see the careful balancing of separate interests within the one body, so characteristic of Benedict. The brothers are to care for the sick; the sick are not to distress the brothers by their demands: both are to offer themselves to each other in mutual obedience. The brothers are to serve generously; the abbot is to supervise them wisely: obedience carries obligations on both sides. The weak are to receive special privileges; it is not to be presumed by the healthy that such privileges have established a precedent: life is best lived in the context of sufficiency and frugality.

Finally, Benedict raises an important concept from the Gospel of Matthew: reward.[86] Today we often think that Christian behavior should be "altruistic," that is, with no expectation of reward. Benedict and Matthew would have been startled by such thinking. For them, our behavior ought to be motivated by our desire for God's reward, illustrated by phrases like "kingdom of heaven," "children of the Father," and "life in abundance." Benedict invites, indeed encourages us to reflect deeply upon God's promised rewards (see especially Chapter 4:46, 76) so that they may increasingly form our aspirations and our behavior.

Reflection

Benedict insists that I take our Lord seriously in Matthew 25 when he says: "[I]n so far as you as you did this to one of the least of these brothers of mine, you did it to me." In other words, Benedict tells me that the normal encounters of each day provide an opportunity to receive Christ. In relationship with one another, we may receive Christ. Lest I miss the point, he emphasizes that receiving Christ involves things like taking care of a sick and cranky relative!

As he suggests to me when he balances interests against one another, every relationship has its high and low moments. No matter how glorious, loving, or even "spiritual" the relationship, it does not take me very long to become aware of certain weaknesses and inadequacies in the other. Shall I then withdraw part of me from this all-too-human person? In some respects, it is easier to take refuge in the "real" thing, Christ unmediated. But the "scandal" of incarnation (now, in my sisters and brothers, as well as once for all in Jesus) has its positive dimensions as well as its negative ones.

Recently, I have discovered that if I continue to risk myself with another in the presence of Christ, quite wonderful and unexpected outcomes may occur. In other words, when I try to be fully present to the actual person in front of me—in light of the fact that Christ is here with us—a new quality of relationship becomes possible in which I learn more about love than I ever dreamed existed.

The wedding rings that my husband and I wear have crosses cut out of their centers, so that sunlight daily burns Christ's symbol into our flesh. When we chose the rings I was speechless with the sudden awareness that with Christ so central, we could really risk what otherwise would have been impossible to us. What happens when we believe that another person "embodies" Christ for us? My hunch is that what "happens" is both very ordinary and nearly miraculous. And my hunch is that Benedict lived that ordinary-miraculous life every day. Can I as well?

Prayer/Response

Chapter 37, The Old and Children
(ENTIRE)

Although human nature of itself is drawn to feel pity and consideration for these two times of life—the elderly and children—yet the authority of the Rule should also provide for them. Let their weakness be always taken into account, and do not allow the full rigor of the Rule as regards food to be maintained in their regard. Rather, let kindly consideration be shown to them, and let them eat before the regular hours.

Comment

This chapter is characteristic of Benedict's constant care for human weakness and limitation. Never a matter for shame or disgust, it is always an opportunity for stewardship and charity. Concern and love are to be expressed not only by those giving care, but by those receiving it.

How strict is the Rule generally in the matter of food? Soon we shall come to Chapter 39, "The Proper Amount of Food," which indicates that there were many days of one meal only, late in the afternoon. On other days there were two meals, a heavier one at midday and a lighter supper in the evening. This is a somewhat meager regimen by our standards, but generally it was the norm even in the secular world in Benedict's day. As monasteries moved farther north from the equator, adjustments were made to provide heartier fare, in accordance with Benedict's general principle that there was to be sufficiency within frugality,[87] because an alert and responsive body is a needed support in the Christian life of service and love.

Reflection

It occurs to me that monastic practice has not been all that success-ful in attaining this balance recommended by Benedict—either in the matter of strictness of diet, nor in the matter of taking lack of strength into account. That gives me some comfort as I realize that neither have I! In food, I alternate between self-indulgence and self-punishment; and in the matter of lack of strength, I generally am embarrassed by it.

As I reflect on the themes that seem to recur in these chapters, I see that there truly is an important connection between humility, stewardship, and sacramental awareness. Both self-indulgence and self-punishment are poor stewardship. Both are undoubtedly rooted in lack of self-acceptance: they are a refusal to acknowledge the way things actually are. I have already confessed my discomfort with my own occasional lack of strength, with my creatureliness. Yet here for the first time I realize that by refusing humility (acceptance of my body and my limitations), I am actually closing myself off from the awareness of the presence of God within my situation. I am refusing the opportunity to receive the strength and assistance of those who would give it.

Perhaps "kindly consideration" is the mark of a humble per-son, of God's person. To give and receive kindliness is a mark that one belongs to a community, the body of Christ. I need to ponder this further.

Prayer/Response

Chapter 38, The Weekly Reader
(ENTIRE)

hen the brethren are taking their meals there should always be reading. Yet no one shall spontaneously presume to take up the book and read; rather let the one who is to read throughout the week begin on Sunday. Let this brother, when beginning his service, ask all after Mass and Communion to pray for him, that God may keep from him the spirit of pride. And let this verse be said three times in the oratory by all, he, the reader, first beginning: O Lord, open my lips, and my mouth shall declare your praise (Ps 51:17). And so, having received the blessing, let him begin his reading.

The greatest silence should be kept at table, so that no whispering or voice, except the voice of the reader alone, is heard there. Whatever is required for eating and drinking the brethren shall offer to one another so that no one need ask for anything. Should anything be wanted, let it be asked for by an audible sign of some sort rather than in words. Let no one ask any question there about anything else, lest occasion be given [to the evil one] (Eph 4:27; 1 Tim 5:4); unless, perhaps, the superior should wish to say something briefly for the edification of the brethren.

The brother who is reader for the week shall receive some mixed wine and water before he begins to read, on account of the Holy Communion, and lest it be too hard for him to fast so long. He shall take his meal afterwards with the weekly cooks and servers.

The brethren, however, are not to read or chant according to their rank, but only as may edify the hearers.

Comment

This chapter is about hearing and receiving the Word of God, but in Benedict's usual way, that idea is stated not in a theological treatise, but within the framework of the ordinary routines of the community; not in terms of the text, but in terms of the responsibility of the human channel for communication of God's Word.

Silence at meals was routine in monastic communities of the time, but Benedict's emphasis is quite different from most of his peers. For him, silence is not introduced for the negative purpose of stopping conversation (which might give rise to arguments or bawdiness), but rather for the positive purpose of listening to the Word of God.[88] The silence at meals is because God is speaking in the scripture and the Fathers, and the monks are to listen eagerly and attentively.

Notice, however, that the written word is not the only source of God's Word. The brothers are to be attentive to each other's needs as they eat and drink and to the superior's words of instruction. And they come to dinner immediately following Holy Communion.[89] This community meal is thus both a highly sacramental and a deeply ordinary moment, to be attended to with all one's heart. The reader during the meal must understand that his work is essential for this communal action of praise and thanksgiving.

Reflection

This moment is both highly sacramental and deeply ordinary. In a sense, that is what Benedict is saying in many different ways in this whole section on domestic arrangements. Do I see my domestic setting that way?

Occasionally, I do. There are mornings when I look out the window above the sink, while my hands are in the hot, soapy suds, and my heart leaps for joy at the sun and the trees and the birds. There are moments when I look at my husband's funny fingernails on his thumbs, and I'm dizzy with happiness at the tangibleness of him. But they are fleeting moments.

It's odd, though. Moments of that sort do seem to involve a specific attentiveness to something ordinary and concrete, as well as an awareness that it is an opening to something else. If I start out looking for God, I seem to get confused and lost. Whereas, if I start out really attending to what is actually given in this moment, I discover God.

Prayer/Response

Chapter 39, The Appropriate Amount of Food
(ENTIRE)

*W*e think it sufficient for the daily meal, whether at the sixth or the ninth hour, that there be at all the tables two dishes of cooked food on account of the variety of weaknesses: so that one who may not be able to eat of the first may make his meal of the other. Therefore let two cooked dishes suffice for the brethren; and if there are any fruit or young vegetables, let a third dish be added. Let a good pound of bread suffice for each day, whether there be only one meal or both lunch and dinner. If they are to have dinner let a third part of the pound be kept back by the cellarer and given to them for dinner.

If however their work has been greater, it shall be according to the will and in the power of the abbot (if it is desirable) to make some addition [to the meal], provided that excess be avoided above all things, and that no monk suffer from overeating. For nothing is more contrary to any Christian life than overeating, as Our Lord says: Take heed that your hearts are not heavily laden through overeating (Luke 21:34). To children of tender years the same quantity should not be allotted; rather they should receive less than their elders, frugality being observed in all things.

But let all abstain from eating the flesh of four-footed animals, except the very weak and the sick.

Comment

In Benedict's time, the general practice among persons consecrated to God was severe abstinence regarding food and drink, often surpassing these "natural austerities" in his Rule. Benedict adopted moderation as his pattern, seeing in severe physical abstinences the danger of spiritual pride, as well as the possibility of a weakened body incapable of being a supportive partner in the life with God.

Benedict's approach to disciplining the body and its appetites is given boundaries by three concepts in this chapter: abstinence (a very limited practice, here only relevant to flesh meat); overindulgence (a sin to be avoided at all costs); and sufficiency (the moderate amount that will suffice for all). Sufficiency is his standard, and one useful for us to consider in many contexts.

Why is overindulgence such a sin? Luke 21 reveals the context not only of this quotation, but also of the whole Christian life, so far as Benedict is concerned: preparation for the great day of judgment. In all we do, we are preparing (whether we know it or not) for that glorious day when Christ will come into his own. Overindulgence minimizes our capacity to be alert, to be responsive to the Christ in our present environment as he brings us into that future one.

Reflection

What is sufficiency? How do I know when I have enough? In every area of my life, this is an important question. I have already reflected on the issue of enough food, but there are also the issues of enough talent, enough self-esteem, enough love, enough security, enough money, and on and on.

I think our society generally operates on the principle of scarcity, so that each of us feels we must claim and hoard to get our fair share. This stance is a startling contrast to the principle on which Jesus seems to operate, abundance, so that there is always more than is needed. I see this in Jesus not only when he feeds the five thousand, but also in his parables, and in such words as "to the one who has will more be given" (Matt 13:12).

Sufficiency must have something to do with Christ's abundance. Can I be satisfied with what is sufficient for now, because I trust in the Lord who clothes the lilies? I wonder if I can begin to experience what I am already receiving not only as sufficient, but also as abundant.

Prayer/Response

Chapter 40, The Appropriate Amount of Drink
(ENTIRE)

veryone has his proper gift from God: one this, another that (1 Cor 7:7). And therefore it is with some reluctance that we determine the measure of another's living. Yet, making due allowance for the weakness of some, we think that a "hemina" of wine a day is sufficient for each. But let those to whom God gives the gift of abstinence know that they shall receive their proper reward.

If either local necessity, the work, or the heat of summer require more,
it is in the power of the superior to grant it, care being taken in all things
that satiety or drunkenness not creep in. Although we read that wine is
by no means a drink for monks, yet, since in our days they cannot be per-
suaded of this, let us at least agree not to drink to satiety, but sparingly:
because wine causes even the wise to fall away (Sir 19:2).

But where the place is such that not even the aforesaid measure can
be supplied, but rather much less or none at all, let those who dwell there
bless God and not murmur. This above all we admonish, that they refrain
from murmuring.

Comment

Here as we deal with matters of food and drink, we are probing the
nature of human desire, its value and its restraint, in the whole of
the spiritual life. Here Benedict draws on many sources,[90] weaving
together a moderate approach that honors the human body and its
construction yet keeps the central orientation on God. As we look at
the two passages of scripture cited here and at Benedict's use of
them, we understand his approach as something like this:

> A person dedicated to God must always be thinking of the hour of
> death and the day of reckoning. Consciousness of that reality helps
> us remember always that who we are and what we do does matter. An
> essential element in this regard is to restrain our desires. Unchecked
> expression of desire for many things dilutes the formative power of
> our great desire for the One. And yet each person will find that the
> spirit of wisdom guides him or her differently in the choice of disci-
> plines and expression of vital energies. We need discernment as we
> seek knowledge of those elements in our makeup that are gifts and
> those that are indulgences. The orientation that best guides the whole
> process is to love God above all.

Benedict summarizes his thoughts in the last paragraph of this
chapter: wherever you are, whatever the conditions in which you
find yourself, bless God and be thankful. This is so central that murmuring may be a greater sin than occasional overindulgence,
because murmuring is the opposite of thankfulness.

Sirach says: seek wisdom. Paul says: live by the Spirit. Benedict
says: bless God. In Benedict's hands, all this advice on spiritual
essentials has an earthy quality, a kind of fullness of delight in what

actually is. It is far removed from the kind of shriveled-up prudery or harsh penitence that I so often associate with spiritual discipline. How much I would like to live in a community where these constraints-infused-with-glory provided the daily rhythm! And yet, no doubt even in such a place, I would have to learn to recognize what was actually there.

I'm reminded of a song fragment: the joy of the Lord is my strength! What a paradox that moderation is the natural outcome of joyous living! I wonder if it's better to start with the joy, or start with the moderation? Maybe a little of both.

Prayer/Response

Chapter 41, At What Hours the Community Is to Take Meals
(ENTIRE)

From the holy feast of Easter until Pentecost the brethren should have lunch at the sixth hour and dine in the evening. But from Pentecost throughout the summer, if the monks do not have to work in the field and are not inconvenienced by excessive heat, let them fast on Wednesdays and Fridays until the ninth hour and take their meal on other days at the sixth hour.

Should they have field labor, or should the heat of the summer be very great, let a meal at the sixth hour be the norm, at the discretion of the abbot. Let him likewise modify and arrange all things so that souls may be saved and that the brethren may fulfill their tasks without any justifiable murmuring.

From September thirteenth until the beginning of Lent let the brethren always take their meal at the ninth hour. During Lent, however, until Easter let them dine in the evening. But let the evening meal be so arranged that they do not need lamps while eating, and that all things may be finished while there is still daylight. Indeed, at all times of the year let the hour for lunch or dinner be so arranged that everything can be done by daylight.

Comment

Patterns of consumption are to be frugal and yet moderate. Although monks are encouraged to stretch themselves by fasting until a later meal, this is to be offset not only by the reasonable needs of the body (relating to hard labor and heat) but also by a concern not to be wasteful of candles as well as food.

We notice the term "justifiable murmuring." On several occasions, Benedict has referred to murmuring as a severe disobedience to the spirit—if not the letter—of the Rule. And yet here he mentions that there might be occasions that justify such grumbling. Again, as always, responsibility is mutual: monks are not to grumble; superiors are to arrange external circumstances to minimize unnecessary distress.

But unquestionably, the most important point about spiritual disciplines occurs in the first verse: for the Christian, fasting must be in relation to feasting. The joy of the resurrection is to be celebrated; the banquet table is prepared by Christ's victory; all are to partake in the feast! Everything in Christian life, including discipline, must take its place in relation to this joy.

"The mystery of Easter is the crux on which (everything) hangs. . . . Everything is done in relation to the resurrection; even the midday meal becomes a way of celebrating it."[91]

Reflection

In what ways do I integrate intentional feasting with intentional fasting? How do I know myself served and loved by the Lord, as well as loving and serving him? A friend of mine starts each day by asking: How will God love me today? At the end of the day, she asks again: How has God loved me today? Having reviewed that, she gives thanks.

I suggested that pattern to another friend who was utterly startled by it. She had often pondered how she was loving God, but had never thought of how God was loving her. It seems almost "sinful" at first. Yet I think there is good evidence to suggest that the human Jesus was empowered by God's ongoing word to him: "I love you!" In a sense, that was the word both at Jesus' baptism and at his transfiguration. And we are certainly invited to participate in both, as we are drawn into Christ's life. What more wonderful feast than that!

Prayer/Response

Chapter 42: That No One May
Speak after Compline
(ENTIRE)

*A*t all times silence should be cultivated by monks, but most especially during the hours of the night. And this shall always be the
case, whether on fast days or ordinary days. If it is not a fast day, as soon
as they have risen from supper all are to sit down together and one is to
read the Conferences or Lives of the Fathers, or at least something else
which may edify the hearers; but not the Heptateuch, nor the Books of
Kings: for it will not profit those of weak understanding to hear those
parts of Scripture at that hour; they are to be read at other times.

If it is a fast-day, then shortly after Vespers they should assemble for
the reading as we have said; four or five pages being read, or as much as
time allows, so that during the interval provided by this reading all may
come together, even those occupied in some assigned project. When all
are gathered together let them say Compline; and when they come out
from Compline no one shall be allowed to speak further to anyone. If
any are found evading this rule of silence, let them be punished severely;
unless the presence of guests necessitated it or the abbot needed to give
a command to someone. But even this must be done with the greatest
seriousness and proper moderation.

Comment

Benedict is often less systematic than organic, using a free-flowing
style to address issues as they come to him. This chapter is about
silence, as well as about meals, reading, community. In short, it is
about listening to and responding to God. In a sense, that has been
the theme of all the chapters about domestic arrangements: God is
here and now in the routine matters of our day. Let us notice and
respond to that presence.

Benedict reminds us in these chapters that material things are
sacraments, that is, outer signs of an inward presence. We are to treat
things tenderly and attentively, that they may reveal God. If we see
only the outer, we may seek to possess rather than care for things. If
we see only the inner, we cease to value and tend the lovely created

world that God has given into our charge. In all we do, no matter how frail or ordinary it seems, we are seeking to listen and respond to God. This is possible because God in Christ is giving Godself to us all the time. All the arrangements of the domestic setting are designed to bring us continually into contact with these truths.

If we are to practice this task of listening for God in all, silence is an essential framework. In the Rule, silence is always about hearing God's Word.[92] Night silence brings rest and allows the Word to take root in the monk's heart, that he might truly open his lips and pour forth God's praise in the morning (Chapter 9:1).

Reflection

Benedict's fluidity in his organization of the Rule forces me to encounter it less with my mind (and analysis) than with my heart (and receptivity). If I stay with the Rule, I find myself being opened to the unknown, and I discover that I am transcending myself.

In a new way, I sense that is exactly what the Gospel is and does. It offers a gentle but steady invitation to grow beyond myself and what I can "know" with my mind so that I might come to be "known" in the ancient Hebrew way: penetrated intimately by the abundant Love who already knows me better than I know myself. And this wonderful process seems in fact to happen in my ordinary daily round of waking and sleeping, eating and eliminating, sickness and study, weakness and work. Astonishing!

Prayer/Response

Interlude VI
A NOTE TO THE READER

Are you finding that it's hard to keep up your *lectio* when you're doing it alone?

Many people are very interested in keeping a regular routine of meditation but find it hard to sustain interest without companionship. They often are energized and stimulated by the conversation and ideas of others, and they simply don't have the heart to keep up a discipline absent that vital exchange. If this describes your situation, it's a good idea to make the *lectio* a group endeavor.

A group *lectio* process might work something like this. Several individuals (anywhere from four to eight is a good number) would commit to each other to do a certain number of private *lectio* meditations between the meeting times. Then, when you meet together, you have a free-flowing discussion of individual insights, questions, wonderments. Say you had agreed to complete three *lectio* units during the week. When you gather, you could review all three units systematically, or instead jump right in to a place where one of you got stuck, or had a great insight, or the like. In the process of sharing, you build on one another's wisdom and gain support for your own process.

For the group meeting times, it's a good idea to begin and end with prayer, either spoken or silent. As you do your sharing, one person might want to bring outside resources explaining the history or context of the Rule in that section. But, in general, the emphasis should be on your own perceptions. That is, the point of the devotional effort is to cooperate with God's work deepening your spirit, so the focus is not on information as such, but on the way it impacts your life. Try to concentrate on "I" statements rather than on "they" statements. Stay centered in your own strong attractions and repulsions. Pay attention to places where the text resonates in you. Listen to one another.

For such sharing to be fruitful, it's good to trust one another and commit to confidentiality. Whatever is said in the group should not be mentioned outside it without specific permission. Trust grows slowly and should not be forced, but gently allow it to bloom among you. Most of us don't have the words to speak of our relationship with God, and we recognize that we experience great vulnerability as we try to do so. A supportive response from others is enormously helpful in claiming our own reality.

If you begin or join such a group, be aware that God is in your midst, and is giving you to one another in love.

Lukewarmness and Its Remedies

Chapter 43, Those Who Arrive Late at the Work of God or at Table
VERSES 1–9

At the hour of the Divine Office, as soon as the signal is heard, each one is to lay aside whatever he may be engaged on and hasten to [prayer] with all speed; yet with seriousness, so that no occasion be given for levity. Indeed, let nothing be preferred to the Work of God. Should anyone come to Vigils after the Gloria of the ninety-fifth psalm (which for this reason we wish to be said very slowly and deliberately), let him not stand in his usual place in the choir, but last of all, or in the place set apart by the abbot for such negligent ones. There they will remain, visible to all and to himself, until the Work of God being ended, he makes penance by public satisfaction. The reason why we have judged it fitting for them to stand in the last place or apart is that, being seen by all, they may amend out of shame. For if they were to remain outside the oratory, there might be one who would return to his bed and sleep, or else sit outside and give himself to idle tales, and so give occasion to the evil one (Eph 4:27; 1 Tim 5:14). Rather let them come in, that he may not lose the whole and may amend for the future.

Comment

This chapter and the next three are known as the minor penal code of the Rule: Benedict is here concerned about minor offenses, offenses of incomplete observance representing a lukewarmness or slackness in behavioral commitment to the consecrated life.[93]

It is fitting that Benedict begins these chapters with a reminder of what the consecrated Christian life is: response to the call of God (compare Prologue 9). God calls; we hear; and we respond at once, immediately. This work of response to God is the only work we do, whatever else we are doing. Notice especially here the use of the word so characteristic of the Gospel of Mark: immediately! The good news of Christ is given, and the human heart leaps in response.

But the intensity of initial fervor is not often matched by the consistency of persistent response. What Benedict presents in these chapters is a profound view of the nature of the whole spiritual life, a layered view building upon the moral theology not only of St. Paul, but also probably of St. Augustine.[94]

Why does lukewarmness matter? Being late for office is not such a grave matter, after all. Why even address it in this formal document? Because it gives occasion to the evil one (here and also RB 38:8). The ascetical life consists of the building up of a habitual response to God, characterized by Paul as putting "on the new self that has been created in God's way, in the goodness and holiness of the truth" (Eph 4:24). This is strenuous and challenging work, which requires constant attentiveness. While it is true that the first suggestion of sin is innocent, or even that an occasional tardiness is minor, it is also true that such a slip represents a first step away from God, and there are so many steps toward God, steps that help us grow. Thus, even for these minor offenses, making "satisfaction"— in the sense of an inward turning of heart, expressed in outward behavior—is a valuable and necessary response.

Reflection

It occurs to me that if I were to take these ideas seriously, I would value every moment of my life in a way vastly beyond my present behavior and attitudes. Do I really matter that much—in each action I take, in every thought I entertain? And am I really that important to God? That takes some pondering.

It seems also to require a growing attentiveness to what is actually going on, both in me and around me, and a constant re-offering of all of it to God for consecration. I want to look further at how that might actually work.

Prayer/Response

Chapter 43
VERSES 10–19 (END)

At the Day Hours, anyone who comes to the Work of God after the verse and the Gloria of the first psalm which is said after the verse, must stand in the last place, as stated above. Nor should he presume to join the choir in their chanting until he has made satisfaction, unless the abbot allows him: yet even so he is to make satisfaction for his guilt.

One who does not come to table before the verse, so that all may say it praying together and sit down to table at the same time, must be corrected once or twice if this be through negligence or fault. If after this he does not amend, let him not be allowed to share in the common table, but be separated from the company of all and eat alone. His portion of wine should be withheld from him until he makes satisfaction and amends. Anyone who is not present at the verse which is said after meals is to undergo the same punishment.

No one should presume to take any food or drink before or after the appointed time; but if something is offered to one by the superior and he refuses it, and afterwards wishes to have what he had rejected or something else, let him receive neither this nor anything else until he makes proper satisfaction.

Comment

Benedict includes tardiness at worship and at the dinner table in the same category. Tardiness, then, reveals a laziness about or an indifference to the community of faith. In this sense, it is an assertion of pride or self-will above the common and shared aspects of life together. It is in effect saying: "What I was doing is more important than what we do together." Setting oneself against or apart from the community, even in small things, is a danger less to the community than to one's own salvation. For it is through the common life that we enter salvation; it is as we come to experience our commonality with our family that we claim our true membership in Christ's body.

Satisfaction is the term used by Benedict to express a concrete and external action designed to effect a deepened humility.[95] It is thus an outward sign completed in cooperation with an inward movement or intention, so like the sacramental reality of the ordinary that we saw so frequently in Benedict's "domestic arrangements." Again, Benedict points to the sacrament of the present moment, seen even in a common act of sin and repentance.

Reflection

The Christian concept of community *(koinonia)* has always been greatly mysterious and greatly attractive to me. Yet it also has always seemed out of reach. Benedict is helping me to see more clearly how great the distance is between assertive individualism and *koinonia*.

He makes me rethink some of my basic values, because I have always understood that it is good to stress my individuality and to differentiate myself from the common. I think with what disdain I used to say: "But he's so common." And yet "common" is the root meaning of *koinonia,* as well as of community and communion. It is an affirmation of our kinship, in contrast to our distinctions.

It seems to me that so much in my environment supports the impulse to be uncommon. Even much Christian talk encourages me to believe that salvation itself is a singular and solitary experience.

Yet Benedict challenges that. I believe he suggests that salvation itself is a participative experience, a sharing not only in God's life but in one another's. How far out of reach that seems! And yet, today brings many concrete opportunities for me to try it.

Prayer/Response

Chapter 44, How the Excommunicated Are to Make Satisfaction
(ENTIRE)

*O*ne who is excommunicated for graver faults from the oratory and the table must lie prostrate in silence before the door of the oratory at the end of the hour at which the Work of God has been celebrated. He should say nothing, lying face down at the feet of all as they leave the oratory: this he should do until the abbot judges that satisfaction has been made. Then, when the abbot bids him, he is to prostrate himself at the feet of the abbot, then at the feet of all the brethren, that they may pray for him. And then, if the abbot orders, he may be received back into choir in the rank the abbot assigns: however, he should not presume to lead a psalm, a lesson or anything else in the oratory unless the abbot again commands him. Moreover, at every hour, as the Work of God is ending, he must prostrate himself on the ground in the place where he stands until the abbot again bids him cease from this satisfaction.

But those who are excommunicated for less serious faults from the table only must make satisfaction in the oratory as long as the abbot commands. This they do until he gives his blessing and says: It is enough.

Comment

This chapter seems very harsh to a modern reader—unnecessarily humiliating, we might say. But we must consider it in two contexts. The first is in relation to other sources of the time, which emphasized corporal punishment (even beating to near death), regarded sinners as heretics, even Judases, and routinely called for intensive Lenten penitential periods even in congregational settings.[96] The second is Benedict's overall purpose in establishing the monastic community, in which humiliations facilitate humility, which is essential for salvation.

The modern reader must struggle with three primary questions in response to this chapter. They are:

1. Are there any moral offenses that can jeopardize eternal life and, if so, what are they?

2. What constitutes true repentance, and how can it be embodied and tested?

3. What process permits forgiveness to flow and be acknowledged by the sinner so that personal and communal restoration may be effectively received?

Most of these issues are simply ignored in modern times. Consider for a moment the last one. Absolution, that is, full restoration, is a concept utterly foreign to the experience of most of us. We frequently express confession in the context of the psychiatrist's couch, but there is no mechanism by which sin can be acknowledged, repented, and removed. One real advantage of Benedict's procedure is that the penitent can fully and joyfully receive the word "Enough!"

Reflection

Two strong images are evoked for me in reflecting on this chapter. The first is a memory of an event that occurred when I was about eleven years old. I had been writing plays that my teacher invited my classmates to perform. One day, when I brought in a new one, she stopped me for a moment and said: "Norvene, in each of these plays, you have written in a star character which only you can play. Why not write some in which others can take the lead?" I flushed and momentarily denied that intention, but I knew at once that what she said was true. I think of that as the moment I became an adult; my teacher gave me real dignity by treating me as a person capable of choosing my ego or the community.

The second is a scene from the movie *Mission,* in which a man has killed his brother in anger and now wants to die himself. He is restored to new life by a priest, who encourages him literally to carry his penance until the moment he is freed to weep and laugh as he hears "Enough!"

Prayer/Response

Chapter 45, Those Who Make Mistakes in the Oratory
(ENTIRE)

If anyone makes a mistake while reciting a psalm, responsory, antiphon, or lesson and does not make satisfaction, humbling himself there before all, let him be subjected to greater punishment, as one who would not correct by humility what he did wrong through negligence. But children for such faults are to be whipped.

Comment

Perhaps we are again reminded here of the disciples' words in John 6:60: "This is intolerable language! How could anyone accept it?" In that context, Jesus is talking about giving them his flesh to eat— harsh words indeed. Is there something of redemption also present here, in these harsh words of Benedict?

Benedict is drawing here, as he often does in the Rule, on the Rule of the Master, in which the rationale for such actions is spelled out more clearly. As regards the whipping of children, the Master says:

> Young boys up to the age of fifteen, we prescribe, are not to be excommunicated but whipped for their faults. After the age of fifteen, however, it is proper not to whip but to excommunicate them, because then they understand that they must do penance and correct what wrong they do as adults. For it is right that one who sins should repent in his heart, and not be physically whipped for it, because we live under the soul's rule . . .[97]

The Master's language illuminates the key issue of this chapter, which is the internalization of the Gospel. This "taking in" of the Gospel is done in obedience to the community's Rule and the abbot, so that the habitual response of the mature Christian to sin becomes self-accusation and spontaneous satisfaction. A small action such as a mispronunciation of the Word of God becomes important because it is a frequent opportunity to train oneself into that spontaneous orientation toward God known as purity of heart.

For children and novices, this training must initially be presented externally, because that is the form in which it is understood. In the *lectio* on Chapter 30, we referred to the contemporary work of Lawrence Kohlberg, which is basically a modern statement of this same point, that at different developmental stages, different behaviors are necessary to influence moral behavior. And the goal of the Rule is the movement toward moral maturity, in which God's law of love is known interiorly as the law of one's very being (see Chapter 7:68–69).

Reflection

So many questions arise for me. Is there a place (and if so, what kind) for an "objective" moral standard against which all actions must be measured? Our society is so oriented toward "situational ethics," and I myself am inclined to consider context highly important in the evaluation of moral behavior. Then, too, most of the "strong moralists" I know have such a narrow and dried-up view of acceptable behavior. On the other hand, I am increasingly aware of the terrible loss of a communal framework within which moral choices can be judged. Surely, there is some limit on acceptable behavior, no matter what the context.

Is it really true that corporal punishment (whether self-inflicted or otherwise) is necessary to bring the bodily appetites and willfulness into harmony with the soul's deepest desire? What about the "strategy" of warm affection and loving regard as attracting us toward good, instead of punishment pushing us away from evil? Are both needed at different times? I confess that I am confused and uncertain on these points. Benedict invites me to ponder and pray and study more reflectively in these areas.

Finally, I realize afresh how very difficult humility is. My pride and ego would so much rather ignore the small errors and sins so I can think highly of myself, rather than attend to them and recognize my utter and every-moment dependence on my God.

Prayer/Response

Chapter 46, Those Who Offend in Other Matters
(ENTIRE)

If anyone while engaged in any sort of work, whether in the kitchen, the cellar, the office, the bakehouse, or the garden, in any craft, or in any place, shall do anything amiss—break or lose anything, or offend in any way whatever—he must go at once before the abbot or the community, and of his own accord do penance and confess his fault. But if this becomes known by means of another, let him be subjected to greater punishment.

If, however, the cause of his sin is hidden in his own soul, let him manifest it only to the abbot or to the spiritual seniors, who know how to heal their own wounds and not to disclose or make public those of others.

Comment

Benedict was a sturdy realist, and he continually makes clear that he does not expect frail human beings to live without error. Why then make such a "production" about repenting for these sins we cannot avoid? First, we are to use these faults to keep us always aware that we are finite creatures, something we prefer not to know, yet something that actually is a source of bonding to our Creator. Second, we are to confess these faults at once, because if they are kept "secret," they fester in our hearts and do internal damage.

Recall that in Chapter 4, Benedict urges us to "dash down at the feet of Christ your evil thoughts . . . and lay them open" (verse 50). This chapter is a practical application of that principle. There is danger to our souls in keeping secrets, even from ourselves. Modern Jungian scholars talk about the negative effects of the undisclosed "shadow" sides of our personalities.[98] Benedict is acknowledging a truth about human nature that runs along those lines: the more we allow ourselves to be blind to our true nature, the further we are moving away from God, who is Truth itself. And when we are also trying to hide our personal weakness from others, there is a tendency to become self-justifying and proud.

In a sense, then, this routine repentance for normal external and visible faults sets a pattern to guide us in matters of deeper inward sin. Everything is to be brought at once into the light, revealed in humility to those who will respond in love. This pattern reveals great wisdom about how the soul's wounds are received and healed. What great freedom there is, always living transparently. Evil is unable to gain strength in disclosure, whereas in hiddenness it can hold our spirits in bondage. A sin once disclosed is deprived of its power to harm.

Notice that Benedict allows such confession to be offered to any of the spiritual elders, rather than reserving this role for the abbot exclusively. This option suggests his recognition that inner healing of the soul is best accomplished in the context of a special human bond of love and regard.

Reflection

Some mornings I wake up under a dark cloud. Who knows why, but it occasionally occurs. Quite often, the "cloud" takes the form of voices accusing me of inadequacy, incompetence, and lack of charity. Sometimes simply noticing the voices as nuisances, like buzzing flies with a monotonous tone, is sufficient to cause them to dissipate. Sometimes that doesn't work. However, I have become aware that if I simply mention to my husband what I am thinking, the specific issue that is bothering me, it quickly fades to realistic proportions that I can handle in some rational way. Taken out of the "hiddenness" of my inner world and exposed in connection with another, it loses its frightening power to compel me.

From another perspective, I have also noticed that if I fail to care for my children in the manner I expect of myself (however valid the reason for my temporary negligence), I tend to justify myself by mentally finding something that irritates me about them! I can have worked myself into quite a snit before I notice what's happening and laugh at myself.

Finally, I reflect ruefully that those who know me best—and love me most—have long since been aware of my weaknesses and limitations. I can vividly remember the time I finally had both the insight and the courage to confess a habitual weakness to my husband, who graciously accepted my confession about something he had known for years! It didn't bother him half as much as it bothered me!

Prayer/Response

Interlude VII
A NOTE TO THE READER

Are you getting discouraged because you seem to be dealing with the same issue over and over?

Perhaps you have noticed that my reflections often seem to repeat the same material. Perhaps you have observed that in your own ponderings. Sometimes it seems like we simply can't get beyond a certain issue. We look at it this way and that; maybe we even understand mentally how to get out of it, but our emotions are blocked and we feel like the interior struggle won't let up.

I have often thought that the message of the Gospel can be told in very few words indeed. Learning to live it fully is what takes a lifetime.

Each of us brings to Christ specific temperaments and predispositions. Benedict is teaching us concrete ways to practice re-channeling (converting) our dispositions into the mind of Christ. It should not surprise us that, as we undertake those practices, we find ourselves coming up against the same barriers time and again. Because, after all, it is the same self we bring to the process each day. A friend of mine says that confession is not a matter of offering up the "flavor of the month," but rather of offering the same old thing (ourselves) for its gradual redemption.

Two points here deserve special attention: first, the value of the struggle; second, the importance of release.

During those moments when it seems to us we are deeply involved in interior struggle (perhaps it even feels like we're wrestling with God), we are cooperating with God in the work of interior formation. As long as we are struggling, we need to be struggling. By this, we are keeping firm the tension between what we are and what we are growing to be, and such tension is creative. I have often thought that the story of Jacob wrestling all night with the angel of God (Gen 32:24–31) is given to us as a symbol of the creative struggle.

But struggle is not the last word. The freedom of resurrection living comes after a breakthrough. A tremendous sense of liberation and wholeness is given to us as we are able to release our concerns and resistances to God. One major meaning of "consecrated" is that which is offered up. The consecrated gift is one that is offered to God. The consecrated life is one that is daily offered to God. We struggle, we cry, and then we offer. We sing, we celebrate, and then we offer. All things, good and bad, are offered back to God, in the recognition that God is the giver of all.

We are privileged daily to practice this offering of our lives to God.

The Consecration
of Mundane
Activities

Chapter 47, Announcing the Hours for the Work of God
(ENTIRE)

*L*et it be the abbot's care to announce the hour for the Work of God day and night: either by giving the signal himself, or assigning this task to a conscientious brother, so that all things may be done at the fitting times.

The intoning of psalms and antiphons is to be done by each after the abbot, according to his rank. No one should presume to sing or to read unless he can fulfill this office in a way which edifies his hearers; let this be done with humility, earnestness and reverence, and by the one whom the abbot has appointed.

Comment

This is a fitting chapter to begin a section called "The Consecration of Mundane Activities." We have already suggested that a central meaning of "consecrated" is something offered to God. Such a definition seems more helpful in understanding Benedictine consecration than that of "set-apartness" from the worldly or the mundane. The Rule does not rigidly classify things as holy and unholy, pure and sinful. On the contrary, it always sees them as a continuum, only asking whether we are attentive to the presence of God in them. The Rule routinely expresses such a sense of continuity between the sacred and the ordinary that we can best understand its call for consecration as an invitation to offer up the ordinary so that it reveals God.

This chapter charges the abbot with responsibility to assemble the community for an important occasion. Nowadays when we have standardized hours and individual watches, such a responsibility does not seem as crucial as it was in Benedict's day. Just what is this important occasion, so important that it alone is nominated "the Work of God"? Of course, it is the Daily Office (see Chapters 8 to 20 above), but let us inquire further.

The Daily Office establishes a rhythm of corporate prayer that provides the framework for each day. The essential context and reason-for-being of creation is the praise and worship of God. The Rule schedules specific times of prayer and praise, but not to suggest that all times are not times of prayer and praise. Rather, the purpose of the office is to establish a formative routine that informs all other times. It sets apart special moments that all moments may increasingly be known as God's.

Reflection

Some days, like this morning, I awake to the song of the birds and my heart floods over with joy. I long that my own song might be as exquisite. And also, I am simply content, glad to be part of the moment, even as one who only hears.

Some days I awake joyful and some days I awake gloomy. But every morning I say the office. Some days my mind is in harmony with my voice, and sometimes not (RB 19:7). But I think that one of the important benefits of the office is that gradually it forms my heart so that I know the song of the birds is there, even when I don't feel it.

Prayer/Response

Chapter 48, The Daily Manual Labor
VERSES 1–13

Idleness is the enemy of the soul. Therefore the brethren should be occupied at stated times in manual labour and at other fixed hours in sacred reading (lectio divina). *We think, therefore, that the times for each may be arranged as follows: from Easter to the first of October, on coming out in the morning let them labor at whatever is necessary from the first until about the fourth hour. From the fourth hour until about Sext let them apply themselves to reading* (lectio). *After Sext, when they rise from table, let them rest on their beds in silence; or if anyone wishes to read to himself, let him read so as not to disturb anyone else. Let None be said rather soon, at the middle of the eighth hour; and then let them again work at whatever has to be done until Vespers. If, however, the needs of the place or poverty require them to labor themselves in gathering in the harvest, let them not grieve at that; for then are they truly*

monks when they live by the labor of their hands, as our Fathers and the
Apostles did. But let all things be done in moderation for the sake of the
faint-hearted.

From the first of October until the beginning of Lent let the brethren
devote themselves to reading (lectio) *until the end of the second hour.*
At the second hour let Terce be said, after which they shall all labor at
their appointed work until None. At the first signal for the hour of None
all shall cease from their work, and be ready as soon as the second signal
is sounded. After their meal let them occupy themselves in their reading
(lectio) *or with the psalms.*

Comment

This chapter is about the use of time, that is, about the balance of
activities within the day. Each day is to include something of several
crucial components, which together are expressive of the wholeness
of human gifts and needs. This is a proposal for the establishment
of daily priorities that manifest one's faith.

The rhythms established by this chapter relate both to the year
and to the day. The whole year is organized in relationship to Easter
and to the pattern of the liturgical seasons (as also expressed secondarily but complementarily in the natural seasons), and the daily
pattern varies in harmony with those seasonal shifts.

The day itself is structured to contain a balance of physical work,
mental work, and spiritual work, although such distinctions are
somewhat sharper in our time than they were in Benedict's. At any
rate, Benedict encourages physical labor, based on the example of
our Lord and the disciples, and grounded in the practical matter
that somebody has to grow the food. He likewise requires mental
labor, which is the process in which we have engaged here, the
labor of *lectio divina*. Finally, of course, the day is framed by the
offices of prayer.

In Chapter 16, we observed that Prime refers to the first hour of
daylight and thus the designation Sext (six) refers to about noon,
and so forth. The details of Benedict's daily schedule show a design
which both 1) maximizes working time available in the fields when
the harvesting needs to be done; and 2) gives the earliest and optimum reflective hours of the day to serious study/*lectio* on scripture.

Reflection

I used to struggle with when (to find time) to pray. Finally, I decided to start the day with prayer, and let other things fall into place as they would. How astonishing to discover that there is always "enough" time left! The best hours can be given to study/prayer and behold! exactly the appropriate hours are left for needed attention to the crops! No doubt this model reflects Benedict's particular genius, but even more it reveals God's goodness, generosity, and gentle caring built into not only my own physical constitution but also into the way things really are. What an opportunity is thus presented to relax and enjoy what is given!

In pondering the way Benedict has organized the day, I see more ways than one in which it invites relaxation. For not only have I worried about when to find time to pray, I also worry about how to make my work time more like my prayer time. What I sense Benedict might say about that is, "Be gentle with yourself and your expectations." Everything in the day has its own natural value, its own natural rhythm. There is no need to make work feel the same as prayer; each has its own value and each can be consecrated according to its own inherent qualities.

I see that whatever I can offer to God, God will take. And it is in the momentary offering that the ordinary elements of my life truly become consecrated. I might take a quick moment when I go to the bathroom or shift from one document to another to offer that moment to God. It almost makes me giggle to think of it, it seems so ordinary, so non-pious. I could take five minutes before lunch to look back on the morning to ask, "How's it gone?" (meaning, where was God in it?).

Can everything in my life be given to God?! I think it could be! I want to try.

Prayer/Response

Chapter 48
VERSES 14–25 (END)

*I*n Lent, however, from the morning until the end of the third hour they should devote themselves to reading, and afterwards work at their appointed tasks until the end of the tenth hour. In this time of Lent let them each receive a book from the library, to be read consecutively and straight through. These books are to be given out at the beginning of Lent.

Above all, let one or two seniors be deputed to make the rounds of monastery at the hours when the brethren are engaged in reading, to see that there is no slothful (acediosus) brother giving himself to idleness or to gossip, and not applying himself to his reading; so that he is not only useless to himself, but a distraction to others. If such a one be found (which God forbid!) let him be corrected once and a second time; and if he does not amend, let him be subjected to the chastisement of the Rule, in such a way that the rest may be warned. Moreover, one brother shall not associate with another at unsuitable hours.

On Sunday let them devote themselves to reading except those who are assigned to the various offices. But if anyone is so negligent and slothful as to be unwilling or unable to read or meditate, he must have some work given him that he is not idle.

For weak or delicate members let such work or crafts be assigned that they will not be idle, and yet will not be oppressed by heavy labor so as to be driven away. The weakness of such members must be taken into account by the abbot.

Comment

Because the language of this chapter appears to be easily comprehensible, we may not realize at first exactly how extraordinary is the subject of this section. Two words in particular give us a clue. One is *lectio* (reading); the other is *acedia* (apathy/indolence/idleness).

We who have been engaged in reading the Rule are coming to have a growing appreciation of the work of *lectio*. As we are discovering, it is a profoundly personal and engaging process of allowing oneself to be formed into the mind of Christ through encounter with the living Word, especially in the scriptures and the Fathers.[99]

As such, *lectio* is strenuous work, requiring great concentration and receptivity. Notice that Benedict treats "reading" in a similar manner to "excommunication" in one respect: it is to be applied primarily to those mature enough to understand it. The weaker or more immature monks must sometimes be challenged with the less complex methods of manual labor (verse 23) or physical punishment (RB 23:4–5).

The opposite of work is idleness or apathy. In general, our society frantically avoids idleness, but there exists among us (and within each of us, at various periods) a kind of utter boredom, which is oddly enough more like workaholism than like true work. For both idleness and workaholism express a refusal to be engaged with the truth of one's life. Idleness, apathy, and workaholism are ways of avoiding ourselves and God. Very likely, they hide the fear either that God does not exist, or that God is not loving. Both apathy and workaholism are the masks of despair.

Reflection

Sometimes I am astonished at how strenuous is this life of faith. It is hard work to be truly engaged—not only with God, but with God-in-the-midst, that is, with my own given life. It is costly to be engaged in open vulnerability, willing time and again to let my assumptions and biases be smashed that I might grow ever more into God's fullness for me. There is often very little to show for it superficially. But what a joy it is to be engaged in such a life!

It's funny, too, how the depth of it "sneaked up" on me. I remember when I first started doing *lectio* on scripture—being surprised that a phrase seemed to attract me, and that the phrase seemed directly to speak to something going on in my life. As I continued, it became more and more clear to me that God was in fact speaking to me each day—in a very ordinary way, nothing spectacular. Nonetheless, I felt invited to change my ways in the small, routine, daily issues that have emerged so often in these pages.

Then one day I realized how much a miracle this is—a startling, life-changing shift in me and in my effect on those around me! Yet it all happened so gradually and so normally that on any given day, it didn't seem all that important.

Prayer/Response

Chapter 49,
The Observance of Lent
(ENTIRE)

*A*lthough the life of a monk ought to be a continuous Lenten obser-vance, yet since few have strength enough for this we exhort all, at least during the days of Lent, to keep themselves in all purity of life, and to wash away during that holy season the negligences of other times. This we shall worthily do if we refrain from all sin and give ourselves to prayer with tears, to holy reading, compunction of heart, and abstinence. During these days, then, let us add something to the usual measure of our service: such as private prayers, and abstinence from food and drink, so that everyone of his own will may offer to God with the joy of the Holy Spirit (1 Thess 1:6), something beyond the measure appointed.

In other words, each should withhold from his body something of food, drink, and sleep, refraining from talk and mirth, and awaiting holy Easter with the joy of spiritual longing. Let each one, however, make known to his abbot what he offers, and let it be done with his blessing and permission: because what is done without leave of the spiritual father shall be attributed to presumption and vainglory, and will merit no reward. Every-thing, therefore, is to be done with the approval of the abbot.

Comment

This chapter is one on which we might meditate fruitfully for many days. Here Benedict presents, in summary, a whole outline of the ascetical life, the life of Christian discipline.[100] Benedict mentions the strength required for this challenging work, the importance of openness with a spiritual director, the centrality of purity of heart (that single-focused longing for God), and the priority of the goal of salvation. Of interest, too, is his suggestion that the deeper disci-plines of Lent, while they involve self-denial, are more fundamen-tally a matter of self-offering. At their best, disciplines are a means of consecration, that is, ways of deepening our capacity to give our-selves body, mind, and spirit to God.

For Benedict, disciplines are oriented toward joy, toward over-flowing celebration of the mystery of Easter.[101] The point of disciplines is to allow expectancy to build in us, that we might more fully apprehend that, in his death and resurrection, Christ makes known to us that we are "loved by God and that (we) have been chosen" (1 Thess 1:4).

Reflection

The phrase that touches me in this passage is "everyone may offer to God . . . something beyond the measure appointed." We have been reminded so often in these pages that consecration means offering that there might seem to be nothing new left in it. But just today, it really touches me that God would want something I might offer. Perhaps God is waiting, eagerly, for my offering.

The offering is to be "beyond the appointed measure." In other words, it's not just the standard, the usual thing. It is to be something perhaps that only I could offer. That means something special from my life, from my self. I suppose the special thing could be either something in which I rejoice or something that burdens me. I could offer my joy in that wonderful tree that stands just outside my window, so solid and so vital every day of my life. Would God then take it away? Might it come back to me even better? It's unknown, except in faith, given what I know of my God.

I could offer my pain in that broken friendship, that betrayal of trust. In this case, I hope God would take it away, but perhaps it might be given back! Again, it's a matter of trust: I don't think God plays mean games, so if it was given back apparently still broken, then there must be something else given with it to make it bearable, or to serve some good unknown to me.

This "offering to God" seems so fragile, so risky. Yet I must say that since I have begun to offer things to God, the overall feel of my life has changed. I am so aware of great goodness, and always as undeserved gift. So even if I can't see exactly the "how" of it, I'm glad to be learning this way of offering.

Prayer/Response

Chapter 50, Those Working at a Distance from the Oratory or Traveling
(ENTIRE) AND
Chapter 51, Those on a Short Journey
(ENTIRE)

*T*hose brethren who work at a great distance and cannot come to the oratory at the proper time (the abbot judging such to be the case) should perform the Work of God there where they are working, bending their knees in reverent awe. In the same way the appointed hours should not pass them by who are sent on a journey: but insofar as they can, let them perform them there and not neglect to offer their due service.

[Chapter 51] A brother who goes out on any business and expects to return to the monastery on the same day must not presume to eat outside, even though he is asked by someone, unless permission has been given by his abbot. If he acts otherwise let him be excommunicated.

Comment

At first glance, it appears that Benedict is giving two opposite instructions: 1) pray when you are away from the monastery; and 2) do not eat when you are away from the monastery. Perhaps we might think this is because prayer is holy, and food is worldly. But as we look deeper, we see it is because of a deep unity between the spiritual and the material, the prayer and the meal. Both instructions are about the nature of the Christian family, which for the monk is the monastery.

The two central points of the family's life together are the prayer hours and the meal. Benedict is making clear that the monks are present in the community's heart and life, whether or not they are physically present. They can lift their voices to join in prayer, crossing space and time and affirming the bond in Christ. But when they eat outside, they break rather than affirm the communal bond expressed in the gathered community.

Whether we are in a monastery or not, it is true for each one of us Christians that we have a particular place of belonging in the whole Christian community. That particular place has an incarnated given-ness, a specific and limited context, while it also transcends any limitations of space and time. Benedict is insisting on the central role of this community/family life in affirming and building the consecrated life of each member. The Rule's emphasis here is an invitation for each one of us to pay attention to what community and/or family has been given to us to nurture our growth in Christ, and to practice living in fidelity to that family.

Reflection

The mental picture of monks away from home reminds me of a couple of my favorite paintings, although neither one is actually about monks! One is *The Angelus,* with the farmers stopped in the fields, heads bowed at dusk as the church bells ring, joining their prayers— and their lives—to the whole community. The other is a sketch of a friar, sitting alongside the road beside his donkey, saying his rosary as he rests. What for me connects both with the monks is the feeling in the paintings that a host of angels and saints fill the air with their songs of praise, since the one who prays seems somehow to be joining a mighty multitude.

Last summer I overhead a conversation between a young mother and a Benedictine nun. The nun was talking about the discipline of arising for the 2 A.M. office, and the mother exclaimed: "How good to know there is someone else awake and praying in the dead of the night when I often feel so alone feeding my baby!"

Our community is indeed a giant one. How extraordinary that something which so transcends space and time should also be so localized and situated!

Prayer/Response

Chapter 52, The Oratory of the Monastery
(ENTIRE)

L et the oratory be what it is called; and let nothing else be done or kept there. When the Work of God is finished all should go out with the utmost silence and with reverence for God; so that a brother who wishes to pray by himself will not be hindered by another's insensitivity. But if one wishes to pray by himself, he should go in with simplicity and pray, not with a loud voice, but with tears and fervor of heart. And let one who is not similarly occupied not be permitted to remain in the oratory after the Work of God, as has been said, lest another be hindered.

Comment

What is the subject of this chapter? Oratory means "place of prayer," stemming from the verb *orare*, to pray. So the chapter is about the place of prayer, and thus in part about praying. Indeed, many commentators turn to this chapter as one of two in the Rule specifically on private prayer. They point out that Benedict takes it for granted that monks will pray privately as well as during the Daily Office.

But Benedict has such regard for the variations and inspirations of private prayer, that he leaves those largely to individual development, under the guidance of a spiritual elder. The Rule simply provides a guide to regulate the external life of the community and also those individual behaviors that offer a sacramental framework for inner purity of heart. Thus, here he is concerned chiefly with those subjects that impinge upon or affect the interactions and relationships among the family. It is fascinating that his expressed concern about the oratory is not primarily the prayer that goes on there, but the "mundane" matters, that is, the way each person's behavior might support or distract others.

In this connection, we note two key words: "insensitivity" and "hindered." As always, Benedict shares responsibility: both the one praying and the one not praying have duties toward one another. The one not praying is to honor the silence of the oratory; the one praying is to keep silence also, even in tears of devotion. This "humdrum" and "external" matter of everyday thoughtfulness for one another is often where Benedict locates "spiritual" progress. Again, we see the interpenetration of the ordinary and the holy.

Reflection

My reflections tug me in two directions, as perhaps Benedict intends! I often find it difficult to be generous in that practical love of neighbor called for when I feel my "rights" are being infringed upon. Indeed, not infrequently I want to be "at prayer" in an utterly peaceful and serene setting, when someone else's "agenda" interrupts that. On the other hand, even the noise and flutter of tourists cannot erase the privilege of presence in a "holy place" when it carries centuries of prayer offered there. Several friends observed that the "Way of Sorrows" in Jerusalem today is filled with shouting vendors . . . and then reflected that it probably was the same way on the day when Jesus carried his cross there.

As I reflect, I glimpse the direct relation between love of neighbor and purity of prayer. The love I receive in prayer is truly the only thing I have to offer my brother and sister in the day to day. I cannot hoard it, for then it disappears; when I give it away, it multiplies! And the wonder of that abundance sends me back to prayer in gratitude for God's goodness made flesh.

Prayer/Response

Chapter 53, The Reception of Guests
VERSES 1–14

*A*ll *guests who come should be received as Christ, for he will say: I was a stranger and you took me in (Matt 25:35). And let fitting honor be shown to all, especially, however, to such as are of the household of the faith (Gal 6:10) and to pilgrims. When, therefore, a guest is announced, let him be met by the superior and the brethren with all signs of love. Let them first pray together, and thus associate with one another in peace; but the kiss of peace must not be offered until prayer has first been said, on account of the delusions of the devil.*

And in the salutation itself let all humility be shown. At the arrival or departure of all guests, by bowing the head or even prostrating the whole body on the ground, let Christ be adored in them, who indeed is received. When the guests have been received let them be led to prayer, and then let the superior or anyone he may appoint sit with them. Let the divine law be read to the guest for his edification; and afterwards let all kindness be shown him. The superior may break his fast for the sake of the guest, unless it happens to be a principal fast which may not be broken. The brothers, however, shall observe their accustomed fast. The abbot is to pour water on the hands of the guests, and both the abbot and the whole community are to wash the feet of all guests. When they have been washed let them say this verse: We have received your mercy, O Lord, in the midst of your temple (Ps 48:10).

Comment

As for the Jew in the temple of Jerusalem (Ps. 48), so for the Christian in the person of Christ: God is received. The awesome majesty and the sure strength of God is actually received. Benedict takes seriously the words of our Lord that he himself will be received in the stranger; indeed, he regards these words as a promise. By our kindness to the stranger and to the sick, in mundane situations, we greet Christ.

Hospitality has come to be known as the "fourth vow" of the Benedictines, so seriously do they take this instruction to honor all who present themselves. The monks share the best of their lives with their guests, especially their prayer and the Word of God in scripture. It is as if they bring out all their treasures in eagerness that the newcomer might appreciate them too. In this way, they honor the guest especially, for they invite him or her to consider and respond to God's call.[102] They offer the guest "all kindness," which no doubt means a meal,[103] and in this and in the foot-washing ceremony, the liturgical aspect of hospitality is heightened, reinforcing the extent to which the monks are to be aware that they are in fact receiving Christ in this stranger.

Reflection

I confess myself mystified and captivated by the implications of finding Christ everywhere. Insofar as Christ is my Lord, when I find him, I am to be obedient to him, honoring the power and authority he carries, as well as being strengthened by his presence. So, receiving Christ, I am receiving one who nourishes me. Yet also, I am to serve him and minister to him, as to one in need, the guest or the sick person. In this sense, receiving Christ is receiving one whom I am to nourish. Such a mixture of response is quite beyond my power to imagine, in large part because I want to stay in control, know precisely how things stand, and be master of the situation rather than servant to it.

When I consider the potential of receiving Christ in every situation and in every person, I realize that I have been experiencing others only at the most superficial level. How might I begin to see Christ in this very specific human incarnation in front of me? . . . who has dirty feet, and is weary and hungry, and maybe has foreign clothes and an odd accent and an irritable manner? Or, who is so familiar that I see her every day and I know exactly her weaknesses and habits and passions and moods?

I see that it begins by being open to the possibility of true relationship with this person now before me. There is no room for categories (this is a such-and-such type!) and none for preoccupation (how will I ever manage to prepare for tomorrow's schedule?). It involves allowing myself to be moved by the impulses of love and joy that burst from Christ's indwelling in me, rather than by the more constrained impulses of my own ego-safety. Such relationship means openness to the possibility that I will be changed, essentially, by something this other might do or say. It involves being willing to encounter irresistible grace and power in this person who carries Christ. I think such openness, such relationship, must be the work of a lifetime . . . as well as a spontaneous response to the sufficiency of grace presented now!

Prayer/Response

Chapter 53
VERSES 15–24 (END)

*S*pecial care and thoughtfulness should be shown in the reception of the poor and of pilgrims, because in them Christ is more especially received. For the very awe we have of the rich assures them of respect. The kitchen for the abbot and guests should be set apart by itself so that guests, who are never lacking in a monastery, may not disturb the brethren when they arrive at uncertain hours. Let two brothers who are able to fulfill this duty well be placed in this kitchen for the year. If they need it, let help be offered them, so that they may serve without murmuring. On the other hand, when they do not have much to occupy them let them go out to other work, wherever they are assigned. And not only with regard to them, but also in all the offices of the monastery let this consideration be shown: that when [the monks] need help it is given to them; and again, when they are less busy they should do whatever is assigned them.

Moreover, let a brother whose soul is possessed by the fear of the Lord have the guest-house assigned to his care. There should be sufficient beds provided there. And let the house of God be wisely governed by those who are wise.

Those who are not required to do so should on no account associate or converse with guests. But if (a monk) happens to meet or to see guests, he should, after humbly greeting them as we have said, ask their blessing, and then pass on, explaining that he is not permitted to talk with a guest.

Comment

The second half of this chapter is a great surprise. Considering that the principle articulated in the first half is that guests are to be received as Christ, most of us moderns would interpret that in an "absolute" way; we would give ourselves unstintingly until we exhausted ourselves in the service of the needy who carry Christ.

But Benedict takes the incarnation more seriously than that, both positively and negatively. He knows how seductive "worldly" things can be if they are not placed in their proper context through prayer, reverence, and silence. So he limits contact between the guests and the monks in general. But this has the effect not only of protecting the monks against worldly influences, but also of protecting them against their own misguided instincts: no one is to exhaust himself. Flesh is to be cared for, according to its requirements. A sufficient number of people are to be assigned so that the work of caretaking can be accomplished within the context of the normal daily routines of the office, the *lectio*, and other matters.

The overall rhythms of the house of God that the Holy Spirit has shown to be essential are to be honored as well as the guests, for Christ is revealed in both. And unless the daily rhythms that teach us how to see Christ in the ordinary are sustained, we will lose touch with him in both places. No person can truly serve Christ unless he or she is also continuously nourished by Christ in prayer, silence, community life, and regularity of food, rest, and study.

Reflection

What a difficult lesson this is for me! How easily I slip into a pattern of exhausting myself in constant busyness, rather than following that pattern of harmonious stewardship of self that involves balance and rest. In a sense, I suppose, what is usually happening for me is the opposite of consecration, of offering up: what I am usually doing is holding on!

If consecration is to be meaningful, it must be possible to offer things up when I don't feel like it, when demands become excessive, when I seem to be very far from God. How might I go about that?

It seems to me that Benedict suggests here that I need to honor my own limitations. If I have developed certain rhythmic patterns for the day, knowing that those patterns are beneficial for me, then it is well to stay with those patterns even and especially in times of crisis. Obviously, there will be moments when I must let them go, but I need to return to them as soon as possible, knowing that without them, my strength is limited.

Whatever helps I have found in the Rule, I need to be faithful to them. Maybe it is daily "silence breaks," maybe morning and evening prayer, maybe a time for *lectio:* whatever is found to be valuable is to be honored. Indeed, *lectio* is a good example. If I leave my *lectio* with a prayer word or phrase, I might take that phrase into the day, using it to bless everyone and everything all day long.

All this is a reminder that I am not Christ, all by myself. I can begin to bring Christ and receive Christ only insofar as I am rooted in those daily patterns that enable me to offer whatever I encounter in the press of the day.

Prayer/Response

Chapter 54, Letters or Gifts for Monks
(ENTIRE)

*O*n no account is it allowed for a monk to receive, either from parents or anyone else, or from brethren, letters, tokens, or any little gifts whatsoever; nor may he give them to others, without the permission of his abbot. And if anything is sent to him, even by his parents, he should not presume to receive it, unless it has first been made known to the abbot.

If [the abbot] orders it to be received, it remains in the abbot's power to decide to whom it shall be given; nor should this grieve the brother to whom it has been sent, lest occasion be given to the devil (Eph 4:27; 1 Tim 5:14). Should anyone, however, presume to act otherwise, let him be subjected to the discipline of the Rule.

Comment

At first this seems an unnecessarily cruel chapter, condemning as it does the "harmless" human habit of sharing gifts as an expression of special relationship. Let us observe that such restraint was a standard practice in monasteries of the time,[104] and then turn to the question of its general relevance.

The principle behind this instruction can be found both in the cited scripture and in the Rule's Chapter 33 on the evil practice of private ownership. The procedures of the Rule are intended to build a solid center for the soul, a keen awareness of the Source and course of one's whole life (Gal 5:25) that penetrates every moment. This is the positive pulse. The negative pulse is the devil's effort to distract us from this awareness of God, generally by misdirecting our own good instincts. Benedict is convinced that pride of ownership is one of the main reasons we abandon God, and thus every impulse to say "This is mine" is to be rooted out.

For example, as this chapter follows immediately after the one on guests, we can imagine that a rich visitor, who had been well served on a recent stay at the monastery by one of the brothers assigned to the guesthouse, might offer a costly token of affection as thanks. If the brother were to accept such a gift and keep it secret, silently telling himself what a fine chap he is, he would be beginning to build a small wall between himself and his brothers through his own sense of superiority. Whereas, if he offers it at once to the abbot, it might be sold and the funds used to improve the irrigation system, so that all might eat better. This example is overdrawn, perhaps, but nonetheless shows the danger to the soul of a spirit of separation.

Even gifts from parents can be a major cause of separatism, because Benedict sought to build an integrated community, without reference to the rigid clear class system then prevailing in the countryside.[105] Costly gifts from some parents could be a major obstacle to such an integrated community of faith.

Reflection

I don't like it. I rebel against such a narrow-minded, tight-fisted view of acceptable behavior! And having said that, I realize just how deeply ingrained is the spirit of pride in me that wants to see myself as better than my brothers and sisters. I realize how tied I am to certain possessions that give definition to my personality. It is not easy to know myself to be precious and loved, apart from these external things. And yet I know the external things don't convey genuine care at all. Such a muddle!

It occurs to me that there is a place for the offering up, or the consecration, even of anger. It does make me angry to think that gifts might endanger my soul. And I realize as I gently probe my anger that I cannot altogether sort out exactly why I am angry, or what is the remedy. So, there is nothing I can do today to "fix things," whatever that might mean in this context. But what I can do is to offer this to God: that I am angry, that I am confused, that I can't find a solution. And then I can trust that because this offering really comes from the center of my concerns at this moment, God will be pleased to accept it.

Again, it is the psalms that help me believe in the value of my anger-offering. Frequently the psalmist seems to shake his fist at God! In the psalms, it seems more important to offer any concern to God rather than worrying whether the concern is "appropriate." Treating concerns this way means that when I have finished analyzing things as far as I can, I release the whole thing. I give up my concerns; I give them all back to God.

Prayer/Response

Chapter 55, The Clothing and Footwear of the Monks
VERSES 1–12

*T*he clothing given to the brethren should be suitable to the nature and climate of the place where they live; for in cold regions more is required and in warm regions less. It is the abbot's duty, therefore, to consider this. We think, however, that in temperate climates a cowl and a tunic should suffice for each monk: the cowl to be of thick wool in winter, but in summer worn and thin: likewise a scapular for work, and sandals and shoes to cover their feet.

Concerning all these things, as well as their color or coarseness, the monks should not complain; rather they should use whatever can be eas-

*ily obtained in the region where they live, or can be bought cheaply. The
abbot should be careful about the measurements, so that these garments
are not too short for those who wear them, but fit well.*

*When they receive new clothes they should always return the old ones
at once, to be stored in the clothes-room for the poor. For it is sufficient
for a monk to have two tunics and two cowls, to provide both night wear
and convenience in washing. Anything beyond this is superfluous and
ought to be taken away. In the same way let them give back their sandals
and whatever else is worn out when they receive new ones.*

Comment

At first we are surprised that the Rule should concern itself with
such apparently minute and unimportant matters. But, again, we
see that the "mundane" reveals Benedict's spiritual theology.

As we note the care to be given to clothing—in terms of attention, careful cleaning and storing for the poor—we are reminded of
the principle set forth in the Rule's Chapter 31: everything is to be
regarded as a consecrated vessel of the altar; nothing is to be neglected. And yet again, this realization of the sacramental quality of
the material world is balanced by awareness of the sometimes exaggerated attraction of things in themselves.

We should be attentive to the things immediately in front of us.
We are to reverence them and give them care according to their
nature. The specific form of things is important and not accidental,
because God is Creator. But we are not to stop at the surface level.
The form is like a window opening up onto a beautiful vista. If we
spend all our time looking at the window frame, what joy we miss!
We are to let our enjoyment of things be a lesson in joy, leading us
even further in, to the very fullness of Joy Itself.

And Benedict says all this as he talks about clothing, and dishwashing, and care of the sick, and greeting visitors, and similar matters. In all things, may God be glorified (Chapter 57:9), even in the
matter of daily dress.

Reflection

Esther de Waal remarks of the Rule's guidance that it is utterly simple
(beyond the reach of no one), and yet utterly demanding (requiring
the most strenuous and continuous discipline).[106] This chapter on

clothing is a good example of that. It makes me realize how far I am from being aware that every single thing I do has the potential to glorify God or not. It is not a hard thing to remember, in the sense of complexity. But it is so hard, in the sense of difficulty. I'm dumbstruck at how far I am from loving God with my whole heart.

For Benedict, the mundane reveals God. It's such a paradox. I have always thought of God as being apart from the earthy, the ordinary. It's hard to make this shift to seeing everything as a prism that shows forth something of God. And yet, when I can see it this way, how lovely it is! A simple dish becomes a precious vessel; an ordinary hand becomes a thing of wonder. My life itself becomes full of glory.

One of my favorite meditations is to imagine young Mary of Nazareth, sweeping the floor on a hot day, hearing the sound of flies buzzing, and suddenly having the sense that the whole small house was filled up with the amazing presence of Gabriel, whose next words will change not only her life, but the course of the world! I have recently discovered a modern novelist whose books convey that same sense of potency inherent in every encounter.[107] Something like that is what Benedict communicates to me in this careful stewardship even of clothing. Something like that must be what consecration means.

Prayer/Response

Chapter 55
VERSES 13–22 (END)

*T*hose *who are sent on a journey should receive underclothing from the clothes-room, and on their return, return them washed. Let their cowls and tunics also be a little better than those they usually wear; they are to receive these from the clothes-room when setting out on their journey, and restore them on their return.*

For their bedding let a mattress, blanket, coverlet, and pillow suffice. These beds must be frequently inspected by the abbot because of private property—lest it be found there. If anyone is found with anything he has not received from the abbot, he is to be subjected to the most severe discipline. In order that this vice of private ownership may be cut off by the roots let the abbot supply all things that are necessary: that is, cowl, tunic, sandals, shoes, belt, knife, stylus, needle, handkerchief, and writing tablets; so that any excuse of necessity may be taken away.

Yet the abbot must always be mindful of those words in the Acts of the Apostles: Distribution was made to everyone according to his need (Acts 4:35). Let him, therefore, consider the infirmities of those in want, and not the ill-will of the envious. Nevertheless, in all his decisions, let him reflect on the judgment of God.

Comment

For the second time, Benedict speaks severely of the "vice of private ownership" (compare RB 33:1), and immediately thereafter quotes Acts in the description of the first Christian community in Jerusalem (see RB 33:6, 34:1).

Careful reading of that whole section of Acts (4:23 to 5:16) reveals a Christian community empowered by the Holy Spirit, a community filled with awe and wonder and love and thanksgiving and praise—a community whose life was wholly turned in gratitude toward God the Savior. Thus, the sharing of goods in common was not so much a discipline for its own sake as it was the natural expression of hearts so full they could not contain their love. Benedict's discipline of common ownership is intended to work backwards toward the goal of the disposition of charity. His intention is to establish a framework for practicing charity day in and day out in small things, so that hearts gradually open to the fullness of true charity, which transforms the whole personality from within.

Reflection

I am drawn by the phrase "every excuse . . . will be taken away" (verse 19). A friend of mine argues that was the main purpose of the life-death-resurrection of Jesus: to take away our excuses that we can't be good enough for God. That's where I "live"! I know myself to be flawed, and I keep insisting I need this or that improvement before I can really give myself to God. All of which talk simply turns out to be an excuse not to risk myself to the awesome out-of-control-ness that involves abandoning myself to the glory of divine providence.

And the wonder is that such abandonment can take place in such ordinary, workaday environments! Perhaps until now I have avoided seeing the simplicity of this because it does make abandonment/offering to God so remarkably easy. I can do it while making beds, washing clothes, buying shoes, taking out a handkerchief. I can, of course, even do it while thinking how much "better" I need to be before I am suitable for God. Everything can be offered, any time and any place.

And the truth is that all along and anyway, I am upheld even in my very breathing—and in everything else I "possess"—only by that loving Providence. What joy when I can truly rest in that love!

Prayer/Response

Chapter 56, The Abbot's Table
(ENTIRE)

*T*he abbot's table should always be with guests and pilgrims. But when there are few guests, it is within his power to invite any of the brothers he wishes. Let him take care, however, always to leave one or two seniors with the brethren, for the sake of discipline.

Comment

We recall from Chapter 51 that the table is a symbol of monastic (Christian) unity, second only in importance to the oratory (chapel). So, despite its great brevity, this chapter reveals important principles.

First, the abbot is to welcome and receive as those-who-belong the strangers and guests of the community. The abbot joins the guests as a sign that they are also brothers and sisters, that is, also children and co-heirs of God.

Second, the abbot is free to share his bread with every member of the monastic community, much like the family in which young and old freely interact. This viewpoint is particularly apparent in Benedict by comparison with his main source, where only senior monks and "those who know the psalter" are privileged to share the abbot's table.[108] Wherever possible, Benedict emphasizes the affirmative motivation: that our lives are a joyful response to God's love, rather than primarily a fearful avoidance of punishment. The abbot may invite monks to share his meal out of care for each person as specially loved by God. Such privileges need not be reserved as a special reward for "good behavior." Each one of us can share and receive the daily love of God in such concrete events of daily life.

Reflection

Who are the people I encounter in a day? Often I stay at the most superficial level, making judgments based on dress or manner or behavior, distinguishing between them and myself. I have been slow to learn the deep joy that comes from recognizing and responding to the spirit in every person. The sacramental awareness of things can be extended to a sacramental awareness of people. I'm learning to be attentive to the person as he or she is externally, while also being open to his or her deeper inner reality. As I let the Spirit guide my knowing of persons, I am privileged to see great beauty.

I am learning to see Christ in those who are given to me. And as I have begun to appreciate that gift, I have come to a startling realization. I can see Christ in others far better than they can in themselves. The reverse is also true: others can see Christ in me better than I can in myself. So one of the great gifts of belonging to the community, to the body of Christ, is that others can help me have faith in Christ dwelling in me, especially at those moments when I have completely lost sight of that possibility. When we hold out this vision to one another, in some way we help bring the kingdom into being. It's like that image of heaven as a long banquet table, piled high with food, with forks three feet long. So the only way to eat is for everyone to feed his or her neighbor across the table. We are essential to one another because together we become Christ's body.

What does Christ's body look like? Sometimes, on Sunday mornings I watch people coming back from the communion rail, saying to myself: "This is Christ's body; these are God's people." They are in some ways as strange to me as an earlobe might be to an elbow; and in some ways as familiar as one human cell to another.

Prayer/Response

Chapter 57, The Artisans
of the Monastery
(ENTIRE)

If there are craftsmen in the monastery, let them practice their crafts in all humility, provided the abbot gives permission. But if one of them becomes conceited on account of one's knowledge of craft, believing that he thereby confers some benefit on the monastery, he is to be taken from it and not permitted to exercise it again, unless having humbled himself, the abbot bids him resume.

If any of the work of the craftsmen is to be sold, let those through whose hands the business has to pass not presume to commit any fraud. Let them remember Ananias and Sapphira (Acts 5:1–11), lest perchance they and all who deal fraudulently with the goods of the monastery should suffer in their souls the death which these incurred in the body.

In the establishing of prices the vice of avarice must not creep in; rather, the goods should always be sold a little cheaper than by those living in the world, that God may be glorified in all things (1 Pet 4:11).

Comment

This chapter is a reflection on giftedness and stewardship. The passage from 1 Peter begins with these words: "Each one of you has received a special grace, so, like good stewards responsible for all these different graces of God, put yourselves at the service of others . . . that in everything God may receive the glory."

This whole section has been concerned with the fact that the mundane and the ordinary elements of each day are in fact gifts of God. It is when we see them and treat them in that way that we become God's stewards and co-participants in the bringing forth of the kingdom.

In particular, the artisan—or one who works skillfully in a craft—is one gifted by God. The gift is not his or hers to possess, hoard, or exploit; rather, it is something given by God for the purpose of extending God's creation. The reference to Ananias and Sapphira is a reminder that all things are God's gifts—physical possessions such as land, property, and money, no less than personal skills. When God gives, it is for use and enjoyment, but God also expects a return on the investment (Luke 19:11–23): stewardship, enjoyment, offering, and thanksgiving are the appropriate responses to gifts. Fundamental to the consecration of life is awareness of all life as gifted: we are offering back to God what originally was given to us by God.

All this is congruent with the overall tone of the Rule about possessions in common (Chapter 33), service to one another (Chapter 35), and reverence for the ordinary as filled with the holy (Chapter 31). This chapter is a fitting summary of this section on the consecration of the mundane: everything is to be done that God may be glorified!

Reflection

Conceptually, who would disagree with Benedict? But again, I see a great gulf between what I know and what I do. I see how important it is to practice what I believe in my daily life experience.

Recently, I have thought frequently about the place where my husband and I live. It is a kind of wooded haven, which is entered by an ambiguously public/private street, thus often inviting the curiosity of strangers. Regularly people drive or stroll down our driveway, sometimes cutting through a dirt pathway to the street above our canyon, sometimes turning around sheepishly to drive out the way they came. Not long ago a small commercial outfit wanted to use our place to film an advertisement, and our outraged neighbor insisted they compensate us financially for the use of our "private property." My first instinct is to assert ownership and drive out the stranger, but then I wonder if the truth is not rather that we are simply stewards of a gift that rightfully belongs to many besides us.

Perhaps this is a model for me of the process of consecration. Our home is such a rich blessing, for which I am daily thankful and to which I give daily care. But underneath both care and thanksgiving is offering up of everything I have, acknowledging regularly to myself that all of it was first a gift.

Prayer/Response

Interlude VIII
A NOTE TO THE READER

Do you sometimes wish for a deeper and more complete interaction with the material than these brief *lectio* meditations offer?

Perhaps you have been doing this process mentally, and have never actually written down your responses. Perhaps even if you have written, you have stayed within the confines of this book, or within your regular limited *lectio* time. And occasionally, that's just not enough.

You might want to start a separate "spiritual journal" where you can explore at your leisure some of the themes you have noticed during your *lectio*. A spiritual journal is as unique and flexible as your own personality. The only required elements are paper and pencil, your reflections, and actually writing them down. Like so much in the spiritual life, it sounds so simple, and yet it is capable of producing much fruit.

From your *lectio*, you already know how to start the reflection process, and that is the key to good journaling. You pay attention to what is going on in your life, and then you reflect on it. In the reflection, you look at it from different points of view to deepen your awareness.

First, write down a life incident, of any sort: a dream, a personal encounter, something you noticed that bothered or attracted you, a nagging feeling of dissatisfaction about something. Then, if you can, try to find a metaphor for it. Say to yourself, "It feels like _____." Fill in the blank. It feels like a bud about to open. It feels like clinging to a tiny branch above a deep canyon. Or, to use an example we cited earlier, it feels like wrestling with God.

Then, let the metaphor lead you into other perspectives. What image does the metaphor evoke for you from scripture? from the culture? from your own opinions and beliefs? For example, the bud about to open suggests to me Mary and the Angel Gabriel. It also suggests to me the eager hopefulness in the Philippines a few years ago when people brought a new democratic government to birth. Oddly, perhaps, it also evokes in me Grandma's favorite phrase about nipping fleshly desires in the bud.

In other words, bring to bear on your life incident the additional perspectives of scripture, culture, and personal values, journaling about whatever seems pertinent. Let these additional perspectives expand your reflection on how God might be speaking to you in your present situation. The point is to become more deeply aware of our own perspectives so that we can more fully offer all that we are to God. It doesn't matter how formally or informally we do that, so long as we are seeking to let Wisdom penetrate our inmost being, that it might bring healing, transformation, wholeness. and love.

Membership and Governance within the Community

Chapter 58, The Procedure
for Receiving Members
VERSES 1–8

To those who are beginners in this way of life an easy entrance should not be granted; rather, as the Apostle says, Try the spirits whether they are of God (1 John 4:1). If, therefore, the one who comes perseveres in knocking, and after four or five days seems patiently to endure the wrongs done to him and the difficulty made about his entrance; and if he persists in his petition, let entrance be granted him, and let him stay in the guest-house for a few days. Afterwards let him stay in the novitiate, where he is to meditate, eat, and sleep.

There should be assigned to him a senior monk skilled in winning souls who will watch him with the utmost care. The concern is whether the novice truly seeks God, and is zealous for the Work of God, for obedience, and for humiliations. It should be clearly laid out for him how hard and rugged are the ways by which we walk towards God.

Comment

With this chapter, Benedict shifts attention to matters of membership within the community and its governance. This chapter in particular, dealing as it does with the primary process for admission to the community, provides a marvelous image or metaphor for the initial steps of the consecrated Christian life.

The phrase "perseveres in knocking" appears to be taken from Luke 11:8, where Jesus is teaching about perseverance in prayer, which is certainly a crucial ingredient of consecration. Hardships all along the way are a test and a strengthening of our endurance. Endurance, or perseverance, is a primary method by which our many desires become purified into the one central desire for God. What we find as our desires are purified is the presence at the center of our being—the presence of Christ. Our waiting and our longing will ultimately bring us to him, for he is the inspiration of our most fundamental desire.

But it is by no means the case that the individual seeking God is doing all the work. As the person refines his or her intention, the community lends all its support, wisdom, and skill, eager to assist the new arrival.[109] This interdependence between the newcomer and the community is suggestive of the way God is present here, supporting every impulse of love as the kingdom is built by many hands.

Above all, we should not miss the language of verse 8. There will be many hard and rugged ways. But that is not the point. The point is that by them "we walk towards God." Within the community of faith and the tradition of prayer, hardship is known as a natural part of the path to Life.

Reflection

However long we have been Christians, it seems to me that we are always encountering new beginnings, new life, deeper conversion. These "initial stages" do indeed seem to have certain patterns, though I seldom notice them at the time. One regular pattern is the appearance of a period during which I know there is a new step to take, but I haven't quite decided with my whole being to take it. (My longing needs to intensify first!) Oddly enough, at this point, if someone tries to help me along, I'll have a thousand reasons why now is not the right time. I must take the first step alone, and only when I am ready.

After that step has been taken, there is often an initial period of intense and joy-filled awareness of God. But following soon thereafter is a time of frustration and difficulty. This period seems to be characterized by a superficial sense of God's absence along with a peculiar certainty that I am being faithful to my own particular call. Eventually, an internal synthesis seems to occur in which I experience a deepened awareness of God's presence and love. But it is very important for me to have a spiritual friend or director as I negotiate that middle passage. Otherwise, I may convince myself that I am being totally untrue, not only to God but to myself, and I might abandon the difficult and "blind" work of purification. I can read books about this middle stage, but it has been essential for me to supplement such impersonal knowledge with the help of someone who knows me and can affirm the rightness of my path and the importance of persistence in it, even when there seems to be nothing happening.

Prayer/Response

Chapter 58
VERSE 7 (SAME PASSAGE)

*T*he concern is whether the novice truly seeks God, and is zealous for the Work of God, for obedience, and for humiliations.

Comment

It seems worth breaking our usual pattern to dwell formally for two days on this rich text about the initial steps in the consecrated Christian life, particularly verse 7.

Here Benedict is advising the novice master and the community on the qualities that are the marks of one likely to endure in the monastic commitment, one likely to strengthen and contribute to the monastic community. What qualities does he emphasize?

1. "truly seeks God": This is a frequent theme not only in monastic literature generally but also in scripture. For example, it is keenly expressed in Psalm 27: "One thing I seek: to live in the house of Yahweh all the days of my life." "My heart has said of you, 'seek his face.'" "This I believe: I shall see the goodness of Yahweh, in the land of the living" (verses 4, 8, 13). Benedict is unquestionably familiar with the patristic thought on this phrase and probably is reflecting on his own prayer experience. The phrase is a shorthand expression for a specific longer meaning that is implicit in the Rule's Prologue (verses 14–18) where we are reminded that it is God who seeks us.[110] Thus, the one who truly seeks God is one who has heard and responded with his or her whole heart to the voice already calling.

2. "is zealous for the Work of God": This phrase "Work of God" refers specifically to the Daily Office, as we have previously noted. The monk is one who finds his or her life rooted in regular prayer. The prayer is a source of nurture and a formative influence; the monk is open to the prayer in such a way that he or she becomes docile to God's Spirit in and through it. Daily prayer with the community shapes one's life with the community and with God. (See for example Chapter 13:12–14; 19:3–7.)

3. "is zealous for . . . obedience": Such language almost seems a contradiction in terms to us, but it probably means something like this: the novice is to show evidence of awareness of the limits

of his or her own knowledge and an eagerness to be taught. Learning involves life skills and not just mental knowledge. Learning involves sometimes not understanding the purpose of certain practices, but being willing to consent cheerfully nonetheless.

4. "is zealous for . . . humiliations": "Humiliations"—that wonderful source of humility! This quality might be discovered through questions like this: Does the novice have a "chip on the shoulder" or a neurotic need to be right all the time or in control all the time? Is there in this person some recognition that life often brings hardships that cannot be prevented and a patience to bear with them? Does the novice have a sense of humor that can laugh at and bear with his or her own foolishness, receiving mistakes gratefully as good teachers?

Most of us don't have the opportunity to be objectively tested by such questions in modern lay life. Even marriage and family settings are often a way to avoid rather than face these issues in ourselves. Yet how important these matters are for our psychological health, not to mention for our spiritual health! And if we have eyes to see and ears to hear, many ordinary opportunities give us the chance to practice simplicity of heart.

Reflection

As I reflect on this list, it seems to me that these are qualities needed to be part of the body of Christ, wherever and however it is incarnated. If I live alone, I can fool myself in many ways about my charitable disposition. When I live with others but refuse them permission to confront me with these issues, I can still be blind to the truth about myself. But if I really long to live in loving Christian community, then these true tests of intimacy are a wonderful gift to me, as they wear away my pride.

Benedict's list includes no consideration of like-mindedness or common table manners and so on. This suggests that it doesn't really matter whether or not I am attracted to, agree with, or feel friendly toward a fellow Christian. What matters is that we both earnestly seek God and try to live in faithfulness to God. How seldom I look at my brothers and sisters in that pure light!

Prayer/Response

Chapter 58
VERSES 9–16

*I*f the novice promises to persevere in his stability, after the lapse of two months let this Rule be read to him straight through, then let him be told: "Behold the law under which you choose to fight: if you can keep it, enter; if you cannot, freely depart." If he still stands firm, let him be taken to the aforementioned novitiate, and again tried in all patience. After the lapse of six months, let the Rule be read to him again, that he may know what it is he is entering. Should he still stand firm, after four months let the same Rule be read to him once more. And if, having deliberated within himself, he promises to keep all these things and to observe everything that is commanded him, then let him be received into the community, knowing that it is decreed by the law of the Rule that from that day forward he may not depart from the monastery nor shake off from his neck the yoke of the Rule, which after such prolonged deliberation he was free either to refuse or to accept.

Comment

Another extraordinarily rich passage! Here Benedict is dealing with the root issues of longing, freedom, and obedience—of human will enfolded in God's will.

The evident tension that Benedict presents here is expressed by Paul in Romans 7: That for which I most long is that which in isolation I am utterly unable effectively to choose. And yet I can choose with that part of me which carries my deepest intention, that is, where the gift of my strong longing attracts me to God. And I can then back this choice up with perseverance and self-acceptance. It is this choice which God's grace (mediated by scripture, prayer, community, abbot, and Rule) rewards richly. But it is well to know at the start that it will require both patience and grace. (Compare Prologue 41.)

Presenting the opportunity for acceptance three times is reminiscent of Jesus' questions to Peter in John 21:15: "Simon, son of John, do you love me?" That is the question: Do we love God? And it is the question we need to be asked repeatedly, until we realize how paltry our love is, and how richly and helpfully God knows that. We are told that Peter was grieved that Jesus asked the third time, because he knew the limits of his own love, but he also knew that Jesus knew them as well. And therein lies the hope that enables any true commitment.

Reflection

I notice especially that Benedict encourages and indeed requires a "prolonged deliberation" to inform this important commitment. Just as I realize how important this daily process of reflection is— laying side by side both my aspirations and my behavior, and ever freshly discovering both the longing and the humility that keep me eager for sweet dependence upon my God.

Reflection helps me get more deeply in touch with who I am and what I long for. Several years ago I was irritated and then amused when someone asked me, "Who are you?" and after I had answered, he asked me again! After the second answer, the question was posed yet a third time. At first, I thought I was not being heard, but then I realized the repeated question was intended to evoke deeper and deeper reflection, until I was able to hear myself at a vastly more authentic level than at first.

My life with God is always going on at those deeper levels, but sometimes I lose awareness of it by my failure to reflect.

Prayer/Response

Chapter 58
VERSES 17–18

*T*he one to be received is to make in the oratory before all, a promise of stability, faithfulness to monastic life (conversatione morum suorum), and obedience. This is done in the presence of God and the saints, so that, if the monk should ever act otherwise, he will know that he will be condemned by God whom he mocks.

Comment

Benedict emphasizes that the monk's promise contains three elements: stability, *conversatione*, and obedience. These "are not to be understood to be three distinct vows, as the vows of religious life later came to be understood. Rather, the phrase describes the content of the monk's promise."[111]

We can understand this content as a commitment to the whole way of life spelled out in the Rule. Special emphases of Benedictine life embodied in the promise are these:

1. stability: This is not running away from yourself or from God. It is staying put and allowing yourself to be purified in the fire of God's life growing within.

2. obedience: This is simple obedience to the Rule, the abbot, and your brothers and sisters, in the context of the deeper obedience of attentive listening to all of life for Christ there revealed.

3. *conversatio:* This is ongoing conversion to God, as expressed in the whole monastic manner of life (simplicity and humility, for example), and deepened formation of the heart toward virtue and grace.[112]

Benedict also clarifies that the monk's promise is made in the presence of the community, but to God. The word "mock" is the same word used in Gal 6:7: "Don't delude yourselves into thinking God can be cheated (mocked): where you sow, there you reap."

Thus, we see the great seriousness of the promise, the great importance of the commitment. We understand that here is one who has solemnly declared, in the presence of God, the angels and saints, and human brothers and sisters, that he or she is committed each day to listen to the voice that calls out: "do not harden your heart!" (Prologue, verse 9–10).

Reflection

I wonder whether, in the life of the laity, there is such a solemn moment as this. Is there a point at which, supported by a community of peers, we declare our intention to love God with all our heart and mind and soul and strength? It is certainly implicit in Baptism, because this monastic commitment is an intentional living out in full of the baptismal covenant promise. Perhaps many young people and adults experience some comparable degree of solemnity and personal commitment in adult baptism and/or in Confirmation.

But even if the moment itself was not marked by a specific ritual, for me there was a growing conviction, a growing longing, which increasingly found its expression in the daily self-offering of my life to God. And although I experienced a special time of consecration as an oblate, it seems to need daily renewal. Also, for me, the evolving consecration typical of my life needs to be nourished among a community of fellow disciples, even if we are only three friends who meet regularly in prayer, or a director and a directee, or a Bible study group at church. How much I need the presence of others who are also trying to live out this daily self-offering to God! For me, it is largely in the context of life together with a few others that I am empowered to deepen my personal discovery that God still calls and still provides the resources necessary for my daily response.

Prayer/Response

Chapter 58
VERSES 19–29 (END)

*C*oncerning this promise, the monk is to make a petition in the name of the saints whose relics are there, and of the abbot who is present. He is to write this petition with his own hand; or at least, if he is illiterate let another write it at his request, and let the novice place his mark on it and place it with his own hand upon the altar. When he has placed it there, the novice himself is to begin this verse: Uphold me, Lord, according to your word, and I shall live; let not my hope be put to shame (Ps 119:116). The whole community is to repeat this verse three times, adding to it the gloria. Then the novice is to cast himself at the feet of all, that they may pray for him; and from that day let him be counted as one of the community.*

If he has any possessions he should either first bestow them on the poor, or by a solemn deed of gift donate them to the monastery, keeping nothing for himself; knowing that from that day forward he will have no power, even over his own body. Immediately afterwards in the oratory he is to be stripped of his own garments which he is wearing, and be clothed in those of the monastery. Those garments which are taken from him are to be placed in the clothes-room to be kept there, so that if ever by the persuasion of the devil he consents (God forbid!) to leave the monastery, he may be stripped of the things of the monastery and cast forth. The petition, however, which the abbot received on the altar will not be given back to him, but will be kept in the monastery.

Comment

Here Benedict directs certain physical actions to express specific theological convictions.

1. Body of Christ: The new monk expresses his awareness that trust and interdependence are essential to salvation as he offers the prayer from the Psalms, which the community joins, and asks for their prayers to support his promise.

2. Baptism and Christian life as a dying-and-rising with Christ: The monk offers his whole self and indeed is stripped of his clothes and possessions, then to be robed with the new clothes symbolizing new membership in this communion of God's people.

3. God's grace in everything: Even when things go wrong, they are not beyond God's mercy. The provision to retain the monk's pledge paper is an ironic form of reassurance that even when the devil tricks us into believing we have passed beyond God's mercy, there is grace enduring beyond our flight. (See Chapter 29.)

Reflection

I am so drawn to the words of the prayer of consecration! "Uphold me, Lord, according to your word, and I shall live; let not my hope be put to shame." I make the promise to the community and to God with all my heart and soul. Yet even as I do so, I know it is beyond my power to keep. How can I turn toward God in every moment, when I know I can't do it more than five minutes in twenty-four hours? How can I be humble at all times, when I know the power of my pride? Even with the prayers and support of the community, it is beyond my power to keep this promise.

So, what is it that I am doing in this promise? I am asking to be received. I am asking God to take me into the divine life. I am, in short, expressing the hope that is my deepest longing. And I place my faith in that longing and in my God, and not in any power of my own.

Prayer/Response

Chapter 59, The Offering of Children by the Noble or the Poor
(ENTIRE)

*I*f a nobleman offers his child to God in the monastery, and the child is not old enough, the parents are to make out the petition of which we spoke before. And, together with the offerings, let them wrap that petition and the hand of the child in the altar-cloth, and so offer him.

With regard to their property they must in the same petition promise under oath that they will never, either directly, through an intermediary, or in any way whatever, give him anything or the means of having anything. Or else, if they are unwilling to do this and desire to give something for their advantage as an offering to the monastery, let them make a donation to the monastery of the property which they wish to give, reserving to themselves, if they so wish, the revenues. And so let every way be blocked, that the child will have no sort of expectation by which he might be misled and perish (which God forbid!), as we have learned by experience may happen.

Those who are poorer are to do the same. But those who have nothing whatever shall simply make the petition, and offer their child along with the offerings and before witnesses.

Comment

The last chapter and this one set forth the two major methods of entrance into monastic life, and in a sense form a parallel to adult baptism/confirmation and infant baptism, the latter involving a parental commitment on behalf of the child.

The context of entrance is expressed by the phrase "together with the offerings," referring to that moment in the eucharistic celebration known as the oblation, or offering. The eucharistic oblation is the offering to God for consecration of the ordinary elements of daily life—bread and wine. Indeed, even as ordinary things, they are gifts of God. We offer them back to God in thanks; God returns them to us transformed. In this exchange, we are given the necessary nourishment for true life.

This offertory exchange is a metaphor for monastic profession. A life is offered to God, which in the first place was God's own gift. In

God's hands, that life is transformed. It is received yet again, filled with God's own presence and guiding care. This offering occurs not only once, but is reenacted daily. This is consecration.

The metaphor suggests why it is so important not to presume to possess anything. The awareness that all is gift lies at the heart of the consecrated life. Nothing is possessed; in all that is important, the Christian is receptive. Any hint of ownership or entitlement is a basic refusal of this essential disposition toward the Giver of life.

Reflection

I ponder what seems to be Benedict's formula for consecration:

1. Receive life as gifted;

2. offer the gift in return to God;

3. receive the transformed gift, which carries the presence and nourishment of the Giver;

4. repeat the process each day, with everything.

This formal description of a moment of consecration serves as a model for the daily process of consecration seen so often in the Rule's section on "Consecration of Mundane Activities." Yet it seems much easier to say the formula than to live it.

As I try to practice consecration in my daily life, I encounter resistances in myself. When thinking about that resistance, I realize that I prefer to have something I can claim as my own, something well defined and "reliable," something I can possess and manage comfortably. At first, it feels very frightening to become aware that the only "constant" is ongoing relationship (not material possession in any of its forms). Yet as I practice, gradually I sense the release of fear and a growing sense of comfort with One who is trustworthy. I realize that I do not need to cling to my ideas of God, nor even to my ideas of myself. Certainty lies not in those static pictures, but only in the dynamism of the love that we share. As this becomes real for me, I am free to enjoy everything!

Prayer/Response

Membership and Governance within the Community ✦ 231

Chapter 60, Priests Who Wish to Live in the Monastery
(ENTIRE)

*I*f anyone ordained to the priesthood asks to be received into the
monastery, assent should not be granted him too quickly; but if
he persists strongly in this request, he should know that he must keep
all the discipline of the Rule, and that nothing will be relaxed in his
favor, for it is written: Friend, for what have you come? (Matt 26:50).
Nevertheless, it may be granted him to stand next to the abbot, to give
the blessing, and to celebrate Mass, if the abbot asks him to do so. Otherwise, he should not presume to do anything, knowing that he is subject to
the discipline of the Rule; but rather let him give an example of humility
to all. Should there arise a question of an appointment or other matter
in the monastery, he is to expect the position due to him according to the
time of his entrance, and not that which was granted to him out of reverence for the priesthood.

Clerics who similarly desire to be admitted into the monastery are
to be placed in a middle rank: but this only if they promise observance
of the Rule and stability.

Comment

Perhaps this whole chapter seems odd to you, since we are familiar
with monasteries composed chiefly of ordained persons. However,
in Benedict's time, the monastery was a lay community, and we
believe Benedict himself was a layman.[113]

The emphasis on the importance of being subject to the Rule and
observing humility and stability is a reminder that the Rule is designed
to facilitate a certain kind and depth of Christian formation, which is
not necessarily found even in priestly formation! Even today, with the
emphasis on academic qualifications in seminaries, many priests are
hungry for solid spiritual formation. However, if the entering priest is
one who has deeply integrated, say, the steps of humility (above in
Chapter 7), then he or she will have no difficulty entering harmoniously into the community life. But if he has not previously had such
training, then the monastery will become for him what he ought to be

seeking there—a way to shatter the arrogance of pride on the anvil of the Rule's daily disciplines of finding Christ in all.

It may seem strange that Benedict cites this specific passage from Matthew, which of course is the question Jesus poses in Gethsemane to Judas, who has come to betray him. Benedict again reveals his even-handedness. by honoring the priest as one who carries Christ, especially in his capacity to consecrate the bread and wine, even while warning that same priest that the call of every Christian is to enter fully into the mind of Christ, a call to which the Rule is response. The Rule grants exemptions from this call neither for any weakness nor for any strength. Those closest to Christ may yet betray him, if they trust primarily in their own self-will.

Reflection

What a hard word this is! My need is so great for security and comfort. I want so much to be able to say, "Well, I know I am a disciple; I've been with Jesus and I understand his mind; I am able and deserving of God's generosity." It's interesting that this happens for me especially around the issue of ordination. Occasionally, I will be overwhelmed by an impulse to seek ordination. Every time, when I track it down, I discover it to be an impulse for certainty and for security. Sometimes I want a tidy little box that will give me a "code-word" I can use for others and myself to "verify" that I'm alright-with-God. Yet I'm always brought back to the realization that ordination describes a function and not a relationship. The relationship may or may not coexist with the function, but they are separate issues. And ordination is no assurance of relationship; often, in fact, it's a distraction from it.

My call, like the monks of old, is to be a consecrated layperson. It's an unsettling call that never fits into any tidy categories and must be renewed each day. A friend of mine says: "Each morning when I wake, I must reaffirm my vocation to be a monk." That's what it's like for me; each day I must reaffirm my self-offering in response to God's call. It involves a deepening realization that I have an important relationship with One who loves me, and that alone is my secure point of reference in good times and bad.

Prayer/Response

Chapter 61, How Visiting Monks Are Received

VERSES 1–4

If any visiting monk comes from a distant place and wishes to remain in the monastery as a guest, and if he is content with the customs of the place as he finds them and does not trouble the monastery with any unreasonable requests, but is simply content with what he finds; he should be received for as long a time as he wishes. Indeed, if he offers criticism or makes suggestions reasonably and with humble love, the abbot should consider the matter prudently; for perhaps God sent him for this very reason.

Comment

One of the main ways balance is expressed in the Rule is by the complementary obligations that Benedict places on co-participants in any situation.[114] For example, in Chapter 36 the monks are instructed to care for the sick, and then the sick are instructed not to make excessive demands on their caretakers. A similar complementarity is expressed in this chapter. Guests are to be received by the monks as Christ (see Chapter 53:1–2), but a guest himself is admonished to be "content with the customs of the place as he finds them and . . . not trouble the monastery with any unreasonable requests." To deepen this complementarity, Benedict also invites the abbot to be aware that sometimes discomfort and disagreement express a point of view we really need to hear.

Perhaps we find it odd to have contentment stressed as a Christian virtue, as Benedict does with visiting monks. Ordinarily we may think of contentment as an expression of lukewarmness, which Benedict emphasizes is at odds with the Gospel. But we may better understand contentment as the opposite of that discontent so typical of our age. Our discontent is like that *acedia* mentioned in Chapter 48, which is an idleness of spirit, revealing a fundamental inability to be present to the moment before us. Thus, the virtue of contentment expresses attentive presence, the ability to see God in the midst of things as they are, a receiving of what is offered to us as a necessary prelude to offering it back to God. Such a contentment enables the abbot to be receptive to the criticisms and observations of strangers.

Reflection

I wonder if contentment is really a virtue? Like balance, it can so easily slip over into indifference or fence straddling. And I know there are times, say when tempers get hot at a party, that I am glad to be neutral about a particularly distressing issue. Yet surely contentment must be more than merely lukewarmness.

Again, my prayer begins to teach me about this. I find that the more seriously I pray, the less able I am to be opinionated about issues; I listen more keenly to both sides of an argument and hear the wisdom represented in each. In fact, I often think it was much easier to know what I thought and what I wanted before I began to take prayer seriously. Oddly, though, today my sympathy and interest are more likely to be piqued by suffering of all types, and my intercession in "hopeless" cases has become much more fervent.

I've begun to realize that this "middle place" may not just be a temporary stop on my way to a fixed opinion. It may indeed be right for me to feel constantly tugged between two competing points of view, now closer to one and now another. I think, in fact, that what I must hold fast to is the sense of tension.

One clear example for me is that I am called at this moment both to love the monastic life and to be an active layperson in the world. At first, it seemed that the tension was unbearable, and that I should "fish or cut bait"! I ought to choose between one or the other, and give up the longing/desire for the unchosen one. Yet I was unable to choose, and gradually I began to see that, right now, God calls me to have a foot on both sides. It may look like fence straddling to some, but to me it feels like a bridge, a conduit through which communication becomes possible in a way it would not without someone like me, someone content being "mixed." The tension continues, but the contentment predominates.

Prayer/Response

Chapter 61

VERSES 5–14 (END)

*I*f after some time he wishes to fix his stability [in the monastery]
this desire should not be denied, especially since his manner of life
could be well ascertained during the time he was a guest. But if during
that time he was found extreme or prone to vice, not only should he be
refused admission as a member of the community, but he should even
be told courteously to depart, lest others be corrupted by his misery.

If, however, he is not the sort who deserves to be sent away, he should
not merely be received as a member of the community on his own request;
rather, he should be persuaded to stay so that others may be taught by his
example, and because in every place we serve one Lord and fight under
one King. And if the abbot perceives that he is a man of this kind, he may
put him in a somewhat higher place. Not only a monk, but also any of the
aforesaid priests or clerics may be put by the abbot in a higher place than
they would be accorded by the time of their entrance, if he perceives that
their lives merit it.

But the abbot must take care never to receive permanently a monk
from any known monastery without the consent of the monk's own abbot
and letters of recommendation; because it is written: What you would not
have done to yourself, do not do to another (Tob 4:16).

Comment

Benedict is suggesting that the quality of life of the visitor also affects
the community in very deep ways. The "presence" of this newcomer
may be beneficial or toxic. If we who serve the same Lord are members of one another, then the persons we are have a profound mutual
influence for good or evil. Therefore, it behooves us to develop the
discernment to recognize those who are negative influences and
those who are positive ones, and respond accordingly.

This is not the same as refusing the company of sinners; it is
awareness that among the self-proclaimed righteous, some will be
life-giving and some will be death-bringing for this specific human
community.

How interesting that Benedict chooses to cite the negative form
of the Golden Rule from Tobit rather than the positive form set

down in Matthew 7:12. Perhaps he does so to heighten the teaching of Jesus in Matthew that this rule-of-life wisdom is one (even) Jesus received from the faith tradition.

Reflection

What do I want done to myself? Well, I really appreciate beneficial presences, and I really suffer from "toxic" persons. So I would like to be a beneficial presence. I imagine that sometimes I am, and that sometimes I'm pretty toxic. How do I become more beneficial and less toxic?

I suspect that the elements Benedict has emphasized in recent chapters can help me. First, I need to pay attention to what is actually going on around me, really to receive what is given in the here and now, both the good and the bad. That's a big first step and involves a kind of allowing things to be what they are while also recognizing God in the midst of them.

But the crucial question is: What kind of God is in the midst? I was quite astonished recently by the statement: "[I]t is of far more consequence what kind of a God than whether a God or not."[115] But in a sense, that's one of the main elements I hear Benedict emphasizing in these sections on membership in Christ's body. God is love. Maybe I have a distorted or inadequate idea of what God is, or of what love is, but as I really pay attention to what is in front of me, looking for God here, then my whole self—perspectives, values, behaviors—begins to be shaped by Love Itself. Conflict, differences, inadequacy: all these are grist for the mill of God's redeeming love. My own presence becomes beneficial as I allow myself to be formed by the beneficent Presence in the heart of all things.

I remember that benefit means to "make good" or "do good." The goodness is God inside things, groaning to be freed. I've begun to wonder if my main task is not simply to notice that goodness. My paying attention, actually looking for God in the midst, somehow helps to release a goodness ready to emerge. Is such a simple vision close to the truth? I don't know, but I will try it and watch.

Prayer/Response

Chapter 62, Concerning the
Priests of the Monastery
(ENTIRE)

*I*f any abbot wishes to have a priest or deacon ordained for himself, he should choose from among the monks one who is worthy to fulfill the priestly office. Let the one who is ordained beware of arrogance and pride, and not presume to do anything that has not been commanded by the abbot, knowing that he is now all the more subject to the discipline of the Rule. His priesthood must not become the cause of his forgetting the obedience and discipline of the Rule; rather he should advance ever more and more in the Lord.

He is always to keep the place due to him according to his entrance into the monastery, except with regard to the duties of the altar, or if the choice of the community and the will of the abbot should promote him on account of the merit of his life. Nevertheless, he is to know that he must keep the rules for deans and priors. Should he presume to do otherwise he must be considered not as a priest, but as a rebel; and if after frequent admonition he does not amend, the bishop is to be brought in as a witness. If even then he does not amend and his guilt is obvious, he must be expelled from the monastery; only, however, if his insolence is such that he will not submit or obey the Rule.

Comment

Benedict is inviting us to consider our own model of personal holiness. Do we have an image of what a holy person is like? How do we go about assessing the spiritual quality of our own lives, and assisting others in their spiritual journey? This is what Benedict is referring to when he speaks of some who are more "worthy" than others, and of those who "advance in progress" toward God. It's ironic that our culture praises many kinds of progress but has an inadequate concept of what progress toward God might look like, in an individual or a community. We tend to focus on external standards, with little understanding of true holiness. Yet the idea of an increase in holiness is basic to monastic life.[116] Indeed, here Benedict clearly associates spiritual progress with the three elements defining cenobitic life (Chapter 1:2): obedience to the abbot, obedience to the Rule, and belonging to the community. The point here is that the priest must move more deeply into the interior practice that has made him worthy of the honor, and not draw away from it at this critical juncture.

At first, it may seem paradoxical that Benedict speaks of progress in the spiritual life in the same chapter in which he describes flagrant violation of its principles. Clearly, Benedict has encountered these problems repeatedly, because the tone of this and several subsequent chapters suggests long-suffering. The problem is captured in the words "presume" and "arrogance." All too often, when we see ourselves as spiritually adept, pride begins to presume on the relationship with God and arrogance replaces humility. It is important to be aware of particular danger points in the spiritual journey; Benedict emphasizes that "promotion" due to spiritual "worth" is always a dangerous moment.

Far from being dismayed at Benedict's attention to such problems, we can find comfort in it. Even for one with Benedict's vision, the spiritual life in community is hard work. There are many "potholes," especially for those who are "advanced," which we all fall into from time to time. Simple prudence suggests we be aware of these dangers, and increase rather than decrease our reliance on God. If we are willing to acknowledge our probable vulnerability, the remedy of humility is readily available.

Reflection

I find it extraordinary that Benedict suggests in verse 6 that the whole community (as well as the abbot) might choose to give a priest/monk a higher place among them! This is such a strong statement of communal discernment, and I seldom have experienced even the possibility of a community so "in tune" with itself and with God that such a thing could be considered. Yet, as I think about it, I see that in some sense it is a logical outgrowth of the idea (presented in the last chapter) that the quality of each life influences the lives of others. As a practical matter, it suggests to me the importance of paying attention to my own call from God, as well as accepting help and strength from others who are attending to theirs. The holiness of each affects the holiness of all, in indirect ways I'll never fully understand. But I can begin to live into this awareness.

"Progress toward holiness" is such an awesome phrase. I realize that as I think about such a thing in my own life, almost immediately I become muddled. How do I know when I am becoming more holy? And what do I do with the information when I do know? It seems to me that Benedict has given me two good tests. One is, how is my relationship with God? Do I feel near to God or far from God (or indifferent)? The quality of intimacy in that relationship is a far better test than any personal assessment of holiness.

The second test from Benedict lies in community life. While it does have its ups and downs, as Benedict knows only too well, there is something sacramental about a community with Christ at its center. It is difficult to see that from inside the community and just as difficult to see Christ inside myself for myself. In both cases, loving "outsiders" can often see with greater clarity.

I know, however, that when I begin to act as if Christ is (invisibly) present, remarkable things happen.

So holiness does seem intimately connected with relationships, with life in community. I rarely thought so before. I want to watch for that holiness now, and cooperate with it.

Prayer/Response

Chapter 63, Rank in the Community
VERSES 1–9

*M*onks are to observe their rank in the monastery which the time of their entry and the merit of their lives determines, or as the abbot shall appoint. The abbot is not to disturb the flock committed to him, nor by the use of arbitrary power establish anything unjustly; but let him ever bear in mind that he will have to give an account to God of all his judgments and of all his deeds.

Therefore, in that order which [the abbot] has appointed or which they hold themselves, the brethren approach to receive the kiss of peace and Communion; and in the same order they intone psalms and stand in choir. And in absolutely every place, age is not to decide the order or be prejudicial to it; for Samuel and Daniel when but children judged the elders (1 Sam 3; Dan 13:44–62).

Excepting, therefore, those whom (as we have said) the abbot has pro-moted for very good causes or degraded for solid reasons, let all the rest take the order of their entry; so that, for example, one who enters the monastery at the second hour of the day must know that he is junior to another who came at the first hour, whatever may be his age and dignity. But children are to be kept under discipline in all matters and by everyone.

Comment

A discussion of this passage could take many directions. But since the responsibilities of the abbot and disciplinary procedures have been discussed elsewhere, let's concentrate on what Benedict reveals in this chapter about the constitution of the community. The issue of rank may be seen as one of hierarchical order or as one of rela-tionships among persons. The latter view has considerable relevance to the Christian life in general. From that perspective, the question here is about fraternal relations, that is, how to relate to one's peers.

Benedict deliberately turns his back on two ranking methods common in his time. He mentions and discards age. He does not mention social class except indirectly ("dignity"), but obviously he has also declined to use social rank as a governing factor in the monastic community.

What does "order of entry" suggest about Benedict's basic yardstick for rank? It suggests precisely a choice for monastic standards and a turning away from worldly standards. It reminds us of Jesus' language in Matthew 20:26. Jesus advises his disciples that when they look at the way worldly people order their relationships, they should be aware that "it shall not be so among you." The standard that governs rela-tionships among monks can only be that all are one in Christ (Chap-ter 2:20). While there are many differences of temperament and giftedness, relationships are to be arranged based on kinship in Christ.

Like the abbot, each of us has the power to do as we wish, but it may conflict with our commitment to God. From the day we make our first decision to give our whole selves to Christ, we give up that power. But we are given the opportunity to choose Christ again and again, each day, in the way that we relate to each other.

Reflection

What standard governs my relationships with others? I'm afraid that all too often it is exactly the same as the world's, that is, very superficial. Perhaps I judge based on how people feed my ego, that is, how similar they are to me, or how helpful to me. But there is another way: the daily recognition that we are all one in Christ. How might that look?

I am privileged to have a close friend who is indeed a beneficial presence. Recently I observed with interest the way he dealt with an important colleague. The colleague had been coldly furious with him, actually because of a misunderstanding. But, before it was cleared up, many harsh words had been directed at my friend. The next day, I overheard him speaking about that colleague, gently concerned that "Joe" might recover speedily from a bad cold. I reflected on this incident with some amazement; I became aware that my friend had made a deliberate choice not to be drawn into the whirlpool of anger and accusation. Rather, he had intentionally turned his emotional energy to matters where he could be loving to the one who had hurt him. He is not naive about "the way things are," but he is utterly convinced that Christ is to be found everywhere. In such ordinary matters, he makes the choice to seek him. And, wonderfully, in many contexts, his gentle presence has indeed revealed the Christ in themselves to many people.

Prayer/Response

Chapter 63
VERSES 10–19 (END)

*L*et the younger brothers, then, reverence their elders, and the elder love the younger. In calling each other by name, no one is to address another by his simple name; but the elders are to call the younger brethren "brother", and the younger call their elders Nonnus, which means "reverend father". But the abbot, since he is considered to represent Christ, is to be called "Lord" and "Abbot"; not that he receives this himself, but out of honor and love of Christ. Let him reflect on this, and act so as to be worthy of such honor.

Wherever the brothers meet one another the younger is to ask a blessing of the elder. And when an elder passes by, the younger is to rise and give him a place to sit down. Nor should the younger presume to sit *unless his senior bids him, that it may be as was written: seek to outdo one another in showing honor (Rom 12:10).*

Young children and boys are to be kept under discipline to their rank in the oratory or at table. In other places, too, wherever they may be, they are to be kept under custody and discipline until they reach the age of reason.

Comment

Here Benedict asks us to think about what's in a name? How do we understand the relationship between the inner and the outer, between the spirit and the law? If you whistle in the dark, do you gain courage? If you address your brother and sister with respect, do you gain love?

Somewhere Martin Buber said that education is to establish law and hope that it will become inward order. That is the theme of Psalm 119. That is what Benedict means about children being disciplined physically until they "reach the age of reason" (understanding). That is why we practice exterior, virtuous behavior, hoping that in time our hearts will be formed by our practice and our prayer. But the external practice must be congruent with inner intent, or we have only hypocrisy. However, when external practice is congruent with inner expectancy, we have the transforming power of sacrament.

In these few words of guidance about the names we call each other, Benedict has set forth his vision of Christian community.[117] That vision is rooted in the conviction that we are all one in Christ. The essence of Christian community is the growing recognition that we are the body of Christ in our relationships with each other, that Christ is revealed among and within the "joints," the connective points, of our human interactions. Thus, we are called in a special way to become Christ's body in our daily intercourse.

Reflection

I think about how I use names. In my southern California world of flexible titles, I am sometimes surprised to hear myself spontaneously address a priest as "father" when my heart has learned respect and regard for the beauty of that person. Perhaps it might also work the other way. I suppose I could practice speaking to all those in my immediate environment with respect, thus teaching myself that they are children of God, deserving of my regard. At first, it might seem contrived, as does any new exercise of this kind. But Benedict is inviting me to consider new possibilities for practical ways of seeking God in my actual present environment.

His invitation sounds to me something like this:

1. Everything that is given is a gift of God.

2. The task set for me is to learn to receive the present moment fully, with all its dynamics, as a gift containing Godself. Among other things, that means receiving my sister and my neighbor that way.

3. If I treat the moment and the person as a sacrament, that is, as a precious outer sign bearing the inner gift of Christ, I predispose myself to see something new/transforming in the present situation.

4. I also invite the other to see that something new in themselves and in the situation.

5. Often I will feel very foolish. Occasionally, I will feel high and lifted up, because glory will indeed break through into the ordinary.

Am I willing to try it? What can I lose?

Prayer/Response

Chapter 64, The Appointment of the Abbot
VERSES 1–6

In the appointment of an abbot this principle is always to be observed: he is to be selected abbot who is chosen by the whole community unanimously in the fear of God, or by a part [of the community], however small, which possesses sounder counsel. The one who is to be appointed should be chosen for the merit of his life and the wisdom of his teaching, even though he should be the last in community rank.

But even if the whole community (which God forbid) should elect a person who condones their evil ways, and this somehow comes to the

attention of the bishop to whose diocese the place belongs, or to the atten-
tion of neighboring abbots or neighboring Christians; they are to prevent
the agreement of these wicked men from prevailing, and are to appoint
a worthy steward over the house of God, knowing that for this they will
receive a good reward if they do it with a pure intention and for the love
of God; on the other hand, they will sin if they neglect to do it.

Comment

These words are clear enough. There may be two modes of selection, either by a unanimous vote of the whole community or by a smaller group of sound judgment, with the backup possibility that the bishop or neighboring Christians might intervene if the community selects an unworthy abbot. But if somebody tried to implement this as a formal procedure in an ordinary community of Christians, hundreds of questions would arise. And indeed, today "there is no agreement about the precise meaning" of this passage![118]

The problem arises out of Benedict's primary concern in this process, which is that the abbot (like the prophets and kings of the Old Testament and the disciples in the New) is one chosen and called by God, and it is the community's responsibility to be open and responsive to this divine intention. However, since the discernment of the concrete will of God in any specific situation depends greatly on the depth of the ongoing relationship we have with God, the details of the abbot's selection are less important than overall obedience to the Rule, in which the monks' hearts are continuously formed in Christ's Spirit.

In the context of human frailty and lukewarmness, much can go wrong, and apparently, Benedict has experienced several variations on just how wrong things can go. It is a comfort to realize that even Benedict sometimes can't see the next step clearly, because we are so often in that position ourselves. It is nonetheless a sobering thought that Benedict suggests there will be occasions when true discernment occurs more effectively through the ordinary common sense of those in the neighborhood rather than through the monks themselves. However little Benedict trusts his own principles, or their implementation by monks, he has great confidence that God's purpose will eventually work itself out, through whatever resources are open to God's ways.

Reflection

I notice especially that Benedict says "God forbid" that the community would act out of self-will. His language implies that God intends and desires to enable the community to choose God's will. He sees God as always present and helping to carry out beneficial purposes, so the issue of discernment becomes not so much a matter of trying to figure out correctly what God has already "decided," but is rather a matter of relying on the ever-present help available.

Strangely, Benedict's muddling around here, even to the point of throwing up his hands and suggesting that help might come from the unlikely source of the neighbors, gives me comfort. So often, I look at a situation from all sides, and feel utterly stuck. I can't see any way out of the mess, the brokenness, the terrible hurt that all parties are feeling. I feel quite blind to God's presence and will, wherever it may be! But Benedict's confidence that, even beyond the usual boundaries of our awareness, God's beneficial presence is making itself known, gives me confidence. I realize that I can offer up my burden of lonely responsibility. I can relax and simply do my best, only watching for what wants to emerge.

Prayer/Response

Chapter 64
VERSES 7–15

*L*et the one who has been appointed abbot always bear in mind what a burden he has undertaken, and to whom he will have to give an account of his stewardship (Luke 16:2); and he must know that it is more fitting for him to profit his brethren than to preside over them. He must, therefore, be learned in the law of God, that he may know how to bring forth new things and old (Matt 13:52).

He must be chaste, sober, merciful, and always exalt mercy above judgment (Jas 2:13) that he himself may obtain the same. Let him hate sin and love the brethren. And in correcting others he should act prudently, not going to excess, lest in seeking too eagerly to scrape off the rust, he breaks the vessel. Let him keep his own frailty ever before his eyes, and remember that the bruised reed must not be broken (Isa 42:3).

By this we do not mean that he should permit vices to grow up: on the contrary, he should cut them off prudently and with charity as he sees best for each, as we have said. Let him seek to be loved rather than feared.

Comment

As we have noticed before, it is often the case when Benedict is trying to lay a theoretical framework that his mind turns to scripture. As his spirit flows freely through that holy book he knows by heart, he offers one image after another, so that there is almost an embarrassment of riches rather than a systematic and explicit presentation.

Here he is trying to explain what the abbot should be. Another way to consider this theme is to inquire what "merit of life and wisdom" (verse 2) looks like in a mature Christian. In order to explore his conclusions, we are best advised ourselves to turn to the scripture he cites, and read the verses leading up to and following his quotations, allowing our minds and hearts to resonate to them. This is one possible paraphrase:

> For every gift we receive, we are responsible to Another for its care; this is no less true of our relationships than of our skills or possessions. (Luke 16)

> Key to this care is knowledge of the ways of God, so that we are no longer limited to a narrow and singular view; with God, we may choose old or new, selecting that which is best to reveal the previously hidden, the kingdom in our midst. (Matt 13)

> Justice is born of harmony. Harmony with all creation occurs when we constantly recall that we too are created, we too will be judged, and that we too are frail as a bruised reed. (Isa 42 and James 2)

Throughout this section on membership and governance in the community, Benedict continuously emphasizes who God is and how God works. In concrete details, Benedict reminds us that God is love, and he helps us to see how that is so. Benedict takes the goal of salvation seriously. Yet he knows a salvation that is filled with joy, that is governed by One whose desire is to be loved rather than feared. Obviously, in this behavior the abbot is imitating the one whose name he carries, the Abba.

Reflection

My eyes fill with tears as I think how much the goal of being loved rather than feared expresses my deepest longing. Over and over in these chapters, Benedict has reminded me of the basic questions: Do I love God? And does God love me?

At some level of my psyche, it is much easier to believe in a mean and stern God, who wants to punish me for my shortfalls, than in a God of care, a God who really loves me more than I can ask or imagine. The God of love is still largely a God of my mind, and not yet one of my heart. I lack the innocence simply to reach out to God in trust and faith. But again and again I see that innocence, in practical expression, in Benedict. I am deeply moved by his trust in God and it strengthens my own.

Prayer/Response

Chapter 64
VERSES 16–22 (END)

*T*he abbot must not be violent and anxious, nor exacting and head-strong, nor jealous and too prone to suspicion; for otherwise he will never be at rest. In his commands, whether they concern God or the world, he should be prudent and considerate. Let him be discreet and moderate in the tasks which he imposes, bearing in mind the discretion of holy Jacob, who said: If I cause my flocks to be overdriven, they will all die in one day (Gen 33:13). Therefore, taking this and other examples of discretion, the mother of virtue, let the abbot balance everything so that the strong have something to strive after and the weak are not dismayed.

And he must especially keep this Rule in all things, so that, having ministered well, he may hear from the Lord what the good servant heard, who gave grain to his fellow-servants in due season: Truly I say unto you, he shall place him over all his possessions (Matt 24:27).

Comment

In every respect, Benedict is drawing a portrait of the "faithful and wise servant" of Matthew 24, the one the Master set over the household to give them their food at the proper time.

Notice two things especially about this servant. First, he is the one the Master appointed. The authority of the abbot comes from God, and this is not less true, but more true, because he has been selected by the community. It is the community's act to express the choice of God. This is because the abbot's selection is a sacramental act: an outward sign manifesting the invisible grace of Christ's presence among the community.

Second, notice that the abbot is to be a person "at rest" (verse 16). Nowadays we seem to believe responsible servants are overworked. Such a view might appear to be reinforced by the language of Chapter 48:1: "Idleness is the enemy of the soul." But this chapter adds to that picture the awareness that the soul is also endangered when never at rest. The abbot is to model for the community that fundamental being "at rest" which can only come from singleness of heart. The soul at rest is focused on the One Thing necessary. From this perspective, the multiple concerns of the world fall into their natural order.

Reflection

I am attracted to the passage Benedict cites about Jacob, taken from the chapter in Genesis showing the moving reconciliation of those long-separated brothers, Jacob and Esau. In such a context, "not causing the flock to be overdriven" is clearly a gentle symbol of reconciliation. If I take this symbol for my own, it is a reminder not to push myself too hard, to be gentle with myself and patient with the development of events around me. This is important not just for my own peace of mind (though that is a good reason), but also because "not pushing" becomes a basic method by which I participate in God's reconciling power in the world.

I know many Christians who act as if they had to re-do the crucifixion in their own lives. Usually they are so caring and giving that they are very attractive persons. But I weep for their way of understanding God and Christ, for it seems to me they believe the whole redemption of the world rests on their self-immolation. And it seems to me that Benedict rightly points to another, more true vision of the Shepherd whose own gift of life now provides gentle care for his flock, the restoration of wholeness for each beloved lamb.

Prayer/Response

Chapter 65, The Prior
of the Monastery
VERSES 1–10

*I*t happens very often that the appointment of the prior causes grave scandals to arise in monasteries: for there are some who, puffed up by the evil spirit of pride and deeming themselves to be second abbots, take upon themselves a usurped power, and so foster scandals and cause dissensions in the community. This occurs especially in those places where the prior is appointed by the same bishop or the same abbots as those who appoint the abbot himself. How foolish this custom is may easily be seen: for from the first moment of entering upon his office the prior is given an incentive to pride, his thoughts suggesting to him that he is free from the authority of his abbot since he has been appointed by the very same persons.

Hence are stirred up envy, quarrels, backbiting, dissensions, jealousy, and disorders. And while the abbot and prior are in conflict with one another, it necessarily follows that their souls are endangered through their dissension; and those who are their subjects, favoring one side or the other, run along to their destruction. The blame for this perilous evil falls on the head of those who by their actions originated such disorders.

Comment

In certain respects, this seems one of the most time-bound chapters of the Rule: Benedict is clearly angrily resisting a common monastic practice of his time. Yet Christ's anger in the temple revealed a situation common to human experience—saying "no" to God by a focus on money at the expense of prayer. In a similar way, this matter of concern to Benedict reveals basic human truths.

Basil Hume comments that the Rule almost seems to have been intentionally "written for a monastery that functioned imperfectly . . . [It] almost seems to assume that there will be misbehavior."[119] Time after time the Rule conveys a realistic understanding of human nature. In this chapter, we see great familiarity with the ways of human rationalization—the "internal voices" in the prior's head (telling him what a fine fellow he is) are given almost as a quotation!

A central principle for Benedict is that those in authority have a responsibility to create conditions and environments that will minimize "legitimate" eruptions of pride and self-will. Benedict does not call for, nor assume, the "destruction of self-will; he takes it for granted it is always alive, and he celebrates that as a marvelous vehicle for ascetical discipline."[120] Instead, he creates a setting in which self-will is minimized and constructively channeled. Thus his anger here is directed at those who set up a system bound to evoke pride; those in authority should have a better appreciation of human nature than that!

Benedict understands that we can refuse the offer of divine goodness in two main ways. We can refuse to respond in joy to the call of God to live as the beloved. But we can equally refuse God by ignoring the evident willful tendencies of our human nature and pretending we are able to be gods ourselves.

Reflection

What am I personally invited to do about Benedict's suggestion that I not ignore my own willful tendencies? Well, for one thing, I can pay attention to patterns that are likely to evoke negative reactions in me. Recently, my husband asked me if I would try to let him know when I was becoming weary, rather than buck up bravely until the last possible moment, and then collapse in an hysterical heap all at once! Or sometimes when I am feeling particularly tired, I insist on our trying to make major long-term decisions, even when I know that an argument is the likely outcome.

It occurs to me, too, that there are situations out of my control that are likely to bring out my worst self. Clearly, those are not the times to expect optimum behavior from myself, and then punish myself for not achieving it. Honestly, the most life-giving thing for me to do would be to be patient, both with the situation and with myself.

What brings life? What evokes love? Yet again, Benedict invites me to look clearly at the nature of God in the midst, and to give myself to that reality.

Prayer/Response

Chapter 65
VERSES 11–22 (END)

*W*e foresee, therefore, that it is advisable for the preservation of peace and charity, that the management of the monastery depends upon the will of the abbot. If possible, let all the affairs of the monastery be attended to (as we have already arranged) by deans whom the abbot may appoint; thus, the same office being shared by many, no one person will become proud.

But if the needs of the place require it and the community asks for it reasonably and with humility, and the abbot judges it expedient, let the abbot himself appoint a prior—whomever he chooses, having taken counsel with God-fearing brothers.

The prior is to perform reverently whatever the abbot asks him to do, and nothing against [the abbot's] command; for the more he is elevated above the rest, the more carefully he ought to observe the precepts of the Rule.

If the prior is found to have serious failings, or is deceived by the haughtiness of pride, or proves to have contempt for the holy Rule, let him be verbally admonished up to four times; and then if he does not amend, let him be corrected by the discipline of the Rule. But if even then he does not amend, let him be deposed from the office of prior and another who is worthy be substituted in his place. If afterwards he is not quiet and obedient in the community, he is to be expelled from the monastery. Nevertheless, let the abbot bear in mind that he must give an account to God of all his judgments, lest the flame of envy or jealousy be kindled in his soul.

Comment

Benedict obviously had negative experiences with troublesome priors, and prefers to abolish the office altogether. Yet he does not quite do that. Why not?

One of the most notable characteristics of the Rule is its balance, and this chapter is a good example of that balance at work. We notice that in the last verse Benedict acknowledges the psychological truth that whenever there is severe conflict, both parties are likely to have something at stake in the issue. Under such circumstances, each party is well served by an examination of conscience (and consciousness), both about his or her contribution to the problem and about how he or she benefits by keeping it unresolved.

Benedict applies this principle to his abbot. But Benedict is gracious enough also to apply the principle to himself. He allows for the possibility that his own blindness prevents him from seeing a case where a prior might be a helpful community asset. Thus, he offers his successors freedom to make that independent judgment within their own settings.[121] Undoubtedly, this flexibility has enabled the Rule to be such an effective Christian guide for so many centuries.

Ultimately, Benedict's confidence does not rest in all these "arrangements," even though he has worked hard at them and they reflect the best of his wisdom. His confidence rests in assurance that all is in God's hands, and thus peace and love are the basic conditions of equilibrium to which things (and people) are predisposed to return. His humility is such that he is able to acknowledge the value of his work, even when he is sure he will sometimes be wrong, for even his work is in God's hands. Thus, this rule he writes can be "holy" (verse 18) because it belongs to the whole community of faith—secure in the hands of God.

Reflection

I am in awe of Benedict's confidence in God's vital presence. It involves the courage to act boldly, based on what I see, with the liberty to let all my visions go, in confidence of a truer One.

I am deeply impressed by Benedict's balance. He is so comfortable with the possibility (even probability) of "backsliding" in faith and action. Obviously, this is not just theoretical for him; he is comfortable with his own errors and weaknesses. By comfortable, I don't mean that he wallows in sinfulness. But he doesn't unduly punish himself, and he isn't particularly surprised when he falls short. He is genuinely repentant, meaning he "confesses and accepts his faults with the specific desire to change, in a spirit of peace and tranquility rather than in fear and guilt."[122] In contrast, whenever I get in touch with my faults, I am so overwhelmed by a sense of blackness and ugliness that it is hard for me to do anything other than beat myself. But Benedict helps me see that such an attitude is not genuine repentance, because it separates me from a sense of God's love and hinders my ability to grow in faith and charity.

I am moved by Benedict's way of repentance, which seems to permit him to always stay within the governing reality of God's love for him, even as he remains aware of his continuing challenge to respond to God! I realize how hungry I am for the wholeness of life Benedict models. And hunger itself is a gift for which I am grateful.

Prayer/Response

Chapter 66, The Monastery Porter
(ENTIRE)

*A*t the gate of the monastery let there be placed a wise old man, *who knows how to give and receive an answer, and whose maturity keeps him from wandering. This porter ought to have his room near the gate, so that those who arrive will always find someone at hand to give them an answer. As soon as anyone knocks or a poor man calls to him, he should answer, Thanks be to God!, or Please give me your blessing! Then with all gentleness in the fear of God, he is to answer quickly in the fervor of love. If the porter needs assistance, let him have one of the younger brothers with him.*

The monastery ought, if possible, to be so constructed that all necessities, such as water, a mill, a garden, a bakery, and the various crafts may be contained within it; thus there will be no need for the monks to wander outside, for this is not good at all for their souls.

We wish this Rule to be frequently read in the community, so that none of the brethren may excuse themselves on account of ignorance.

Comment

Several themes are interwoven in this short chapter, and they center around familiarity and routine, that is, stability. The old man will stay put; the monks should not roam; the Rule is to be read again and again.

What do we imagine is the value of stability? Do we believe it "breeds contempt" or even boredom? What positive benefits might stability carry? Why on earth (or heaven) would we give ourselves to one place and one group of people for the rest of our lives? Is this not a narrowing, a denial of the giftedness of all God's creation?

We know that stability is a crucial element in the promise the monk makes on joining the community (Chapter 58:17). Stability was a particular contribution of Benedict to the monastic vocation; it was his insight that it was central. Stability as a virtue is rooted in the concept of a sacramental world. It is based on the view that outer reality (any created outer reality) is a sign of inward grace, if deeply attended to with "all gentleness in the fear of God."

But we humans cannot give this kind of attention to anything at all if we are trying to give it to everything. We must concentrate, and focus, and be centered rather than fragmented. We must be able to wait patiently, with expectancy and love, for Christ to reveal himself in that which we behold. Stability is a precondition for attentive listening to the sacramental reality built into the structure of the world.

The monastic community is a setting designed to offer this kind of stability. In every respect, Benedict has tried to create a routine and an environment that facilitate sacramental presence. This whole section on membership and governance is an extraordinarily complex and fruitful one, because Benedict presents a number of the basic theological assumptions upon which he founds the consecrated life—as always, in the context of ordinary daily experience.

The consecrated person is one who seeks God, that is, one who responds to God's seeking him or her. The continuing questions such a person asks are: "Do I love God?" and "How does God love me?" As these questions are asked within the context of daily experience, certain perceptions emerge. The consecrated person learns to accept the present as gifted and then to offer it back to God. This acceptance and offering are undertaken with the limitations imposed by the specific setting and by human nature. Yet the daily practice of such behavior, combined with an inner expectancy to meet Christ, gradually reveals God's kingdom come.

Probably the two most lovingly drawn portraits within the Rule are those of the cellarer and the porter. This chapter contains a powerful vignette of an "old" monk, who has begun to taste the "unspeakable sweetness of love" (Prologue, verse 49) promised to those who progress in this way of life and faith. The porter's greeting to the unknown stranger, "Please give me your blessing," is telling, because "it is indisputable that a blessing is given by a superior to an inferior"

(Heb 7:7). The porter knows he is inferior to whoever might pass, because for him, the stranger truly carries Christ.

Reflection

I am reminded of one of my favorite quotations from C. S. Lewis: "The world is crowded with God. He walks everywhere incognito. And the incognito is not always hard to penetrate. The real labour is to remember, to attend. In fact, to come awake."[123]

How similar this quotation is to Benedict's comment in the Prologue that it is now time for us to rise from sleep! (verse 8). Am I awake or asleep? I guess probably mostly asleep, but how glorious are my moments of wakefulness!

As I have begun to practice stability, I find it brings great gentleness to my life. I have begun to notice and enjoy the way the sunlight shifts not only from one hour of the day to another, but from one season to another. I delight in the gradual unfolding of a new philodendron leaf. I watch with awe the slow healing of a cut on my finger. I even enjoy the predictable outbursts of adolescent rebellion in my children. I come to know things better in their true context, of ebbs and flows, of death and life, of care in the hands of the Creator.

Prayer/Response

Interlude IX
A NOTE TO THE READER

What have you learned in faithfulness to this daily process of *lectio?*

Perhaps you have realized how much less stress affects you in every area of your life because you have set aside a few moments of peace and quiet regularly in your week. Perhaps you observe that your mind and spirit seem more rested and less irritable as you attend to them regularly. Perhaps, as you have reflected on the Rule, you have recognized certain disciplines that you know to be helpful in keeping your own life centered.

Before you finish this particular process, you might want to honor it specifically by taking time to reflect on what you have discovered about what nurtures you. Then you might wish to make that discovery somewhat more formal by drafting a simple "Rule of

Life" for yourself. Benedict's Rule is a community rule. It is appropriate to supplement that by a personal rule, adopted generally for about a year at a time, to guide your own unique journey.

A personal rule should always be considered within the context of the communal Christian experience, and it may articulate or assume the corporate framework. Generally, there will always be membership in a worshiping community, involving regular commitments of time, money, and energy to that community.

But specifically, what has the Spirit pointed out as regular patterns of faithfulness that are nurturing to your spiritual life? What practices powerfully enable your deepened responsiveness to God's presence in your life? What is good for you? These are the questions a personal rule is intended to answer.

Practical considerations might involve daily, weekly, monthly, and annual rhythms. Look at not only the "spiritual" matters, such as times for prayer, scripture and *lectio*, but also at "ordinary" matters, such as regular physical exercise and mental stimulation. Don't forget the practice of charity, and simple courtesy to those who are given to you as family and friends.

A rule should be selective, containing a few important elements rather than so many items you will be burdened with "oughts." A good way to choose the important ones is to ask: What helps me develop the Spirit's dispositions of love, joy, peace, gentleness, kindness, and so on? (Gal. 5:22). Another way to ask this question is to inquire: What nurtures me? Pick one or two things and give them to yourself as a way of valuing the person you are in God's eyes. Then, watch with awe.

A Few Final
Guidelines for the
Consecrated Life

Chapter 67, Those Who
Are Sent on a Journey
(ENTIRE)

Brothers who are about to be sent on a journey should commend themselves to the prayers of all the brethren and of the abbot; and always, at the last prayer of the Work of God, all the absent should be remembered. The brethren who return from a journey should, on the very day they come back, lie prostrate on the floor of the oratory at all the canonical hours at the ending of the Work of God; they request the prayers of all on account of their transgressions, in case they have seen or heard anything evil on their journey, or have fallen into idle talk.

No one may presume to tell others what he may have seen or heard outside the monastery, for from this comes great destruction. If any so presumes, he is to be subjected to the punishment of the Rule. Also, he shall undergo a like penalty who presumes to leave the enclosure of the monastery, to go anywhere or do anything however small, without permission of the abbot.

Comment

There is some evidence that Chapter 66 was a primitive conclusion of the Rule. However, it is generally agreed that these final chapters are also the work of Benedict, perhaps as an "afterthought." Thus, these last chapters are Benedict's reminders of important points he has neglected so far or wishes to emphasize. They can also be read as succinct summaries-by-example of some foundational elements of monastic life.

This chapter deepens the lesson about the value of stability. It emphasizes that stability involves not only not wandering with the body, but also not wandering with the eyes or ears, the memory, or the imagination. Here Benedict makes an important distinction between the quality of the created order as such, and the problem of the human spirit's response to multiplicity.

The created order is God's and therefore essentially good. Because this is so, brothers may be sent into the world for reasonable and important matters, and strangers from the world may be welcomed into the monastery. There is a natural interface, and indeed interdependence, between the created world and the committed Christian. But the Christian's primary goal is to seek God and to respond to God as God is revealed in creation and elsewhere. Such seeking and responding must set the context for and order one's relationships within the material world.

It is the long experience of those who seek God that the ear or eye that takes in everything finds nothing. Discovery of the sacrament within is a matter of discipline and discernment: it involves allowing our deepest longing to become central so that peripheral or superficial longings may drop away. A sacramental presence involves a deliberate decision not to be captured in the merely superficial in favor of a commitment to union with the ultimate within the daily. Such decisions are most effectively made within the stability of a community sharing that commitment.

Reflection

So often I allow my curiosity to draw me away from my center. Oddly enough, "the news" is one major source of temptation to me. I was reflecting this morning on how little of the "morning TV news" is about anything real. So little context is given from which to understand events; there is so little time for sacramental attention to situations. I often find too large a dose of thirty-second news disorienting.

Another way my curiosity pulls me away from my center is gossip. I realize there are many times when I ask about people simply to be titillated by random details. Usually this is true of the media folk-heroes, but often enough it is true about people in my parish or my club. "Is Jane still going around with that terrible fellow?" is seldom a question I ask out of prayerful concern. These discrepancies become more severe as I am privileged to know what it is to meet the world and the people in it from the vantage point of deep prayer.

Prayer/Response

Chapter 68, Those Who Are Commanded to Do the Impossible
(ENTIRE)

*I*f *a brother is commanded things that are hard or impossible, he should accept the order of his superior with all gentleness and obedience. But if he sees that the burden completely exceeds his strength, he should lay before his superior the reasons for his incapacity, patiently and at a fitting time, without showing pride, resistance, or contradiction. If, however, after these explanations the superior still persists in his command, the subject must know that this is best for him; and he is to obey out of love, trusting in the help of God.*

Comment

This chapter (exploring obedience and humility in a specific context) is surely one of the strongest and most important chapters in the Rule, because it makes utterly clear the radical nature of the consecrated life. Radical means "at the root," and we see here that the Christian's transformation is to extend to the deepest center of his or her being.

The monk is to do "the impossible." He is to accept it, meaning to undertake it, in the same way implied by the Hebrew verb "to hear," meaning already-to-be-in-response. Truly to accept is already to be doing.

And yet, in the doing, we may discover that we have passed beyond our strength. In a sense, this is the prototypical Christian situation. We always find ourselves acting as if transformation were implicit, ready to be released in ourselves and in others, as we sense that we are being utter fools for Christ: we have no true personal power to do that which we intend and desire. And yet, there is also a deep sense of the rightness of this action; it is best for us in some mysterious way. How are we to proceed?

Benedict gives us a summary model of how to be obedient in difficult situations:

1. First, listen. Listen to our superior—to whatever has been given us to do. Listen to the situation—to the nature of the environ-

ment in which the task is set. Listen to ourselves—to what information is provided by our bodies and our psyches.

2. Next, state clearly and fairly how we see the situation. Honor ourselves enough to recognize the value of what we have heard from these sources, and present our view with clarity and openness. The actual statement or presentation may be made only to ourselves (and God) in a journal, or to a spiritual director, or may actually be made to our superior. In any case, at some point, we need to face clearly how we see things and seek to make whatever adjustments seem appropriate.

3. Finally, accept and submit to what is required! Generally, in our modern culture we tend to omit either step two or step three. Seldom do we consider combining them. Among other things, step three seems unfair, unjust, and maybe irrational. But this sequence contains a fundamental insight of Benedict's about when God's power is most effectively released into the world: when a just man goes to the cross. Or when "(we) obey out of love" in the life situation given to us this day.

Reflection

I resonate with the image suggested by the Latin word translated "gentleness." The word is *mansuetudine,* meaning "accustomed to the hand," and refers to training wild animals.[124] I have a vivid sense of a small colt, standing shivering in cold and excitement as an attentive trainer approaches and gently caresses it. I often feel that way in the presence of God: fearful and shivering both with anxiety and eagerness, but willing myself to do all I can to respond, which is often simply not to run away. Instead, I tremble, and await the hand that touches me in love.

Perhaps this is often the way of obedience.

Prayer/Response

Chapter 69, Monks May Not Presume to Defend One Another in the Monastery

AND

Chapter 70, Monks May Not Presume to Strike One Another at Will

*T*he greatest care must be taken that no one in the monastery presumes for any reason to defend another or to take his part, even
*if they are closely related to one another by ties of blood. The monks must
not presume to do this in any way whatsoever, because the most grievous
occasions of scandals may arise from this. If anyone transgresses this rule,
let him be very severely punished.*

*[Chapter 70] In order that in the monastery every occasion of pre-
sumption may be avoided, we ordain and decree that it is not lawful for
anyone to excommunicate or strike any of his brothers, unless he is given
power do to so by the abbot. Those who sin shall be reproved before all,
that the rest may have fear (1 Tim 5:20).*

*Children, however, are to be kept under diligent and watchful discipline
by all until their fifteenth year: yet this too is to be done with all measure
and discretion. For if anyone presumes, without permission of the abbot, to
chastise those who are above that age, or shows undue severity even to the
children, he is to be subjected to the discipline of the Rule; for it is written:
Do not do to another what you would not have done to yourself (Tob 4:16).*

Comment

These two chapters reveal an essential element of monastic (Christian) formation. They convey an important image about one of the
central dynamics of life in Christ: conversion of heart.

As always, the first level of awareness is the material or physical.
The chapters go hand in hand, and in combination make clear the
instruction: neither take the side of, nor side against, one of your
brothers and sisters in Christ, in any matter of conflict. Neither
defend nor strike.

Why not? In part, because it is the abbot's prerogative, but more
deeply because the abbot stands in the place of Christ, who is drawing that person daily toward deeper union with God. The bystander's

observation of the issues involved may be quite wrong; indeed, it may seem things are directly opposed to what is needed for a friend's health at that moment.

The inward reality is that each person stands naked before God, in the essential particularity and uniqueness of their relationship at that moment. The Christian life is to facilitate that relationship with God in Christ. The abbot and the person him- or herself are the only ones close enough to understand how the relationship with Christ will best be deepened at this moment. No one else can take the essential steps of the spiritual life for us. No one can "carry the lamp oil" for us (Matt 25:1–13). No one dare take away from us the good portion we have chosen (Luke 10:42).

Benedict cites Tobit for the third time in the Rule (see also Chapters 4:9 and 61:4). We may perhaps see his intention best by noting its context in Chapter 4, where it immediately follows the phrase "honor everyone." The intention of the quotation is to emphasize that we are to have the deepest regard for each person's life in Christ. We are to be aware that for each of us, life in Christ is the fountain of *conversatione*/the monastic way of life/ongoing conversion of heart. Above all, Christ in us is to be cherished, that our life might be daily recreated in him.

Reflection

One of my earliest memories is desiring to defend my baby brother from what I thought was unjust criticism. Not too many years later, I was forced to cease reading to him, because he had not needed to learn to read for himself. I love my brother deeply and we are very close, but I think in both instances, I was "stealing" from him the chance to be his own person in experiences that tested and strengthened him. I still struggle with the great desire to "do for" others what rightly they can only do for themselves.

This is a twin-headed monster. On the one hand, out of my supposed loving and caring, I am denying others opportunities to interact creatively with their own lives: to develop their own strengths, to realize the value of their own weaknesses, to undertake their own privileged response of formation. Benedict teaches me that conflicts or difficulties or sufferings are always opportunities to choose Christ. Thus, I see that it is a privilege to respond to them, and I as an outsider have no right to intrude.

On the other hand, I realize too that my preoccupation with other people's issues is a neat way to avoid my own problems. By directing my energies outside me, I can pretend that I have no issues or problems of my own that are giving me the opportunity to choose Christ in my life. Even if I am aware of the need to deal with my interior issues, I may manage never to have the time because I am always busy with the care of others.

It's not easy to learn how to "be with" others emotionally. I hope, as a member of Christ's body, to be vulnerable and interdependent. Like everyone, I need the love and care of others, their support and assistance. But I also need to do the work given to me to do, and I must let others proceed to do their own work at their own pace. That way, each of us learns not only to do our own work, but also to ask for help as we discover it is needed. To be human is to be utterly alone and unique, while also to be wonderfully connected and supported. I suspect it takes a lifetime of trial and error to manage a contentment in the midst of tension with those two apparently distinct realities.

Prayer/Response

Chapter 71, They Should Obey One Another
(ENTIRE)

*N*ot only is the blessing of obedience to be shown by all to the abbot; the brethren must also obey one another, knowing that by this path of obedience they go to God. The commands, therefore, of the abbot or the superiors appointed by him (to which we allow no unofficial orders to be preferred) are to be given precedence. For the rest let all the younger brothers obey their elders with all love and courtesy. Anyone who is found to be quarrelsome is to be corrected.

If anyone is rebuked by the abbot or by any superior in any way for however small a cause, or if he comes to believe that any superior is angered or perplexed about him, however trivially; he should immediately and without delay cast himself on the ground at his feet, remaining there to do penance until the turmoil is healed by the other's blessing. But if any one is too haughty to do this, he should be subjected to corporal punishment: if he remains unyielding, he must be expelled from the monastery.

Comment

Is it true that we are all one in Christ? (Chapter 2:20; Gal 3:28). Is it true that Christ is to be found in each one of our brothers and sisters, and that when we truly listen to each other we are listening to God? (Chapter 5:6, 15). Here Benedict is making clear what he has suggested throughout the Rule, that not only is Christ found in the abbot, but Christ is found in all our brothers and sisters. This is a radical extension of the thought in Benedict's time; it is a startling idea in our own. Yet, as we consider it, we realize it flows naturally from the sacramental orientation toward the world: the outer form of created life always and everywhere reveals and leads to the deeper inner reality that is God.

If this is true—that Christ is present in all our brothers and sisters—then what should our attitude be toward them? Obedience. Deep, attentive listening. Expectancy. Obedience to one another is an important way to God, because as we listen attentively to one another, God is revealed in our interaction.

But to say that Christ is present in all is not just to say Christ is present in everyone else. It is also to acknowledge Christ present within ourselves. Each of us is called to deepen our participation in the mind of Christ, who dwells in us. This is what enables us to cast ourselves at another's feet, even as Jesus humbled himself utterly before us (even us!) (Phil 2:5–11).

True, it takes considerable humility for the young monk to cast himself at the feet of an elder he may have offended. But we can be sure that Benedict is not unaware of the humility required from the "offended one" who is subsequently obliged to allow himself to be sufficiently calmed to offer his blessing with generous heart. In such humble exchanges, we are privileged to see with greater clarity the radiance of Christ shining forth.

Reflection

Early in our marriage, my husband taught me about seeing the emerging beauty in another person. He "taught" me by the way in which he did that for me. He listened carefully to me, and then he marveled at the growth of loveliness in me, which I was often less able to see than he was! It was not that he saw his own "agenda" being fulfilled in me: he genuinely saw and responded to an emergent beauty in me in a way that helped me be more faithful to that beauty in myself. What a glorious gift that was and is to me.

I think this sort of thing is what obedience to another person must mean. I see that obedience in this sense is a powerful way to release reconciliation and transformation into our human experience of brokenness. I pray that I will more and more learn to give and receive this gift of seeing and releasing Christ in the ordinary people who are my daily companions.

Prayer/Response

Chapter 72, The Good Zeal Which Monks Ought to Have
(ENTIRE)

*J*ust as there is an evil zeal of bitterness which separates from God *and leads to hell, so there is a good zeal which separates from vices and leads to God and to life everlasting. This zeal then, should be practiced by monks with the most fervent love. That is: they should outdo one another in showing honor (Rom 12:10). Let them most patiently endure one another's infirmities, whether of body or of character. Let them compete in showing obedience to one another. None should follow what he judges useful for himself, but rather what is better for another: they should practice fraternal charity with a pure love, to God offering loving reverence, loving their abbot with sincere and humble affection, preferring nothing whatever to Christ; and may God bring us all together to life everlasting. Amen.*

Comment

Substantively, this is the last chapter of the Rule, the next and final one having the quality of a postscript on the author's purpose. So here are Benedict's final words to us on the consecrated life, his summary of what we are about.

What Benedict does not say is often as interesting as what he does say. If we were to describe the "good zeal," that is, the eager and earnest desire of our hearts that will lead us to God, what might we say? Very likely, we would frame some statement such as "loving God with our whole beings." Unquestionably, that is what Benedict intends, but he understands it to be lived by showing respect for one another. Yet again, Benedict directs our thoughts to something that seems very simple, but which is profoundly transforming if we begin to live it.

For Benedict, God "bring[s] us all together" to everlasting life; salvation is not an individual project, but one we undertake with and among our brothers and sisters in Christ. We work out our salvation not only in fear and trembling, but also in community. It is in our care for, and interaction with, one another that we become the body of Christ, now and forever. That is why Romans 12:10 and the other ethical portions of Paul's letters and Matthew's gospel and the Old Testament Wisdom literature are so central to Benedict's thought in the Rule. Salvation is near at hand! Our goal as Christians is daily growth into seeing and responding to Christ present in the midst of us.

That is why preferring Christ is something we are able to do, in hundreds of ways, each and every day, no matter what our setting. We are given daily choices to accept the love present implicitly in every portion of the created world by abandoning our self-will in favor of that purity of the heart that knows itself to be the recipient of God. The movement toward Christ, in heart and mind and soul and spirit, within daily ordinariness—that is the whole goal and the whole longing of the Rule.

Reflection

Yet again the simplicity and accessibility of the Rule causes me to catch my breath in wonder. Benedict helps me see that living the gospel life is something I can do today, within the setting and among the persons right in front of me. Christ present in the situation draws me; Christ present in my heart and soul helps me respond.

Sometimes as I have meditated the Rule I have wished Benedict would make it more difficult than this, so I would have better excuses for not doing today the simple things that are possible for me to do. But by and large I am thrilled and delighted with the discovery that the little details of my life matter so very much, and that I can respond to such a worthy calling simply by taking up my day today, supported by my brothers and sisters in Christ.

Prayer/Response

Chapter 73, The Whole of Observance Is Not Contained in This Rule
(ENTIRE)

We have written this Rule in order that, observing it in monasteries, we may show that in some measure we have goodness of virtue and a beginning of monastic life. But for those who are hastening to the perfection of monastic life there are the teachings of the holy Fathers, the observance of which brings one to the heights of perfection. For what page or what word is there in the divinely inspired books of the Old and New Testaments that is not a most accurate rule for human life? Or what book of the holy catholic Fathers does not loudly proclaim how we may by a straight course reach our Creator? Moreover, the Conferences of the Fathers, their Institutes and their Lives, and the Rule of our holy Father Basil—what else are these but examples for observant and obedient monks, and instruments of virtue? But to us who are slothful, unobservant and negligent, they bring the blush of shame.

Whoever, therefore, you are who hasten towards your heavenly country, fulfill with the aid of Christ this little Rule for beginners which we have set forth; and then at last you shall arrive, under God's protection, at the lofty summits of doctrine and virtue of which we have spoken here. Amen

Comment

For some time we have been engaged with this Rule, and have found it an intense and earnest manual for the practical living out of a life consecrated to God. We cannot help but wonder if Benedict is not being somewhat coy here by describing the Rule as "only a beginning." But perhaps we can discover his meaning by considering the following:

1. Much of the Rule is synthesized from other sources. Benedict did not intend to do a "new thing" or make an "original" creation in the Rule. His primary intent was synthetic in the best sense of that word. He sought to gather ideas from the patristic writers, scripture, and tradition into a simple guide for daily life. His goal was always to be pointing elsewhere and onward, to fix the monastic's eyes on Christ. In a sense, Benedict is emphasizing that goal here: inviting the monastic to go on from this "secondary" sourcebook to the originals, perusing them in greater depth for the work of the heart.

2. In the Rule, Benedict describes aspects of a quality of life summarized in the phrase "some degree of virtue."[125] The phrase refers to the formation into the mind of Christ that is a lifelong process, enabled by lived familiarity with spiritual and communal disciplines, and involving ever more wholehearted inner receptiveness and response to God's Spirit. It is not like a racetrack, the simple completion of a circuit. It is an ongoing and ever deepening work. The Rule began with an exhortation to earnestly engage in such a life, and that exhortation is renewed here at the end.

Even the words of this chapter are both echoes of and invitations to deepen the words of the Prologue: "Today if you hear his voice, harden not your hearts" (verse 10). Whole observance, as used in the title of this chapter, means something like "fullness of justice," and evokes another phrase from the Prologue: "the one who may dwell in the Lord's temple is the one who works justice" (verse 25). And the phrase from this chapter, "you who hasten towards your heavenly country," is a recalling of the Prologue's discussion of "resting on the holy mountain" (verse 22).

So, the work of the consecrated life is like that of a spiral, or perhaps the three-dimensional helix, ever returning to the beginning to enter more fully into the dwelling of the Lord. In that sense, no matter where we are, we are always just beginning our relationship with Christ.

Reflection

I am reminded of a meditative exercise in which one slowly counts from one to ten, with a full inhalation and exhalation for each number. It is intended as an exercise in concentration, so that the meditator is advised that each time any thought other than the present number enters his or her mind, he or she is to go back and begin again at the number one. But it becomes a spiritual exercise when the meditator realizes that the purpose is not to reach the number ten, but to be willing to begin over and over at number one.

So in my life with Christ, I must begin again and again: that is my work. But the great miracle is that I do not do it alone. Each time I begin again with humility and generosity, Christ rises up to greet me in a new and radically transforming way. And by some miracle not of my own making, I pray I will at last arrive into the depths of love. Amen.

Prayer/Response

An Afterword: The End; The Beginning

If you have completed the journey traveled by this book, then you will have been both encouraged and challenged as you followed the way. Encouraged by the nearness of Christ which the Rule points us towards—indeed God is everywhere and all is holy—but challenged in that to be lived rightly, the Christian life is fulfilled in the relationships upon which the community depends. God both confronts us in everything and cries out for our response in everybody.

Sixth-century wisdom, compiled for the good order and discipline of religious in community, is shown as wisdom indeed when its elements are extended to the wider relevance of any Christian's ordinary way of life. The clue to this discovery is the ancient and yet largely forgotten art of *lectio divina*. This book is in itself a wonderful and effective example of this method. Use *lectio divina* now in your own daily life.

The "text" is before you—in the one you love, in the hurt you suffer, in the joy which lifts you, in the disappointment which drains you. Of such things is the "text" of life comprised.

"Read" the text, in the face of others, in the world of nature, and in the circumstances that build up around you. Having "read," proceed to the applied work of understanding. Your "comment" will be formed by the perspectives that informed understanding gives. Then you will be rightly placed to "reflect"—with God, to relate what is before you to yourself personally. From that relationship flows your "response," presented to God in the affirming openness of your prayer. It is a "response" which will become increasingly wordless and still, in a simple, contemplative offering of yourself.

Texts from the Psalms and the Gospels and the Epistles bubble up all around us as we read the Rule. They indicate to us how behind the one "text" lies another—that of Holy Scripture. Extended Biblical study will show up "texts" behind that. The Rule is a rich deposit, laid down in the evolution of practical, spiritual wisdom.

Norvene Vest's very special contribution has been to give us a stepping-stone, itself very richly made up of clues and understandings. We can use this stepping-stone to bring ourselves within a sustaining tradition that represents a way of Christian life characterized by realism and balance. The stepping-stone is one we can use in two directions. We can step backwards into the Rule itself or we can step forward into its enlightening of our own day-to-day growth.

There is, of course, the originally intended setting in which we can find the Rule being worked through and realized—that of a Benedictine community itself. We can go to those communities as visitors and retreatants, to find some space for ourselves. We can "belong," as members in the world, by becoming oblates. Such a step carries with it formalized obligations and commitment—things we all need anyway as we face up to the journey of life which follows the steps of our Lord and Master.

That of course is not for all. But anyone who has worked this book to the end will have been touched by the Rule indelibly. Again and again we will come back to it—we will come back, as well, to the wealth of exposition Norvene Vest has given us.

Listen, carefully, my son to the master's instructions, and attend to them with the ear of your heart . . . (RB Prologue 1).

Peter Brett
(Retired) Canon Residentiary of Canterbury Cathedral

References/Notes

Introduction

1. Fr. Luke's translation is based in part on a version of the Rule prepared in 1921 by Dom Justin McCann, O.S.B., which accompanied the first English edition of the *Commentary on the Rule of St. Benedict* by Dom Paul Delatte, O.S.B. In cases of doubtful readings, he consulted the critical edition of the Latin text of the Rule, *La Regle de Saint Benoit*, edited by Adelbert de Vogue and Jean Neufville in *Sources Chretiennes* (Paris: *Les Editions du Cerf*, 1971–72), volumes 1–7.

2. This is a phrase used by Helen Luke of Dante's *Divine Comedy* in her book, *Dark Wood to White Rose* (Pecos, NM: Dove Publications, 1975), 5.

Prologue

3. Throughout the commentary, I have not sought to discuss and compare sources, so there is no effort, for example, to attribute certain sections of the Rule of Benedict to the Rule of the Master. Other sources deal with that subject far more fully than would be appropriate for this treatment. I note here simply that most contemporary scholarship assumes that Benedict chose to take much of his prologue directly from the so-called Rule of the Master, translated by Luke Eberle, OSB (Kalamazoo, MI: Cistercian Publications, 1977), and yet abbreviated the RM substantially. I believe it was because of Benedict's practical interest that he selected what RM calls "the performance of our service" as his primary concern in the RB Prologue.

4. For other references to salvation in the Rule, see RB 4:46, 5:3, 25:3–4, and elsewhere.

5. See indications of good desires in RB 49:6 and 61:5.

6. C. S. Lewis, *The Problem of Pain* (London: Collins Fontana Books, 1957), 64.

7. See Jean Leclerq, OSB, *The Love of Learning and the Desire for God,* trans. Catharine Misrahi (London: SPCK, 1978), esp. chap. 5, "Sacred Learning," for a deeper discussion of this method of "scripture by heart."

8. See RB 1980: *The Rule of St. Benedict in Latin and English with Notes* (henceforth called simply RB 1980), ed. Timothy Fry, OSB (Collegeville, MN: Liturgical Press, 1981), for more detail on the importance of this phrase "to see God" in shaping monastic life; see esp. 34–40 and the note on 160–61.

9. Indeed, Benedict is so conscious of the recent Arian controversy that he never uses the name "Jesus" without adding "Christ" or "Lord." See Jean Leclerq, OSB, "The Problem of Social Class and Christology in Saint Benedict," *Word and Spirit,* vol. 2 (Still River, MA: St. Bede's Publications, 1981), esp. 33 and 42.

10. At first it may seem repugnant to think of being used by anyone, even God. But the word is curiously apt if we understand it as rooted in its earliest agricultural meaning. The Latin, *utor,* was a term that originally would have been applied to a fertile field where the soil was rich and the crops would be abundant. So, that which is "used" is fecund, fruitful, and capable of being enjoyed by one who has need of it.

Foundational Matters

11. "Appendix 1: "Monastic Terminology: Monk, Cenobite, Nun," RB 1980, 319.

12. A good modern interpretation of this "battle" is presented in Tad Dunne's extrapolation of the methods of St. Ignatius of Loyola in *Review for Religious* 45, no. 5 (September/October 1986): 709.

13. Wilfred Tunink, *Vision of Peace* (New York: Farrar, Strauss, 1963), 307–8.

14. For details on this shift in the tradition and in Benedict's treatment of it, see RB 1980, 356–63.

15. Compare this with St. Paul's thought in 1 Cor. 4:15–16.

16. For elaboration of this point, see RB 1980, 325–26.

17. George MacDonald, *The Marquis' Secret,* ed. Michael Phillips (Minneapolis: Bethany House, 1982), 143–45.

18. Notice too that Benedict has not included the Fifth Commandment: Honor thy Father and Mother, but has instead added at the end the phrase from 1 Peter, translated "honor everyone." The family here has become greatly extended, because in Benedict's family everyone is kindred in Christ.

19. This wonderful definition of fasting is from a presentation by Dr. Paul Ford at St. Andrew's Abbey on July 12, 1989, during the Benedictine Spirituality for Laity workshop on "Work and Prayer."

20. There is an excellent modern psychological treatment of this daily "training of the will" presented in Roberto Assagioli's work, esp. "Exercise

of the Will in Daily Life," *Psychosynthesis* (New York: Penguin Books, 1965), 133–36.

21. In addition to these two main citations, the preference for the love of Christ occurs another time in Chapter 4 (verse 72: "pray for your enemies out of love for Christ"); in Chapter 7 on Humility (verse 69: "no longer out of fear of hell, but out of love for Christ"); in Chapter 63 (verse 13: the abbot is called father "out of honor and love for Christ"); and indirectly in Chapter 5 on Obedience (verse 1: "obedience, which comes naturally to those who cherish Christ above all"). Meditation on these citations might help give deeper dimension to Benedict's meaning of the phrase "preferring Christ."

22. Benedict refers to Christ as "Lord" at least thirty-seven times in the Rule. For a further discussion of Christ's titles in the Rule, see the thematic index in RB 1980, 560.

23. C. S. Lewis, *Perelandra* (New York: Macmillan, 1944), 68–69: "One joy was expected and another is given. . . . You could refuse the real good; you could make the real fruit taste insipid by thinking of the other."

24. See also RB 19:1 and 7:13 for explicit acknowledgment of this principle.

25. The term is used here as it is used by William James in *Varieties of Religious Experience* (New York: Collier, 1961), meaning those souls whose basic experience of life tends to be tragic. See esp. chaps. 6 and 7; for the terminology once- and twice-born, see p. 80.

26. Pope St. Gregory the Great, *Life and Miracles of St. Benedict,* Bk. 2 of the *Dialogues,* trans. Odo J. Zimmermann, OSB, and Benedict R. Avery, OSB (Collegeville, MN: Liturgical Press), 46–47.

27. Leclerq, *The Love of Learning and the Desire for God,* 94.

28. For example, there is the suggestion that the beautiful Song of Zechariah (Luke 1:68–79), used daily in the morning office of Lauds was made possible because of the enforced silence and contemplation required of Zechariah between the visit from the angel Gabriel and the birth of his son John. Patrick O'Connell, "Worth Pondering," *Living Prayer* 20, no. 6 (November/December 1987): 13.

29. An excellent study of silence and word in the Rule is Ambrose G. Wathen, OSB, *Silence: The Meaning of Silence in the Rule of St. Benedict* (Washington, DC: Cistercian Publications/Consortium Press, 1973). See esp. pp. 195–97 and 230 on the matter of normal discourse among monks.

Monastic Virtues

30. The earlier citations can be found in the Prologue and in Chapter 2 (*lectio* segments on the Prologue, verses 1–2, and Chapter 2, verses 6–10).

31. See RB 1980, note on 187.

32. See also the *lectio* segment on Chapter 4, verses 59–61.

33. Benedict does allow some specific checks on obedience: those of the abbot's own accountability to Christ, as noted in Chapter 2, and the importance of the Rule as known by all the monks as a countervailing influence to the abbot's power. In addition, Benedict omits the passage from the Rule of the Master 2:36–37 that allows monks to impute all actions done under obedience to their superior at the last judgment. See RB 1980, 187.

34. John Cassian (d. 435) wrote *The Institutes* and *The Conferences*, cited by Benedict in RB Chapter 73. (See notes 57 and 124.) Dom Cuthbert Butler indicates that we "must look to Cassian for Benedict's 'system' of the spiritual life." *Benedictine Monachism* (London: Longmans, Green, 1919), 47.

35. As cited earlier, one modern psychologist has done some fascinating work on the will as the "unknown and neglected factor in modern psychology, [even though] . . . the will is the function which is most directly related to the [authentic] self." His description of the training of the will sounds like a page taken out of Benedict's Rule! Assagioli, *Psychosynthesis*, esp. 125–36.

36. See *lectio* segment on Chapter 4, verses 39–40.

37. Wathen, *Silence*.

38. See in particular RB 1980, notes on pp. 186 and 193. Another good source is Emmanuel Heufelder, OSB, *The Way to God, According to the Rule of Saint Benedict*, trans. Luke Eberle, OSB (Kalamazoo, MI: Cistercian Publications, 1983), who uses Chapter 7 of the Rule as the basis for his entire commentary on the Rule. See esp. 116–17 on this point.

39. Note, too, that tradition associates this psalm (114) with David's sorrow as his first child of Bathsheba, conceived in sin, is dying after Nathan's prophecy to David and his admission of guilt.

40. See my *Desire for Life* on the role and importance of desire in the Rule of St. Benedict and in the modern world.

41. Benedict has taken this quotation from the Rule of the Master, whose source was the *Acta Anastasiae* 17.

42. For a fuller exploration of this "inner necessity" in modern terms, see Paul Ricoeur, *Phenomenology of Will and Action* (Pittsburgh, PA: Duquesne University Press, 1967).

43. See *lectio* segment on Chapter 4, verses 59–61, and Chapter 5, verses 1–9.

44. See note in RB 1980, 198.

45. Carl Sagan, *Contact* (New York: Pocketbooks, 1985), 209–10.

46. The phrases "dark night of the spirit" and "dark night of the soul" are, of course, taken from the work of St. John of the Cross. They seem to have been appropriated willy-nilly in modern language to refer to any opacity in understanding or experience.

47. Jim Wallis, *The Call to Conversion* (San Francisco, CA: Harper & Row, 1981), 100–107.

The Daily Office

48. Ernest Becker, *The Denial of Death* (New York: Free Press/Macmillan, 1973), 3–34, 51, 58.

49. Throughout the text I have used the Hebrew numbering of the Psalms, which is the normal usage in most modern Bibles. In contrast, Benedict and the RB 1980, for example, generally use the Vulgate numbering. So the reader who meditates these psalms along with Benedict will have to check the normal usage in his or her own devotional source.

50. David Parry, OSB, *Households of God* (London: Darton, Longman, & Todd, 1980), 56.

51. To see how the hours for the offices are established from this "timetable," see note 55 below. For additional details on this and other elements of the Daily Office, see the helpful appendix entitled "The Liturgical Code in the Rule of Benedict" in RB 1980, esp. 409–10.

52. RB 1980, 388. The Syrian manual called the *Apostolic Constitutions* invites and exhorts the faithful to this celebration with these words: "[G]ive praise to God, who made the universe through Jesus, sent him to us, permitted him to suffer and raised him from the dead. For what excuse will a person make to God if he fails to assemble on that day to hear the saving word concerning the resurrection?"

53. Charles Cummings, OSCO, *Monastic Practices* (Kalamazoo, MI: Cistercian Publications, 1986), 39.

54. Much of the analysis which follows is suggested by Parry, *Households of God*, 60–61.

55. Parry, *Households of God*, commentary on Chapter 15 of the RB.

56. As mentioned in the *lectio* segment for Chapter 10, in Benedict's time the secular day was divided into two twelve-hour periods, from sundown to sunup, and sunup to sundown. "Prime" (or first) refers to the first hour of the day period (or just after sunup), "Terce" (or third) to the third hour, and so on for the other Latin designations. Thus, the "actual" hours of the daily offices were approximately as follows:

Vigils (2 a.m.)	Sext (noon)
Lauds (shortly after Vigils)	None (about 3 p.m.)
Prime (about 6 a.m., dawn)	Vespers (dusk)
Terce (about 9 a.m.)	Compline (before bed)

57. The source here is Parry, *Households of God*, commentary on Chapter 16 of the RB.

58. Benedict's key source, Cassian, has a lengthy dialogue on the power of the short prayer from Psalm 70:1: "Lord, come to my assistance." See John Cassian, *Conferences* (New York: Paulist Press, 1985), esp. Conference 10 with Abba Isaac, 132. Predecessors of the "Jesus Prayer" ("Jesus/Lord, have mercy") were also well known to the desert fathers, tending to be more highly developed in the Eastern Church, as in the Philokalia. A more recent discussion of this prayer and its use is presented in Anonymous, *The Way of a Pilgrim* (New York: Doubleday/Image, 1978).

59. Francis de Sales, *Introduction to the Devout Life* (New York: Doubleday/Image, 1950), 56.

60. Parry, *Households of God*, commentary on Chapter 19 of the RB.

61. Discipline can mean a variety of things in the Rule; prominent among them is the forming of interior disposition. For a study of these and related themes in the Rule, see "Discipline" in the thematic index of RB 1980, 561. As a helpful supplementary study and devotional guide to the Rule, the thematic index of RB 1980 is a marvelous resource.

62. Heufelder, *The Way to God*, 153–54.

63. See Parry, *Households of God*, in his commentary on Chapter 20; and Butler, *Benedictine Monachism*, and esp. chap. 6, "Benedict's Teaching on Prayer," 58.

64. It may be that Benedict is recollecting a moment like this while he writes this chapter, thus accounting for the almost poetic cadences of the Latin text. See RB 1980, 100.

Disciplines of Community

65. For further details on these origins, see RB 1980, esp. notes on 216–17.

66. See Cummings, *Monastic Practices*, chap. 11, "The Monastic Cell," beginning on p. 154, and note regarding John Baptist Hasbrouck, 214–15.

67. See for example the Episcopal Book of Common Prayer, pp. 99 and 123–24, as well as the Compline service in that book on p. 133. As noted earlier, this document is solidly rooted in the Benedictine influences on the English Church.

68. The wonderment was initially expressed by Adalbert de Vogue, *The Rule of Saint Benedict* (Kalamazoo, MI: Cistercian Publications, 1983), chap. 11, 185. In something of an overreaction, an alternative position is well presented by Julian Stead, OSB, "The Penal Code of St. Benedict," *Word and Spirit*, vol. 6 (Still River, MA: St. Bede's Publications, 1984), 58–68.

69. On this point, see Dom Justin McCann, *St. Benedict* (London: Sheed & Ward, 1938), 139.

70. See Stead, "The Penal Code," 59.

71. See the discussion in RB 1980, 421–26, on Benedict's theory of excommunication and salvation as rooted in many of the Pauline letters.

72. See Stead, "The Penal Code," esp. 65.

73. For reference, see the earlier *lectio* segments on Chapter 4:41–43, 74; and Chapter 7:49–50, 62–66.

74. Stead, "The Penal Code," 67.

75. See RB 1980, 100–101.

76. See RB 1980, 430.

77. See RB 1980, 225.

78. Compare, for interest's sake, the stages of moral development outlined in such modern authors as Kohlberg. In particular, notice his "Preconventional Level, Stage I Compliance" category, in which response to authority is chiefly on the basis of force or simple rewards and punishments. Lawrence Kohlberg, *Essays in Moral Development* (San Francisco: Harper & Row, 1984).

79. See for example the Rule of the Master, chap. 14, verses 78–87. The Rule of the Master was Benedict's major textual source, as we have noted, and this brief passage should in no way be construed as characterizing its whole tone and direction.

Domestic Arrangements

80. RB 1980, 226.

81. Very possibly Benedict's thought on this passage was shaped in part by Augustine's (see his Epistle 211:5 and 9), RB 1980, 604.

82. For support of this statement, see Daniel Rees et al., *Consider Your Call* (Kalamazoo, MI: Cistercian Publications, 1980), 59–60, and RB 1980, 167. For an opposing view, see de Vogue, *The Rule of Saint Benedict*, 65–66.

83. For a particularly good brief discussion of the monastic custom of dishwashing as a sacrament, see Cummings, *Monastic Practices*, 82–83.

84. See the *lectio* segments on Chapters 17 and 18.

85. See also Benedict's Chapter 4:15–16 and Chapter 53:1.

86. See esp. Matthew 5:46, 6:1, 7:11, and so forth.

87. For more discussion of these practices, see Tunink, *Vision of Peace*, note 12, 104; as well as Dom David Knowles, *The Monastic Order in England* (Cambridge: University Press, 1949), 688; and Basil Hume, OSB, *Searching for God* (London: Hodder & Stoughton, 1977), 150.

88. See Wathen, *Silence*, esp. 165–72.

89. Eucharist is seldom mentioned in the Rule, probably because it was assumed. There were not necessarily any priests in the monastery, so Mass itself might be infrequent, but daily Communion was probably the norm. For more detail on this point, see RB 1980, 410–12.

90. "We read" apparently refers to the *Lives of the Fathers*. See RB 1980, 241.

91. Esther de Waal, *Seeking God* (Collegeville, MN: Liturgical Press, 1984), 72. This book is a very fine introduction to Benedict's thought for the contemporary layperson.

92. Wathen, *Silence,* esp. 30, 97, 168, and 179.

Lukewarmness and Its Remedies

93. Parry, *Households of God*, in his introduction to these chapters of the Rule.

94. See esp. Augustine's *The Lord's Sermon on the Mount*, trans. John J. Jepson (Westminster, MD: Newman Press, 1948), p. 43, in which he sets forth three steps in the commission of sin: suggestion, pleasure, and consent. Benedict may well have been familiar with this thinking of Augustine, a source on whom he often draws.

95. RB 1980, 435.

96. See "Appendix 4: "Disciplinary Measures in the Rule of Benedict," RB 1980, 415.

97. *The Rule of the Master*, chap. 14, verses 78–82 (our translation).

98. See for example M. Esther Harding, *The I and the Not I: A Study in the Development of Consciousness* (Princeton: Princeton University Press, 1965).

The Consecration of Mundane Activities

99. Some authors suggest the Lenten "books" referred to here are sections of the Bible. See RB 1980, note on p. 251, for example.

100. There is some evidence that indeed this chapter is the fruit of Benedict's own long reflection on the sermons of Pope St. Leo (39–50) on Lent. RB 1980, 253.

101. For elaboration of this point, see Heufelder, *The Way to God*, 161–64.

102. On this point, see de Vogue, *The Rule of Saint Benedict*, 263.

103. See RB 1980, note on 257.

104. This practice is also provided for in the Rules of Augustine, the Master, Pachomius, and Caesarius of Arles. See RB 1980, note 7, and notes on 258–59.

105. Leclerq, "The Problem of Social Class," esp. 35–42.

106. de Waal, *Seeking God,* 152.

107. Namely, Iris Murdoch.

108. The Rule of the Master, chap. 84, 250.

Membership and Governance

109. Verse 7, which is also the subject of the next *lectio* segment, refers to "the concern," suggesting that the whole community, as well as the novice

master, is lending its prayers and presence to this process. See RB 1980, note on 267 and text on 447.

110. See Parry, *Households of God,* 158.

111. RB 1980, note 7, 268. For details on the various interpretations of these vows, see the appendix on "Monastic Formation and Profession," esp. 458–66.

112. Numerous texts discuss this promise in detail. For lay use, see esp. de Waal, *Seeking God.*

113. Indeed, the Master's Rule always considers priests and deacons as "outsiders" to the monastic community. See RB 1980, note on 273.

114. I am indebted for this idea to Martin Cawley, OSCO, "Four Themes in the Rule of St. Benedict," *Word and Spirit,* vol. 2 (Still River, MA: St. Bede's Publications, 1981), esp. 97.

115. George MacDonald, *The Musician's Quest,* ed. Michael Phillips (Minneapolis, MN: Bethany House , 1984), 128.

116. See RB 1980, note on 276–77 and text on 34–41.

117. The brief reference to Romans 12 suggests these verses may be the fruit of Benedict's reflection on the vision of community set forth by St. Paul there.

118. See RB 1980, appendix on "The Abbot," 372.

119. Cardinal Basil Hume, OSB, *In Praise of Benedict* (London: Hodder & Stoughton, 1981), 18.

120. Butler, *Benedictine Monachism,* 50. This statement is presented in an excellent chapter on "Benedict's Teaching on the Spiritual Life" (chap. 5).

121. See also Chapter 18:22 of the Rule for a similar example of Benedict's humility.

122. Adele M. Millette, "Searching for the God of My Heart," *Living Prayer* 21, no. 1 (January/February 1988): 12.

123. C. S. Lewis, *Letters to Malcolm: Chiefly on Prayer* (New York: Harvest/HBJ, 1963), 75.

A Few Final Guidelines

124. RB 1980, 288.

125. This phrase was culled from the patristic and monastic literature, and might be particularly traced to Cassian's *Conferences* and *Institutes* as well as Basil's Rules. I have previously given one reference for Cassian's *Conferences;* another for both of his books is the Eerdmans series on the Nicene and Post-Nicene Fathers of the Christian Church, vol. 11, *Sulpitius Severus, Vincent of Lerins, and John Cassian,* ed. Philip Schaff and Henry Wace (Grand Rapids, MI: Eerdmans, 1986). The standard English translation of Basil's "Long Rules" is *Basil of Caesarea, Ascetical Works,* trans. Sr. M. Monica Wagner CSC, Fathers of the Church Series vol. 9 (Washington, DC: Catholic University of America Press, 1950).